The Political Refugees

A History of Canada's Peoples

The Political Refugees

A History of
the Estonians in Canada

Karl Aun

Published by McClelland and Stewart Ltd., in association
with the Multiculturalism Directorate,
Department of the Secretary of State
and the Canadian Government Publishing Centre,
Supply and Services, Canada.

Catalogue No. Ci44-12/ 1985E

McClelland and Stewart Limited
The Canadian Publishers
25 Hollinger Road
Toronto, Ontario
M4B 3G2

CANADIAN CATALOGUING IN PUBLICATION DATA
Aun, Karl
  The political refugees: a history of the Estonians in Canada

(Generations: a history of Canada's peoples)
Bibliography: p.
Includes index.
ISBN 0-7710-0174-6

1. Estonian Canadians – History.*   I. Title.
II. Series.   III. Series: Generations. (Canada.
Multiculturalism Directorate).

FC106.E7A95 1985   971'.00494545   C84-099726-4
F1035.E85A95 1985

Printed and bound in Canada by John Deyell Company

Contents

Editors' Introduction

Canadians, like many other people, have recently been changing their attitude towards the ethnic dimension in society. Instead of thinking of the many distinctive heritages and identities to be found among them as constituting a problem, though one that time would solve, they have begun to recognize the ethnic diversity of their country as a rich resource. They have begun to take pride in the fact that people have come and are coming here from all parts of the world, bringing with them varied outlooks, knowledge, skills and traditions, to the great benefit of all.

It is for this reason that Book IV of the *Report of the Royal Commission on Bilingualism and Biculturalism* dealt with the cultural contributions of the ethnic groups other than the British, the French and the Native Peoples to Canada, and that the federal government in its response to Book IV announced that the Citizenship Branch of the Department of the Secretary of State would commission "histories specifically directed to the background, contributions and problems of various cultural groups in Canada." This series presents the histories that have resulted from that mandate. Although commissioned by the Government, they are not intended as definitive or official, but rather as the efforts of scholars to bring together much of what is known about the ethnic groups studied, to indicate what remains to be learned, and thus to stimulate further research concerning the ethnic dimension in Canadian society. The histories are to be objective, analytical, and readable, and directed towards the general reading public, as well as students at the senior high school and the college and university levels, and teachers in the elementary schools.

Most Canadians belong to an ethnic group, since to do so is simply to have "a sense of identity rooted in a common origin . . . whether this common origin is real or imaginary."[1] The Native Peoples, the British and French (referred to as charter groups because they were the first Europeans to take possession of the land), the groups such as the Germans and Dutch who have been established in Canada for over a hundred years and those who began to arrive only yesterday all have traditions and values that they cherish and that now are part of the cultural riches that Canadians share. The groups vary widely in numbers, geographical location and distribution and degree of social and economic power. The stories of their struggles, failures and triumphs will be told in this series.

As the Royal Commission on Bilingualism and Biculturalism pointed out, this sense of ethnic origin or identity "is much keener in certain individuals than in others."[2] In contemporary Canadian society, with the increasing number of intermarriages across ethnic lines, and hence the growing diversity of peoples ancestors, many are coming to identify themselves as simple Canadian, without reference to their ancestral origins. In focusing on the ethnic dimension of Canadian society, past and present, the series does not assume that everyone should be categorized into one particular group, or that ethnicity is always the most important dimension of people's lives. It is, however, one dimension that needs examination if we are to understand fully the contours and nature of Canadian society and identity.

Professional Canadian historians have in the past emphasized political and economic history, and since the country's economic and political institutions have been controlled largely by people of British and French origin, the role of those of other origins in the development of Canada has been neglected. Also, Canadian historians in the past have been almost exclusively of British and French origin, and have lacked the interest and the linguistic skills necessary to explore the history of other ethnic groups. Indeed, there has rarely ever been an examination of the part played by specifically British – or, better, specifically English, Irish, Scottish and Welsh – traditions and values in Canadian development, because of the lack of recognition of pluralism in the society. The part played by French traditions and values, and particular varieties of French traditions and values, has for a number of reasons been more carefully scrutinized.

This series is an indication of growing interest in Canadian social history, which includes immigration and ethnic history. This may particularly be a reflection of an increasing number of scholars whose origins and ethnic identities are other than British or French. Because such trends are recent, many of the authors of the histories in this series have not had a large body of published writing to work from. It is true that some histories have already been written of particular groups other than the British and French; but these have often been characterized by filio pietism, a narrow perspective and a dearth of scholarly analysis.

Despite the scarcity of secondary sources, the authors have been asked to be as comprehensive as possible, and to give balanced coverage to a number of themes: historical background, settlement patterns, ethnic identity and assimilation, ethnic associations, population trends, religion, values, occupations and social class, the family, the ethnic press, language patterns, political behaviour, education, inter-ethnic relations, the arts and recreation. They have also been asked to give a sense of the way the group differs in various parts of the country. Finally, they have been asked to give, as much as possible, an insider's view of what the immigrant and ethnic experiences were like at different periods of time, but yet at the same time to be as objective as possible, and not simply to present the group as it sees itself, or as it would like to be seen.

The authors have thus been faced with a herculean task. To the extent that they have succeeded, they provide us with new glimpses into many aspects of Canadian society of the past and the present. To the extent that they have fallen short of their goal, they challenge other historians, sociologists and social anthropologists to continue the work begun here.

Jean Burnet
Howard Palmer

---

[1]   *Report of the Royal Commission on Bilingualism and Biculturalism.*
[2]   Ibid. Paragraph 8.

Estonia and her Neighbours

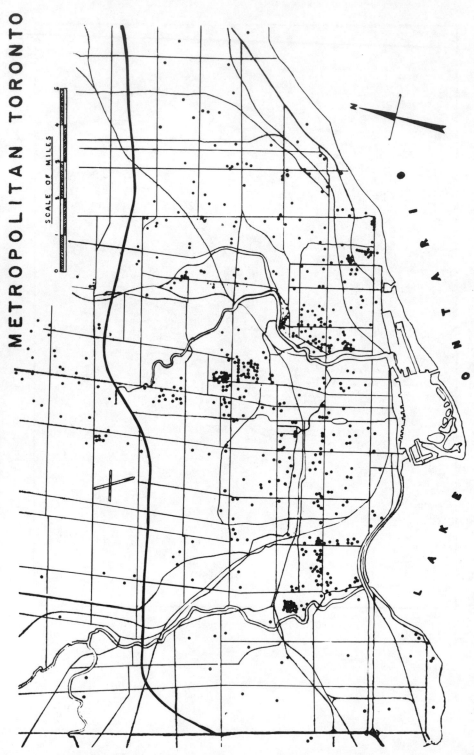

METROPOLITAN TORONTO

SCALE OF MILES

LAKE ONTARIO

N

Settlement Patterns of Estonians in Toronto around 1965|(Owners of Family Houses or Apartments)|Eestlased Kanadas, p. 157

Preface

Although the Estonians, one of the smallest groups in our multicultural mosaic, have been present in Canada since the beginning of this century, they were largely unknown until recently. The arrival of 14,000 Estonian immigrants in less than five years around 1950 brought with it the establishment of vigorous Estonian communities with extensive organizational structure and a very active cultural life in several cities across Canada.

Because Estonians mingled freely with the Canadian populace while maintaining a fierce pride in their Estonian heritage, the group enjoys far greater recognition in Canada than their small numbers warrant. As the author can testify from personal experience, it is no longer an isolated fellow Canadian who knows or has met Estonians. The following incident is now quite common: some years ago in Toronto, home of half the Estonians in Canada, a young Canadian of Scottish extraction asked me whether I was Estonian. To my surprise he explained, "Your accent is Estonian. In high school in Halifax I had an Estonian friend whose home I often visited."

Nevertheless, though Canadians may know Estonians personally or may have met them casually, very few know much about them. Hence, an easily accessible reference source for acquiring more systematic knowledge about Estonians in Canada has become necessary. This book was prompted by the recognition of that need by the Directorate of Multiculturalism of the government of Canada.

The first part of the book gives a brief introduction to Estonia and Estonians in general, both in their homeland and as immigrants adjusting to Canada. The second part deals with Estonians as a distinct ethnic community in Canada, with their own organizations and activities, mainly during the post-war decades following the arrival of the overwhelming majority of the Estonian immigrants in Canada. The final part summarizes the experiences, perceptions, dynamics, and problems

1

faced by the group, from both the point of view of the Estonians themselves and that of Canada as a multicultural society.

Needless to say, the ground covered is complex and the book does not pretend to encyclopedic answers. But the author hopes that a sufficiently detailed yet comprehensive picture emerges to contribute to a better understanding of the Estonians and the multi-ethnic, multicultural structure of Canadian society.

The author wishes to acknowledge his debts to many, both Estonians and others, who have helped in providing data, discussed specific aspects of the project, or read and commented on drafts of the manuscript in whole or in part. Without their help the book could not have been written. For the shortcomings that these many kind friends will undoubtedly find in the book I alone am responsible.

I owe a debt of gratitude to Arvis Oxland and Gail Presley for the onerous task of retyping the manuscript many times, and to my editor, Diane Mew, whose meticulous attention to detail has made the manuscript into a readable book.

A special thank you is due to my colleague, Professor Toivo Miljan, who worked closely with me to bring this book to completion. The generous support of the staff of the Multiculturalism Directorate, Department of Secretary of State, who patiently and gently coaxed the book to completion through long delays, has been the decisive factor in the production of this book.

Karl Aun
Waterloo, Ontario
October, 1984

PART ONE

Immigration and Adjustment

ONE

Who Are the Estonians?

THE COUNTRY AND ITS PHYSICAL GEOGRAPHY

Estonia, along with the other two Baltic states of Latvia and Lithuania, is located on the eastern shore of the Baltic Sea across from Sweden. To the east stretches the continental land mass of the vast plains of Russia. To the north, across the 400-kilometre-long Gulf of Finland, is Finland. Thus, more than half of Estonia borders the sea, and on the map of northern Europe it looks like a peninsula surrounded by many islands, the largest of which, Saaremaa, is half the size of Prince Edward Island. Since ancient times, the location of the country has enabled its peoples to establish contacts with Denmark, Germany, and other west European countries by sea and with the eastern Mediterranean through the river systems of Russia. Indeed, Estonians have found themselves at the cross-roads of many trade routes and many cultures – and many conquests – since the beginning of their recorded history.

Although Estonia is located as far north as Churchill, Manitoba, on Hudson Bay, the climate is much more moderate and similar to that of southern Quebec and central Ontario. This is due to the influence of the Baltic Sea and the warm North Atlantic Current (Gulf Stream) that passes the coastline of Norway about 600 kilometres to the west. The landscape of the country presents the familiar panorama of the Precambrian Shield with white birches standing next to the deep green firs on land penetrated by numerous rivers and dotted by many lakes. By North American standards Estonia is a small country, with an area slightly less than that of the province of Nova Scotia. However, we should note that many European countries are small: Belgium, the Netherlands, Switzerland, and Denmark are territorially smaller than Estonia, and Latvia and Lithuania are only slightly bigger.[1] Most of Estonia's agricultural land, found both on the flat coastal regions and in the hilly central and southern parts of the country, has been under cultivation for many centuries, with the result that although fertility is moderate and varies from area to

3

area, Estonia today forms the northernmost productive agricultural area in Europe. Apart from agriculture the main natural resource of Estonia is oil shale, which covers almost a third of the northeastern part of the country and is found virtually at ground level. Industrial development of the oil shale began in the 1920's and with its intensive exploitation since the Second World War it has become the source not only of industrial energy in Estonia but also of electric power for the northwestern region of the Soviet Union, including the city of Leningrad.[2]

POPULATION AND LANGUAGE

At the beginning of this century the population of the country reached the one million mark and in 1938 it stood at 1.1 million, of whom 88.2 per cent or 970,000 were Estonians, with small minorities of Russians, Germans, and Swedes forming the balance.[3] Three decades later, the 1970 census showed a population of 1.4 million, of whom 68.2 per cent or 925,000 were Estonians, and a large minority of 381,000, or 28.2 per cent of the population, were Russians and other Slavs.[4] Hence, before the Second World War Estonia was ethnically one of the most homogeneous countries in Europe, but in 1970 only two-thirds of the population were Estonians, and the total number of Estonians had actually declined. The census of 1979 reported 1,020,000 Estonians in the Soviet Union, of whom 948,000 were in Estonia.

Ethnolinguistically the Estonians belong to the Finno-Ugrian language group and as such are related to the Finns and Hungarians as well as several other lesser known Finno-Ugrian nationalities in the Soviet Union.[5] Hence, the Estonian language is quite unlike those of its Slavic or Germanic neighbours, nor does it have affinities to the Baltic (the Lithuanian and Latvian) or the Romance languages, which all have a common Indo-European origin. More specifically, Estonian belongs to the Finnish sub-group of the Finno-Ugrian languages, together with Finnish, Karelian, Ingrian, and the now extinct Livish spoken by the Livs who formerly inhabited the northern half of the present-day Latvia. Estonian, along with other Finno-Ugrian languages, does not differentiate between the masculine and feminine genders (for example, there is no "he" and "she" distinction as in English) as all Indo-European languages do.[6] Estonian differs radically from the Indo-European languages in other ways also: it has no articles or future tense; the accent is always on the first syllable; it uses suffixes instead of prepositions; and it has fifteen cases.[7] Its strictly phonetical spelling makes it comparatively easy for the foreigner to learn. The Estonian vocabulary, which is basically different from the Indo-European languages, is very rich, especially in onomatopoetic expressions and nuances, and has a greater frequency of vowel use than most other languages, including other Finno-Ugrian.[8]

There are several dialect groups in Estonia divided roughly into northern and southern dialects. The northern dialect is the basis of the contemporary literary and official language, but it is interesting to note that the southern dialects are closer to the contemporary Finnish literary language. The reason for this, supposedly, is that when Finland was settled from northern Estonia other Estonian tribes from the east moved in between the Gulf of Finland and southern Estonia. Local dialects are still spoken in Estonia and some Estonian poets in Estonia as well as abroad write in dialect. Within the Finno-Ugrian group of languages Estonian and Finnish are sufficiently similar to each other to make it relatively easy for the speaker of one language to learn the other; Hungarian is much more remote due to different geographic and historic variables. The total number of people who speak the Finno-Ugrian languages today is approximately 25 million, of whom the Estonians, both in the homeland and abroad, represent slightly more than one million.[9]

HISTORY AND CULTURE

The ancestors of the present-day Estonians came to Estonia from the east at least 3,000 years ago, but possibly more than 4,000 years ago.[10] Earlier they were a hunting and fishing people, but in Estonia they took up agriculture, trading, and seafaring. By the twelfth century they lived in tribes or nations, but their settlements also included a number of cities that were mainly unfortified trading centres, with the older ones dating from the tenth century. Whether Estonians can be counted among the Vikings is debatable, but it is known that they interacted with the Danes and the Swedes and carried on trading relations with Novgorod in Russia.[11] By the end of the twelfth century Christianity began to penetrate Estonia from Russia in the east and from Sweden and Denmark in the west. But before the Estonians had a chance to adopt Christianity voluntarily they were conquered and Christianized by force in a sequence of wars from 1206 to 1227 by Denmark and the Order of the Brethren of the Sword, recruited mainly from among the Germans.[12] The conquest was promoted by the Pope, who pronounced the country "The Holy Land of Mary," a name by which it was known for centuries.

A century later Denmark ceded her possession of Estonia to the Order and the latter became the dominant military power and the political ruler of the region of present-day Estonia and Latvia for the next 200 years. The clergy, the landlords, and the ruling elites in the cities either were Germans or were Germanized and German-speaking. Economically the country prospered; the lucrative trade of its Hanseatic cities of Tallinn (Reval in German), Pärnu, and Tartu formed the transit depots between western Europe and the Russian hinterland.

After the Lutheran Reformation, which swept Estonia with unusual speed (1523-35) and may well be considered a social revolution, the Order decayed and finally dissolved in 1561. For about a century Sweden, Poland, and Russia vied for the domination of the eastern coast of the Baltic Sea, which brought incessant warfare and military invasions to Estonia, economic decline to the cities, and misery to the countryside. Eventually Sweden prevailed over the other contestants and for the duration of the seventeenth century the Baltic Sea became a "Swedish lake" with the Swedish realm surrounding it to the west, north, and east. The Swedish government introduced economic and social reforms, for its own economic and fiscal purposes, which curbed the power of the German and Germanized overlords and were aimed at promoting the middle and lower classes, including the peasants.[13] Several educational institutions were established and access was granted to students from the lower classes. A university was founded in 1632 in Tartu, an old city of central Estonia.

In the Great Northern War (1700-21) Sweden lost her territories east of the Baltic Sea and south of the Gulf of Finland to Russia. The war was devastating for Estonia since Russia applied scorched-earth tactics to cut off supply lines for the Swedish army campaigning in the Ukraine. This devastation, together with mass deportations to Russia and the plague, decimated the population of Estonia.[14] The German-Baltic nobility who had both resisted and detested the reforms of the Swedish period sided openly with the Russian Czar, in return for which Peter I restored their rights and privileges, which amounted to political autonomy for their corporate institutions in the so-called Baltic provinces (later Estonia and Latvia). Moreover, largely by default the Czarist government permitted these corporate bodies to determine themselves the extent of the "previous" rights to be restored, with the result that many "rights" were added that had not existed before.[15] The Germanic landlords could now sell the Estonian peasants and their families as chattels and impose excessive services and inhuman punishment upon them. This, the darkest age of the Estonian people, lasted for about a hundred years.

This was followed, in the second half of the nineteenth century, by one of the most remarkable periods in the history of the Estonian people. In barely two generations, a modern nation with an economically independent middle class, conscious of its cultural identity and confident of its collective future, emerged from an inarticulate native population. A number of coinciding causes, of which only the most outstanding can be mentioned here, assisted in this quasi-revolutionary phenomenon commonly called the "national awakening." First, serfdom was abolished in the Baltic provinces almost half a century earlier than in Russia.[16] Added to this, the policies of the Czarist government in reforming local government and the judicial system provided the foundation on which indigenous Estonian forces were able to develop as a counterweight to the hegemony of the German-Baltic nobility. Second, widespread financial difficulties forced large numbers of landlords, many of them absentees, to sell or rent parcels of their land to the Estonian peasants, thus assisting in the creation of an economically independent farmer class. At the same time the growth of cities opened up new opportunities and careers for Estonians.[17] Finally, and perhaps most important, because of the centuries of cultural linkage with the West, Estonians were able to respond quickly to Western liberal ideas, and especially to the ideology of modern liberal-romantic nationalism. The University of Tartu, then a German-language university and one of the outstanding universities of Europe with a strong liberal tradition, was the alma mater of the intellectuals and professionals of Estonian descent and thus acted as the main catalyst of the Estonian national awakening.

The two outstanding events in this process of cultural awakening were the publication of the Estonian folk epic *Kalevipoeg* in 1867 and the first national song festival in 1869. These were followed by the widespread use of the Estonian language in a variety of publications and in the theatre. This was accompanied by the collection and publication of Estonian folklore, a vigorous co-operative movement, and the establishment of various civic organizations as well as secondary schools. It is important to note that the national awakening did not establish Estonian as a literary language; it had been that since the sixteenth century, but it had been relegated for use by peasants only.[18] Because of the spread of literature before the end of the nineteenth century, illiteracy had been wiped out for all practical purposes in Estonia, whereas in many Western countries it was still widespread, and in Russia more than four-fifths of the population was illiterate.[19]

Throughout the seven centuries of foreign rule the Estonian people maintained their indigenous cultural patterns and extensive cultural links with Western Europe, often in effect functioning as the northeastern-most outpost of Western culture. Western-style art and architecture, Western ways of life and value systems, the Latin alphabet, and the Lutheran Church are even today the main testimony of this historic legacy in manifest contrast to the Byzantine architecture, Cyrillic alphabet, and Orthodox Church that historically have dominated Russia.[20]

ESTONIA AND ESTONIANS IN THE TWENTIETH CENTURY

After the overthrow of the Czarist government in Russia in February, 1917, the Russian provisional (Lvov-Kerensky) government granted Estonia political autonomy.[21] Following the October Revolution of 1917 an independent Estonian Democratic Republic was proclaimed on February 24, 1918. This was followed by the War of Independence (1918-20) in which the Estonian army defended the independence of the country against both the Red Army in the east and the mercenary German forces, the Landeswehr, in the south.[22] The Landeswehr was defeated and the war with the Soviets ended by the Peace Treaty of Tartu in 1920. In September, 1921, Estonia became a member of the League of Nations.

During the 1920's the nation experienced the aftermath of the ravages of the war and the dislocation of its economy. Estonia's traditional trade market with Russia had been cut off and it was not possible to immediately establish new markets in the West. However, the Land Reform of 1919, which created 56,000 new individual family farms from the former large estates in addition to about the same number of existing ones, provided considerable incentive for intensive and improving farming and marketing techniques. In the 1930's Estonian agricultural products, mainly in form of bacon, eggs, and butter, had become established as quality goods in the highly competitive markets of Germany and England. In addition, the Land Reform had a significant social effect by creating a strong land-based middle class. And, although Estonia remained primarily an agricultural economy, industry reached the take-off stage in the 1930's, particularly in the manufacturing of textile products and chemicals and in the development of the technology and exploration of oil shale. In fact, economic growth was so rapid that by the late 1930's seasonal workers for agriculture had to be imported from abroad.

The political system of Estonia during the 1920's may be characterized as an ultra-liberal multi-party system, which, however, under the pressure of the worldwide economic depression in the early 1930's, underwent a political crisis. The resultant authoritarian regime, after the adoption of a new constitution in 1938, showed signs of eventually returning to a parliamentary-presidential political system.[23] Educational standards advanced rapidly, to such an extent that already during the 1920's there was an "overproduction" of university graduates. This led to the establishment in 1936 of admission by competitive entrance examinations to universities and the emphasis on vocational technical education, especially in agriculturally oriented fields.[24] By comparative indexes of university students and books printed per year per capita, Estonia in the 1930's placed among the leading countries in the world.[25] In one area, that of providing for its ethnic minorities, Estonia was unique: with the support of government funds the ethnic minorities were able to manage their own school systems and teach in their own ethnic languages.[26]

The 1930's were also a decade of intensified nationalism in Estonia with nationalistic civic organizations promoted. Estonianization of first names and surnames, which previously had been largely German, was encouraged. Along with the traditional song festivals, national festivals of folk dance, gymnastics, and open-air drama were held, and new Estonian operas were written and produced.

The Ribbentrop-Molotov Pact of August, 1939, between Hitler's Germany and the U.S.S.R. delivered up the Baltic states to the Soviet Union and subsequently, in June, 1940, the three Baltic republics of Lithuania, Latvia, and Estonia were invaded by the Soviet armed forces. The three countries were annexed by the Soviet Union and its economic and political systems were imposed on their populations. The Soviet version that the peoples of the three Baltic states voluntarily joined the Soviet Union is a hoax; according to Soviet Estonian sources the Communist Party of Estonia had only 124 members in June of 1940.[27] The president of the republic and other leading members of the Estonian government, trade unions, political parties, armed forces, churches, and civic organizations were arrested and many were deported to Russia or killed. [28] On the night of June 13-14, 1941, about 10,000 more people were arrested and deported to Russia. [29] Thus, in July and August of 1941, when the German forces in turn drove the Soviets out of the country, it is understandable that they were awaited as liberators. However, very soon the Germans also created open as well as underground resistance as they exploited the country economically, tried to impose their Nazi doctrines on the population, and began forcefully to conscript Estonian men into their armies. Nevertheless, many Estonian men were conscripted and others volunteered when the Germans were already in retreat; these Estonians fought the Soviet army when it re-entered Estonia in 1944. However, about 4,000 Estonian men deserted the German army in 1942 and 1943, fled to Finland, and volunteered to serve in the Finnish army. [30] On the other hand, more than 30,000 Estonian men had been conscripted in the summer of 1941 into the Soviet army. [31]

When the Soviet army reoccupied Estonia in the autumn of 1944, about 80,000 Estonians (8 per cent of the total population) fled to Sweden and Germany. [32] Many more would have fled if only the means of escape had been available. During the same period about 25,000 Estonians returned to Estonia from the Soviet Union in 1944 and 1945 after having fled or been taken there in the summer of 1941 before the Germans occupied the country. [33] This does not mean that all these people were collaborators or even sympathized with the Soviets or the Germans, but during the Second World War the Estonian people found themselves "between the devil and the deep blue sea."

Since the war, Estonia, Latvia, and Lithuania have remained incorporated into the Soviet Union as the newest three of its fifteen Union Republics. [34] Their economies have been absorbed into the Soviet economy and their politics have been dictated by Communist parties, whose top leaders, more often than not, do not belong to the indigenous population. [35] Hence, politically and economically these countries are treated as colonies of Russia. [36] It must also be noted that Estonia and Latvia, especially, are economically, educationally, and industrially the most developed and modernized Union Republics in the Soviet Union today, mainly due to their advanced development before the war. [37] Also, since the 1960's their intellectual and cultural achievements in the sciences, literature, arts, and music, building upon traditionally high standards, have perhaps even surpassed those before the war. Finally, it may be noted that the United States, Canada, and several European powers have not legally recognized the 1940 annexation of the Baltic states by the Soviet Union. [38]

Although it is not possible to cover the whole of the history of the Estonian people in one chapter, we hope, nevertheless, that the facts covered in this brief introduction will serve as a foundation for a better understanding of Estonians as immigrants to Canada.

NOTES

1. The areas are approximately: Belgium – 30,500 sq. km; Switzerland – 41,000; the Netherlands – 41,000; Denmark – 43,000; Estonia – 45,000; Nova Scotia – 53,000; Latvia – 64,000; Lithuania – 64,000; Prince Edward Island – 5,600; Saaremaa – 2,700. John Paxton (ed.), *The Stateman's Yearbook 1970-71* (New York, 1970).

2. *A Thousand and One Facts about Soviet Estonia* (Tallinn, 1977), p. 80. According to this source 60 per cent of the electric power produced in Estonia is used outside Estonia. According to other sources Estonia "generates 16.7 billion kwh and consumes 6.6 billion" annually. H. Ratnieks, "The Energy Crises and the Baltic," *Journal of Baltic Studies*, XII, 3 (Fall, 1981), p. 247.

3. 92,636 Russians, 16,346 Germans, 7,641 Swedes, and 4,434 Jews. See A. Pullerits (ed.), *Estland* (Tallinn, 1938), pp. 13, 128.

4. 925,157 Estonians, 334,620 Russians, 28,086 Ukrainians, 18,732 Belorussians, 18,537 Finns. The total population of Estonia as of January 1, 1975, was 1,428,708. G. Naan (ed.), *Nõukogude Eesti* (Soviet Estonia) (Tallinn, 1975), pp. 37, 40.

5. Mordvin (1,200,000), Udmurt (700,000), Mari (600,000), Komi (500,000), and other small nationalities like Karelians, Ingeris, etc., with the combined total of over 3.5 million. Valev Uibopuu, *Meie ja meie hõimud* (The Estonians and the Finno-Ugrians) (Lund, 1984).

6. For the English word "man" the Estonian language has two equivalents: "mees" – the man, and "inimene" – the human being; thus "mankind" in Estonian is "inimkond," "meeskond" means a male team, "naiskond" the female team (from "naine" – the woman).

7. A. Saareste, "The Estonian Language," in E. Uustalu (ed.), *Aspects of Estonian Culture* (London, 1961), pp. 161-74; J. Aavik, "Introduction," in P. Saagpakk, *Estonian-English Dictionary* (New Haven, 1982), p. xxvii. Cf. W.B. Lockwood, *A Panorama of Indo-European Languages* (London, 1972).

8. It has been claimed that the frequency of vowel use enhances the melodic quality of a language, which is believed to be the reason why Italian has become known as the premier "language of opera."

9. The total of Hungarians is estimated to be 14 million, the total of Finns, 6 million.

10. Of the sources of Estonian history and culture in English, the following may be mentioned: E. Uustalu, *The History of Estonian People* (London, 1952); V. Raud, *Estonia: A Reference Book* (New York, 1953); J.H. Jackson, *Estonia* (London, 1948); A. Võõbus, *Studies in the History of Estonian People*, 9 vols. to date (Stockholm, 1969-84).

11. It is debatable who destroyed the Viking city Sigtuna in Sweden in 1187, but it is sure that an Estonian fleet from Saaremaa participated in this retaliatory act; earlier, Estonians and Danes both exchanged raids several times, and carried on trade relations.

12. The Order was affiliated to the Teutonic Order, which was created in the Holy Land and conquered and colonized the Prussians, ethnolinguistically a Baltic nation who lived in the area that later was known as East Prussia.

13. The objective of the reforms was to introduce in the peripheral areas of the realm the Swedish socio-economic system; in contrast to all of Europe, in Sweden the peasantry represented an independent and countervailing estate to the nobility and clergy. See E. Heckscher, *An Economic History of Sweden* (Cambridge, 1954); and I. Anderson, *A History of Sweden* (London, 1962).

14. The Russian field commander, Sheremetiev, reported to the Czar: "There is nothing left to destroy, not a cock crows from Lake Peipus to the Gulf of Riga." A. Bilmanis, *A History of Latvia* (Princeton, 1951), p. 214; Jackson, *Estonia*, p. 65.

15. See especially Uustalu, *History of Estonian People*, pp. 95ff.

16. In the province of Estonia in 1816, in the province of Livonia (southern Estonia and northern Latvia) in 1819, in Russia in 1861. On the role of the liberally minded members of the Baltic-German nobility in abolishing serfdom in Estonia, see I. Käbin, "Märkmeid Eesti historiograafiast" (Notes on the Estonian Historiography), *Tulimuld* (Lund, Sweden), 4 (1981), pp. 192-203.

17. Of the other factors may be mentioned the following: the "Estophiles," who were Germans and came from Germany to Estonia as pastors, teachers, or professionals but made the promotion of Estonian culture and language the object of their interest; the example of a similar "national awakening" in Finland, which started earlier; and, most curiously, it may be added, even the Civil War in America, which cut off the cotton supply to the English textile factories and thus opened an unexpected market for Estonian flax growers and small merchants.

18. The oldest found book printed in Estonian is dated 1535, and it is known that at least another one had been printed in 1525.

19. H. Haarmann, *Soziologie und Politik der Sprachen Europas* (München, 1975), p. 179, gives the following information on the literacy in 1897, 1939, and 1959 (in percentages), with the U.S.S.R. percentages for the whole of the present-day (1975) territory of the Soviet Union.

	1897	1939	1959
U.S.S.R.	28.4	87.4	98.5
Ukraine	27.9	88.2	99.1
Belorussia	32.0	80.8	99.0
Lithuania	54.2	76.7	98.5
Latvia	79.7	92.7	99.6
Estonia	96.2	98.6	99.6

Cf. E. Glyn Lewis, *Multilingualism in the Soviet Union* (The Hague, 1972), p. 175, Table 31.

20. For a report on differences between today's Soviet Estonian Republic and Russia, see Priit Vesilind, "Return to Estonia," *National*

Geographic Magazine (April, 1980), pp. 485-511. Similar reports abound from travellers and journalists who visit the Soviet Union and Estonia or Latvia. Historically, Estonia was in the reach of the "Three Great R-s" (Renaissance, Reformation, and [political] Revolution) of the West.

21. In the summer of 1917 the Estonian Diet (Maanõukogu) was democratically elected.

22. The aim of the Landeswehr was to restore the system of large land estates of the Baltic-German nobility, which had been abolished by the Land Reform of 1919.

23. The contemporary writings in Soviet Estonia, for clearly political reasons, portray the independence period as decadent, when the workers were "oppressed" and the government was "a fascist dictatorship" by "lackeys of Western capitalists and imperialists." The contemporary literature of exiles tends to underestimate the deficiencies and overstate the achievements of the independence. The most reliable and balanced analysis of the social change in Estonia, and of the political crisis and stabilization in the 1930's, is T. Parming, *The Decline of Liberal Democracy and Rise of Authoritarianism in Estonia* (Berkeley, 1975). It may be noted that political prisoners (fascist and Communist) were released in 1938 and that four members of the Estonian parliament in 1940 were left-socialist or Communist.

24. In 1935 a new technical university was founded in Tallinn, in addition to the 300-year-old University of Tartu.

25. See Jackson, *Estonia*, pp. 235-6.

26. Cultural autonomy should be distinguished from multiculturalism. In the case of cultural autonomy, the public decision-making power in cultural affairs, including the schools, is delegated to the self-governmental institutions of the ethnic group; in contrast, multiculturalism means recognition of diverse cultural patterns and government aid in maintaining these patterns by private cultural organizations. In Estonia the Germans and Jews had cultural autonomy. The total membership of the Jewish cultural autonomy in 1925 was 3,045, of whom 2,041 had the right to vote, the rest being minors. The Russians and Swedes did not establish their cultural autonomies because they lived in areas where they were the majority of the local population and thus already had the same privileges through local self-governmental institutions. See E. Maddisson, *Die nationalen Minderheiten Estlands und ihre Rechte* (Tallinn, 1930); and K. Aun, "On the Spirit of the Estonian Minorities' Law," in *Apophoreta Tartuensia* (Stockholm, 1949), pp. 240-5.

27. A. Panksejev (ed.), *Ülevaade Eestimaa Kommunistliku Partei ajaloost* (Synopsis of the History of the Communist Party of Estonia), vol. III (Tallinn: Eesti Raamat, 1972), p. 13; O. Kuuli, *Revolutsioon Eestis 1940* (The Revolution in Estonia in 1940) (Tallinn: Eesti Raamat, 1980), p. 47.

28. E. Kareda (comp.), *Estonia the Forgotten Nation* (Toronto: Estonian Central Council in Canada, 1961), p. 31. According to this source, 6,964

men and 727 women altogether. Also, R. Maasing *et al.*, *Eesti riik ja rahvas teises maailmasõjas* (The Republic and the People of Estonia in the Second World War), vol. III (Stockholm: EMP Kirjastus, 1956), especially M. Kuldkepp, pp. 228-34.

29. According to Kareda (comp.), *Estonia the Forgotten Nation*, 5,102 men and 5,103 women.

30. E. Uustalu, *For Freedom Only: The Story of Estonian Volunteers in the Finnish War of 1940-1944* (Toronto: Northern Publications, 1977). After the war about 100 of these men immigrated to Canada.

31. Kareda (comp.), *Estonia the Forgotten Nation*, reports 5,573 men of the Estonian regular army taken to the Soviet Union and 33,304 men conscripted in the summer of 1941. Soviet Estonian sources show from 25,000 to 30,000 men in the Estonian units of the Soviet army, but these figures include also those Estonians who lived in the Soviet Union before the war and were conscripted in the Soviet Union.

32. About 14,000 of these refugees later emigrated from Germany or Sweden to Canada. See Chapter Two.

33. This is the figure from Soviet Estonian sources; the figure from other sources is considerably lower. The Soviet sources must include also deportees and some of those conscripted in the summer of 1941.

34. Estonia, with only 1.4 million people, is the smallest of the fifteen Union Republics within the Soviet population of 270 million.

35. The first secretaries of the Communist Party of Estonia have been of Estonian descent, but invariably they have immigrated to Estonia from Russia after the war and their knowledge of Estonia and of the Estonian language has been limited. The "second secretaries" always have been Russians. See, for instance, *Rahva Hääl* (Tallinn), May 14, 1982. Recently (1980) a Russian was appointed minister of education in the Soviet Estonian government, and several other government members or high government officials are Russians.

36. R.J. Misiunas and R. Taagepera, *The Baltic States: Years of Dependence, 1940-1980* (Berkeley: University of California Press, 1983).

37. T. Parming and E. Järvesoo (eds.), A *Case Study of a Soviet Republic: The Estonian SSR* (Boulder, Colorado: Westview Press, 1978). Cf. A. Küng, *A Dream of Freedom* (Cardiff: Boreas Publishing, 1980).

38. On February 1, 1982, Alexander M. Haig, Jr., the Secretary of State of the United States, wrote to E. Jaakson, the Consul-General of Estonia in New York, ". . . I therefore wish . . . to reaffirm to you that the United States does not recognize the forcible incorporation of Estonia into the Soviet Union in 1940." Quoted from *Teataja* (Stockholm), February 20, 1982; cf. the same statement in Estonian translation in *Meie Elu* (Toronto), February 25, 1982. Also, statement by the Foreign Minister of France on December 17, 1981, in the Senate of France, reported in *Teataja*, May 15, 1982.

TWO

Immigration to Canada

The Estonian ethnic group in Canada is essentially a community of recent immigrants. According to the census of 1961, there were 18,500 Canadians of Estonian ethnic origin. But 14,310 Estonians immigrated to Canada between 1947 and 1960, 11,370 in the four-year period from 1948 to 1951.[1] Hence, of the 18,500 Estonians in Canada in 1961, only about 4,200 were either earlier immigrants or Canadian-born – a total that was smaller than the 4,573 who came in the peak year of 1951.

These data demonstrate succinctly that the overwhelming majority of Estonian immigrants, almost four-fifths of the total, came shortly after the Second World War. More specifically, they belonged to the 80,000 political refugees who left Estonia in 1944 for Sweden and Germany, and re-emigrated from there a few years later to other countries, including Canada. Their arrival occurred within a short time span and they represented a very cohesive ethnic group. The backgrounds of these post-war immigrants, their professional training and experience, their values, attitudes, and behavioural patterns determined the structures of their organizations, the scope of the ethnic activities of the Estonians in Canada, and their adjustment as well as their contributions to Canadian society. Although a few ethnic organizations of Estonians existed in Canada before their arrival there were none that brought them all together.

Furthermore, it must be stressed that, after their arrival, the immigration of Estonians to Canada ceased again. Virtually no emigration has taken place directly from Estonia.[2]

In the 1960's and 1970's only a few Estonian refugees who had previously immigrated to the United Kingdom, Australia, or Latin America later moved to Canada for various reasons. Accordingly, the number of Estonians in Canada has remained constant since the 1950's, as borne out by the 1971 census. In 1971, 18,810 Canadians of Estonian ethnic origin were reported, an increase of only about 300 over the 1961 census. The census data for 1981 show 15,915 Canadians of Estonian ethnic origin.[3]

14

The Estonian ethnic community in Canada has experienced no new immigration in the last three decades. Consequently, the constancy in numbers has been accompanied by an increasing ratio of those who have either grown up or been born in Canada and, therefore, new and different attitude and behavioural patterns manifest themselves within the different generations of the ethnic group. In due course we will turn to these diverse issues.

IMMIGRATION BEFORE THE FIRST WORLD WAR[4]

All we know about the presence of Estonians in Canada before the end of the last century is that there were some Estonian fishermen at Prince Rupert, B.C., in the late 1890's.[5] It seems reasonable to assume that at least some Estonians must have come to Canada even earlier, but we have no evidence to prove that. However, there were more Estonians in the United States and we know more about them.[6] From these sources we find occasional references to Estonian seamen in Canada, but it is not known whether they were transients or had settled here. Considering the number of Estonians already in America and also that many of them were former seamen, we may assume that at least some of the Estonian seamen may have chosen Canada for a permanent home; this, however, cannot be verified.

The established history of Estonians in Canada begins at the turn of the century. In 1899 a school teacher, Hendrik Kingsepp, arrived with his family in Alberta, received a land grant as a homesteader, and started farming near Sylvan Lake. It seems that he had left Estonia mainly for political reasons. He was joined by his brother, a seaman who came from South America. Next year the brother left Canada again for the seas but his family, which came from Estonia, remained at Sylvan Lake. Two years later, in 1901, there were already five Estonian families at Sylvan Lake, and in 1903 the Estonians there had sixteen farms and a population of sixty-one, including children. Thus, Sylvan Lake may be considered the first Estonian settlement in Canada.

Soon, however, most of the Estonians at Sylvan Lake moved to other neighbouring areas in Alberta to which Estonian immigrants were now arriving in increasing numbers. Within ten years separate Estonian settlements developed in Barons, Stettler, Eckville, Foremost, and Walsh. In Barons by 1903 there were already twenty-six families with seventy-seven people. In Stettler in 1910 there were forty-five Estonian farms with about 160 people, and the following year an Estonian community hall (Linda Hall) was built there. In 1916 in Eckville there were about forty farms with 171 people. The Foremost (seven families) and Walsh (twelve families) settlements were less cohesive since the Estonians there were more isolated from each other.

All these settlers did not come from Estonia; some came from Estonian settlements in Russia, and others were seamen. Many had come from

Russia to South and North Dakota and Wisconsin, whence they moved on to southern Alberta.[7] The main attraction of Alberta was the availability of homestead land grants and expectations of other favourable opportunities for successful farming. The number of Estonians in Alberta, however, was constantly in flux; new immigrants came but many also left – for other places in Canada, seamen back to the sea, and a few even back to their former homes in Russia. Nevertheless, we can quite safely estimate the number of Estonians in Alberta around 1916 at almost 100 families and several unmarried men, with a total of about 500 Estonians.[8]

Of the Estonian immigrants outside Alberta we know much less because they were scattered and lived isolated from each other. There were some Estonian farmers in Manitoba, Saskatchewan, and Ontario, a sprinkling of Estonian miners, lumbermen, and fishermen, and a slightly larger number of Estonians in various cities. Usually they neither expected nor tried to meet other Estonians. The immigration statistics are of no help because Estonia was part of Czarist Russia and Estonians were documented as immigrants either from Russia or from whatever countries they came from. Estonia as a country or a nation was unknown in Canada. Therefore, an Estonian immigrant instructed others as follows:

> To get a job you cannot say you are a Russian. But Estonians are unknown. Say you are a German and you will get a job. Russians are the 'spademen' (shovellers) and so are Poles and Italians. The Germans have the better jobs.[9]

Hence, these Estonians easily assimilated with other nationalities, often without trace. For example, in 1912 an Estonian tried to find another Estonian in Toronto and failed; but this does not mean that there were no other Estonians in that city. An interesting case of an "unknown" Estonian in Canada is that of August Masik (Maasik), who came to Canada in 1912. He was involved in the revolution of 1905, fled Russia, and after working as a sailor for a few years settled in the Northwest Territories of Canada and in Alaska. He was a known explorer of the Canadian Arctic, especially in the Beaufort Sea, on his own and with the famous Canadian Arctic explorer of Icelandic descent, Vilhjalmur Steffanson. Though Masik considered himself an Estonian, he was, according to his own testimony, best known by his nickname "Russian Bolshevik."[10]

More by circumstantial than direct evidence we can estimate the number of Estonians outside Alberta in 1916 at close to 1,000.[11] Thus, the number of Estonians in Canada before the First World War was small and many of them did not come to Canada directly from Estonia. It was not because there was no emigration from Estonia: on the contrary, from the middle of the nineteenth century considerable emigration from Estonia had taken place. But it was to Russia and not to the New World.

Russia attracted Estonians not only because of geographic proximity, but because of its fertile soil and the many opportunities for skilled occupations in its growing cities. Since the educational standards of Estonians were much higher than the average in Russia, Estonians could find employment easily in a variety of professions at the middle and upper-middle socio-economic levels. Around 1900 there were more than 400 Estonian rural settlements in Russia with a combined population of over 250,000. [12] In the larger cities there were sizable Estonian communities, such as in the capital city of St. Petersburg, which had a community of about 50,000 Estonians. The 10,000 Estonians living in North America were insignificant when compared to the more than 300,000 Estonians in Russia. The reason for emigration from Europe often had been political; the main reason for coming to Canada was the search for better economic opportunities. The availability of homestead grants and the fertile soil drew many Estonians, particularly those with a farming background, to Alberta.

IMMIGRATION BETWEEN THE TWO WORLD WARS

In the 1920's very large numbers of new immigrants entered Canada, but in the 1930's there was a sharp drop due to the economic depression and Canada's restrictions on immigration. This difference between the 1920's and the 1930's is also reflected in the immigration of Estonians to Canada. But it must be pointed out that the number of Estonians among the total number of immigrants to Canada was extremely small, especially in the 1930's: one Estonian among 3,000 immigrants in the 1920's and one in 6,000 in the 1930's. During the first of two decades of this century perhaps more than 1,500 Estonians immigrated to Canada, but their numbers in the next two decades, during the period of Estonian independence between the two world wars, did not amount to more than 700.

From 1922 on we have Canadian immigration data that show migration from Estonia because Estonia was by then an independent state. According to this data 612 Estonians immigrated to Canada from 1922 to 1930, but in the 1930's (1931 to 1940) their total number was only thirty-six. [13] The highest annual totals were in 1927 (110) and 1928 (107). In the early 1930's Estonian immigration to Canada became practically nil (1932 – 0, 1933 – 1, 1934 – 2), and not until after the war were there more than nine immigrants per year. This pattern corresponds roughly to the pattern of emigration from Estonia in the same period. In the 1930's about 13,000 people emigrated from Estonia, with the peak emigration years occurring in 1925 (2,676), 1926 (2,426), and 1927 (2,322). Total emigration from Estonia in the 1930's amounted to fewer than 4,000 persons. [14]

From these figures, it is clear that there was more reason for emigration from Estonia, as well as more inducement for immigration to Canada, in the 1920's than in the 1930's. In the 1920's the Estonian economy was still in post-war transition, and the country had to absorb a considerable additional population. An estimated 100,000 Estonians returned from Russia during the Revolution, about 40,000 opted for patriation from the Soviet Union in the early 1920's, and more than 10,000 White Russian officers with their families remained in Estonia after the war. In addition, emigration from Estonia could have been much higher than it turned out to be. In the 1930's the Estonian economy had stabilized; although the global economic crisis also affected Estonia, the depression was much more severe in other countries, including Canada. Thus the number of emigrants from Estonia decreased considerably.

The figures also show that the proportion of Estonian emigrants who came to Canada was very low. In the 1920's only one out of every twenty emigrants from Estonia came to Canada, and in the 1930's, one in 100. The low ratio in the 1920's may be explained, at least partly, by the small number of Estonians already in Canada and thus by a lack of knowledge about Canada. The same explanation cannot apply to the 1930's. Consequently, it must be concluded that Canadian economic conditions and the government restrictions were the main causes for the sudden drop.

Of the post-war immigrants only fifty-eight went to the Estonian settlements in southern Alberta, and twenty-three of these left soon for various other places in Canada. About thirty Estonians settled in Peace River, Alberta, as farmers, traders, and entrepreneurs. Some started fruit farming (twelve farms) in the Niagara Peninsula; some raised poultry in British Columbia; others became lumbermen, miners, or entrepreneurs in northern Ontario. The majority remained city dwellers in a variety of vocations and often also changed cities and occupations. The new immigrants differed from the earlier ones: they were usually young and unmarried, many had secondary education, and some were university graduates or acquired higher degrees in Canada.[15] The majority, however, were tradesmen, small merchants, and manual labourers.

Some had left Estonia for the reason called the "foreign policy syndrome" – a fear emanating from the proximity of the Soviet Union to Estonia. This is discernible in Estonian emigration figures for, after the unsuccessful Soviet-arranged putsch in Estonia in December, 1924, emigration doubled for the next three years.[16] Thus, new Estonian immigrants were also more nationalistic about their Estonian ethnicity and through their initiative the annual celebration of the Estonian Independence Day, February 24, became one of the traditional functions of Estonian communities in Canada.[17] But it would be far from the truth to assume that all Estonian immigrants in Canada intended to maintain their ethnicity; many assimilated quickly and completely within Canadian society. A remarkable example is a young Estonian sailor who landed in Montreal in 1924 and turned into a painter-artist, the first Estonian to become a member of the Royal Canadian Academy of Art (1958). He married a French-Canadian girl, assimilated into French-

Canadian society and culture, and also Francicized his name, Oskar Lall, into Oscar Daniel de Lall. He painted portraits of several well-known Canadian politicians, McGill University professors, and other prominent personalities.[18]

On the other hand, among the Estonian immigrants of the 1920's there were those who had left Estonia mainly for economic reasons or because they disagreed with the social or political system in Estonia. Thus, in a sense, the motivations for emigration from Estonia and immigration to Canada were mixed, and certainly not only economic. It also seems that in some cases adventure was the reason. A nineteen-year-old Estonian girl, daughter of a businessman in Estonia, was about to return home from Hamburg after travelling in western Europe. There she met a woman with children who was going to Canada and decided to join her in order to see Canada. Though she later visited Estonia several times, she settled in Canada, married a Canadian minister of Finnish descent, and spent the rest of her life in Montreal.[19] The case is not a typical one, but neither is it unique. In the 1920's there were some who came to Canada only to see the country, yet subsequently settled here.

In Estonian circles the much talked about immigration of Admiral Johan Pitka to Canada is a special case.[20] Rear Admiral Pitka was a national hero in the War of Independence and founder of the Estonian navy. Through his business connections in England and as a Knight of the British Order of St. Michael and St. George (holder of the Grand Cross of the Order) he was in a very special position when he inquired about settlement opportunities from Canadian authorities while touring in Canada. He selected the uninhabited area near Fort Saint James in British Columbia, 320 miles north of Vancouver, for his settlement and immigrated to Canada in 1924 with his family and a few other Estonians, twenty-six persons altogether. Land grants were received and farming and other businesses such as a sawmill and trading post were started.

The reasons Admiral Pitka left Estonia were many and complex. In nature he was ambitious, energetic, and restless. In Estonia he had become disappointed because of his lack of political success. It is not quite clear why he chose such a remote place in Canada, but he himself has referred to his fascination with nature and wilderness, and the northern climate also may have been a consideration. Some sources have suggested that he might have had an ultimate plan to pioneer a new community of Estonians, a "New Estonia" in Canada.

However, the undertaking failed. Perhaps the site chosen for settlement was most to be blamed. The conditions were not favourable either for agriculture or for other lines of business because the area was too remote from commercial centres and lacking in adequate transportation. The approaching economic depression played a destroying role as well. As one historian has pointed out, Pitka had the right ideas but he was at least thirty years too early, before the development of the Canadian North began.[21] According to unconfirmed information the Canadian railroad people had told Pitka that a railroad to Fort Saint James would be built soon. The railroad was built – forty years later.

In 1930 Pitka returned to Estonia where he headed one of Estonia's largest commercial enterprises. Those who had come with him either also returned to Estonia or moved elsewhere in Canada. As a memorial to Admiral Pitka a creek and a promontory of Stuart Lake (Pitka Point) still carry his name and a small lake is named after his daughter Linda. In Estonia much publicity was given to Pitka's emigration and to his return. This publicity must have worked in both ways – first, in the 1920's, it propagated immigration to Canada, but in the 1930's its effect was negative.

IMMIGRATION AFTER THE SECOND WORLD WAR

As already mentioned, the Estonians who immigrated to Canada after the Second World War came from among those refugees who in 1944 had fled from Estonia to Sweden or Germany. More than 9,000 came to Canada from West Germany, about 4,000 from Sweden, and the rest from the other countries to which they had moved in the meantime. The largest group from Germany went to the United States, and the next largest groups moved to Canada and Australia. Only those who were not able to emigrate because of age or sickness, or who were already integrated in the German economy and did not want to emigrate, remained in Germany. The only large group that left Sweden came to Canada; the vastly overwhelming majority of Estonian refugees in Sweden remained there.

By 1960, after all these resettlements, the largest Estonian communities were to be found in the United States (30,000), Sweden (28,000) and Canada (18,500), followed by smaller ones in Australia (7,000), West Germany (6,000), and England (5,000). Before the war there were virtually no Estonians in Sweden, Germany, or England, and there have been no substantial changes in the Estonian communities abroad since 1960.

In Germany the Estonians were among the several million displaced persons who were housed and supported by the United Nations Reconstruction and Rehabilitation Administration (UNRRA). UNRRA's main aim was to repatriate the displaced persons to their home countries, and when most of them had been repatriated UNRRA was disbanded in 1947. It was replaced by another international organization, the International Refugee Organization (IRO), whose task was to resettle the approximately one million refugees who did not want to be repatriated to the Soviet Union or Soviet-dominated eastern Europe.[22] Among this group were the Estonians.

By 1947 the lives of refugees in Germany had become meaningless and intolerable. Since the end of the war they had lived crowded in camps and without gainful employment. Among the mixture of men, women, and children, the adults had a variety of professional skills and experience they had no opportunity of using. The possibility of an outbreak of another war between the U.S.S.R. and the Western powers made Germany even less acceptable for them and they were ready to take any opportunity to be resettled in any other Western country. For most of them the United States was their first choice but since immigration to the United States was delayed and limited, many chose Canada in its place, often with the hope that they could move from Canada to the United States later, which most, however, never did.[23] There were also a few who preferred Canada to the United States, particularly some agriculturalists and farmers, mainly because they expected the social conditions and climate to be more like those of Estonia. But after all, there was hardly any choice; they went to whichever country offered them an opportunity to leave the refugee camps of Germany.

The Estonians in Sweden did not belong to the displaced persons because Sweden was not a member of IRO. Thus they were not included in the IRO resettlement project and could not immigrate to the United States under the U.S. Displaced Persons Act. But in Sweden the Estonian refugees had already been absorbed into the Swedish economy and many had personal savings they could use for immigration to Canada since Canada's immigration regulations required either "independent means" (cash of $2,000) or a sponsor in Canada who could guarantee employment and housing for them. In contrast, the displaced persons in Germany were penniless and had to rely solely upon the sponsor's guarantees. Moreover, the IRO paid the transportation cost for the displaced persons while the Estonians in Sweden had to pay the fare themselves.

Under the IRO project of resettlement, England, Belgium, and Australia were the first countries that accepted the refugees as immigrants. England took single men and women for hospital personnel and for labour in textile factories, coal mines, and on farms. A few thousand Estonians went to England although most of them did not belong to any of those occupational categories. Belgium took coal miners and a few Estonian men, mostly former soldiers, went there. Regulations of immigration to Australia were more liberal than to England and Belgium and again a few thousands, single people as well as families, went to Australia; however, many Estonians considered Australia too far away and waited for opportunities to immigrate to North America.

Soon Canada also began to accept political refugees from Europe as immigrants. In May, 1947, Prime Minister Mackenzie King stated in the House of Commons:

> The government will seek by legislation, regulation and vigorous administration, to ensure the careful selection and permanent settlement of such numbers of immigrants as can be advantageously absorbed into our economy. . . . Among other considerations, it [Canada's policy] should take account of the urgent problem of the resettlement of persons who are displaced and homeless, as an aftermath of the world conflict.[24]

21

But he also pointed out that Canada was under no obligation "to accept any specific number of displaced persons" and added that "the displaced persons admitted to Canada [should be] of a type likely to make good citizens." On this point, Prime Minister King added, "There will, I am sure, be general agreement with the view that the people of Canada do not wish, as a result of mass immigration, to make a fundamental alteration in the character of our population."[25]

This statement was preceded by animated discussion, in government circles as well among the public, about the merits of bringing political refugees to Canada from Europe. Supporters of the plan, mainly the churches and particularly the Canadian Christian Council for Resettlement of Refugees, emphasized the humanitarian motives but also argued it would be to Canada's advantage by enlarging the domestic market and thus enhancing industrial production and economic growth. Opponents were cautious about the capacity of Canada's economy to absorb more immigrants than the small number immediately needed in some occupations, their opinion being dominated by memories of the depression years of the 1930's. In fact, another economic slump was expected to occur after the war. Concern was raised also about the effects that a mass immigration from continental Europe would have upon the British-based Canadian social and cultural structures.[26] Obviously the statement of the Prime Minister took account of these arguments and was aimed at striking a balance between the different views, as was the resultant government policy.

In the summer of 1947 Canadian representatives were sent to Europe to select immigrants from among the refugees, and the first refugee-immigrants began to arrive in Canada during the second half of the year, among them 282 Estonians. But acceptance was narrowly restricted in numbers as well as to the occupations Canada was then short of: lumbermen, farm labourers, construction workers, miners, and women domestics. In addition, only single persons or family heads who were willing to leave their families behind for the time being were accepted. The immigrants had to sign working contracts, usually for one year, with their employers in Canada. The size of the allowable refugee-immigrant group was expanded several times by Orders-in-Council, the upper limit of 5,000 in June, 1947, reaching 40,000 by October, 1948.[27] Already in 1948 about 1,500 Estonians immigrated to Canada from Germany. The occupational categories, however, remained unchanged.

Even though among the Estonian refugees there were almost none who had occupational backgrounds that Canada looked for in refugee-immigrants, they nevertheless applied and were accepted for jobs in Canada that most of them had never held before and for which they were not fitted either by education or experience. Almost without exception their educational and professional skills were far above the demands of these manual jobs. Indeed, many applicants concealed their education and training in order to be acceptable for immigration, and they stressed instead any other experience they might have, for instance, that they had grown up on a farm or had done some manual work in their youth. The reminiscence of one of these Estonian immigrants is worth noting:

> I was born at St. Petersburg in Russia. My parents opted to move to Estonia in the early 1920's when I was a child. We lived in a city [Tartu] where I attended school, including university. Thereafter I was employed by a shipping company in Tallinn. The company's business was international and a knowledge of English was required so that I became fluent in that language too. All I ever had to do with farms was that I spent my summer holidays as a schoolboy on my relations' farms. I never worked on a farm. In Germany I was employed by the American occupation authorities as a store superintendent. When Canada began to take refugees for immigration I applied for farm work in Canada. I was a young man, still in my thirties, and in good health. I wanted to get out of Germany and I wanted to go to Canada. But when I was interviewed by the Canadian immigration officer, a very sympathetic man, he asked me how I could ever expect to be accepted when I had never done any farm work? I didn't have an answer, obviously he was right, he must reject me. I felt myself so foolish – how could I ever have thought that I could be accepted?
>
> My wife, who was with me, was more desperate than I and started to cry. That apparently mellowed the officer. He called his translator, an Estonian girl, and asked her and myself together to go over my curriculum vitae once more. So we did and we inserted my vacations on farms. And so I came to Canada where my first job was harvesting sugar beets near Winnipeg. I had never seen a sugar beet before in my life. My wife, with our three-year-old son, came to Canada a year later when I was already in Kitchener, Ontario. [28]

Though the above shows some peculiar features – good knowledge of English by the applicant, exceptional benevolence by the Canadian immigration officer, and "the tears of a woman" – it was not atypical. In a work team of twenty-two Estonian men in the lumber camp at Longlac two were university graduates and eleven were university students. Later, women were taken on at the same camp as cooks and servants, and in 1948 there were twenty-five single Estonian women at this camp. [29] Among the sixty Estonian men who worked as labourers in 1948 at the hydro construction site in Rolphton, Ontario, were a physician, a senior army officer, a judge, an economist, an architect, a lawyer, and other university graduates who once had had established professional careers. [30] The young women who came as domestic servants, mainly to Ottawa and Montreal, had never done servants' work before, almost all had secondary education, and some had university degrees. [31] The facts varied from case to case, but virtually all the refugee-immigrants had backgrounds quite different from those required by the jobs for which they were hired and which they performed when they came to Canada, whether they worked as farm hands, lumbermen, construction labourers, miners at Kirkland Lake, or labourers at the Algoma Steel Company. Among them were also those who at one time or another had been farmers, and there were people with less education or without any occupational training. Many young men had been soldiers and their education had been interrupted by the war. But most had continued their education in Germany after the war, many had graduated from high school and some continued their studies at university mainly in technical fields, and others learned practical skills. All displaced persons in the camps in Germany, regardless of their previous training or profession, had learned some technical skills, specifically to facilitate their emigration. They had also learned English, although very few had acquired fluency in the language. But all that was irrelevant to their acceptability as immigrants. The question arises why they came to Canada at all and why Canada assumed that, to quote John W. Holmes, "any DPs who would be permitted to come . . . would be selected like good beef cattle with a preference for strong young men who could do manual labour and would not be encumbered by aging relatives."[32] The reason is that they came and were happy to come, because the only other choices would have been either to be repatriated to their home country where persecution or violent death was to be feared, or to stay in Germany where life was meaningless and at that time without much hope for improvement. They had burnt their bridges and the only hope left was to emigrate. They hoped that once in a vast country like Canada, they would find better opportunities sooner or later. And they were not wrong in these expectations. They never thought of remaining lumbermen, unskilled labourers, or domestics.

We should not blame Canada since most other countries did not even offer what Canada did. Immigration to the United States did not get under way until after the passing of the Displaced Persons Act by Congress in 1948, and the demand for "good beef cattle" was greater there than in Canada.[33] Any country would consider its own need first and assign the unsolicited immigrants to jobs its own people would not do. Estonian men who went as coal miners to Belgium realized soon that the work was damaging their health and that they would never have any chance for other kinds of work in Belgium. Almost all of them came to Canada later. And so did many hundreds of Estonians who went first to England, and for the same reasons. Manual work in the new country was not considered the end, it was merely the means to emigrate and to look for other chances that the country of immigration might offer later, and Canada offered more opportunities than most other countries.

There were a few who could find jobs in their former professions if their special qualifications were badly needed in Canada. For instance, three highly qualified Estonian statisticians were brought to Canada and employed as statisticians by the Dominion Bureau of Statistics and other federal government departments. One of them had applied to both the

United States and Canada, and he came to Canada only because the Canadian visa arrived a few days earlier than the U.S. one.[34] But these were the exceptions and they were very few.

In addition, "during the latter part of 1948 and in 1949, Canada was faced with a rather unusual refugee problem in the form of a relatively small but unusual seaborne invasion."[35] The "invasion" embarked in Sweden and almost all the "invaders" were Estonians. They had come to Sweden in tiny and crowded boats in August and September of 1944. Some boats perished in the rough seas of the Baltic and others were captured by either the Soviets or Germans before they reached Sweden, but those boat people who reached Sweden were generously treated by the Swedish government. They were channelled into the Swedish economy and special jobs were even created for the intellectuals. This did not mean that they were employed in their previous occupations, but all were provided with meaningful and gainful jobs. They could integrate into Swedish society very easily after learning Swedish, which most did quickly. Sweden, a country that had not suffered in the war, wisely profited by the variety of skills of the refugees.

But politically the refugees felt insecure. In November, 1945, Sweden had extradited 2,700 German soldiers to the Soviet Union, among them 167 Estonian and Latvian men who had served in the German army. Sweden treated the refugees as Soviet citizens since she had legally recognized the annexation of the Baltic countries by the Soviet Union in 1940. The Swedish government repeatedly announced that Sweden would not object to the repatriation of refugees to the Soviet Union although they were not urged to repatriate. Rumours of a new war in which Sweden would keep friendly relations with the Soviet Union circulated incessantly. Fearing that they might be taken back forcibly to Soviet-occupied Estonia, many Estonians planned to leave Sweden as soon as possible.

Several groups bought boats jointly with their accumulated savings. Captains, experienced seamen, and mechanics were found and forty-six "Viking boats" of various sizes and conditions left Sweden between 1946 and 1949, mostly with Estonians aboard, but with a few Latvians, Lithuanians, and Ukrainians as well.[36] All boats were overcrowded, few were in the best shape for an oceanic voyage, and in most cases it took longer than expected to cross the Atlantic. Typical was an old boat, *Walnut*, with a normal capacity of less than 200 people, which left Sweden in September, 1948, with 355 passengers aboard and arrived safely in Halifax, Nova Scotia, on December 13.[37] Seventeen boats landed in the United States, ten in Canada, six in South Africa, five in Argentina, three in England, one in Brazil. Two perished in the Atlantic and two were lost without trace.[38] The arrival of the first of these boats in Canada took the Canadian authorities by surprise. The passengers asked for permission to stay as they had asked the Swedish authorities a few years earlier and had been accepted as refugees and immigrants. After investigating their background the government admitted them, waiving the current immigration restrictions by special Orders-in-Council in each case. Since in the United States the admission procedure in similar cases was much slower, an additional 466 "Estonian Vikings" came to Canada from the United States, mainly sponsored by the Lutheran Church of Canada.[39] In 1948, 519 arrived in Canada, in 1949, 951, and in 1950, 123, for a total of 1,593 "boat people" from Sweden, of whom about 1,500 were Estonians.[40] Only twelve were denied admission as immigrants.[41]

In 1949 Canada liberalized its immigration policy on refugees from Europe and thus many more Estonians came in the next two years. Instead of being a burden the refugees had demonstrated themselves to be an asset to Canada. More important, the gloomy forecast of the economy changed into an expectation of economic boom. The total number of immigrants was still kept under control but it was continuously revised upwards and restrictions were eased: besides the requirement of good health, only a sponsor in Canada who could guarantee accommodation and work for the immigrant was required. The main problem now became finding a sponsor. As before, the first jobs were manual ones, on farms, in factories and mines, or in construction and service industries. But families could immigrate together and jobs could be changed as soon as better ones were found. Lack of English and unfamiliarity with Canadian social and cultural customs were still problems. However, the more Estonians there were, the more they could assist one another.

The Lutheran Church of Canada sponsored many Estonian immigrants, as did many Estonians who had immigrated to Canada before the war.[42] Eugen Lasn, an entrepreneur in the lumber industry in Port Arthur who came to Canada in the 1920's, gave hundreds of guarantees and so did Villem Kerson, an industrialist in Montreal, and to a lesser extent Jüri Waimel, an engineer in Kitchener who had come to Canada with Admiral Pitka in 1924, and several Estonian farmers in southern Alberta and the Niagara Peninsula. Guarantees were also given by those who themselves had immigrated in 1947 or 1948 to their relatives and friends who were still in Europe and wanted to come to Canada, although the latter guarantors, more often than not, did not actually have either accommodation or employment for those they sponsored. But that was of no concern to either the sponsor or the migrant. Jobs in Canada were easily available, if one was ready to take any job, at least temporarily. Hence, the guarantee often amounted to no more than housing for a few nights and assistance in finding a job. There were cases where the new immigrant never even met his guarantor; instead he contacted a friend who had arrived just a few weeks earlier and had informed him of available jobs.

We should remember that the Estonian refugees were a cohesive community, many knew each other, and all were ready to help one another extensively. It is interesting to note that many Estonians came to Montreal, Toronto, and southern Ontario – Kitchener and Hamilton – even when they had been sponsored somewhere else, because there were many

Estonians in these places who would give advice and assistance. The Lutheran churches in Kitchener put an empty apartment building at the disposal of the new arrivals, rent-free, until they had found jobs and accommodation. Many of those who stayed at this house were not sponsored by the church at all. Some came from overseas, others from other places in Canada, and those who got jobs and accommodation made room for the new arrivals. We shall discuss the extensive migration of the Estonian immigrants in Canada between 1948 and 1952 as an aspect of adjustment in the new country in the next chapter.

It was the publicity created by the arrival of the "Viking boats," the many inquiries by Estonians in Sweden about immigration to Canada, and the urging by the Estonians in Canada that brought pressure upon the Canadian government to consider the immigration of refugees from Sweden also, although they were not displaced persons and thus not included in the IRO resettlement project.[43] In the summer of 1948 Dr. Hugh Keenleyside, then Deputy Minister of Mines and Resources, on a fact-finding tour in Europe visited Stockholm and met with Estonian representatives. Although he was sympathetic, as were many others in Canada, including members of the Senate Committee on Immigration and Labour, the issue turned out to be more complicated than expected.[44] The Swedish government did not want to have any Canadian immigration agencies operating in Sweden because it feared that this might provoke the Soviet government; but Swedish authorities agreed that they would not object if the immigration screening were done without any publicity by the Canadian embassy in Stockholm. Back in Ottawa Mr. Keenleyside presented a memorandum recommending that approval be given to admit up to 5,000 Estonian refugees from Sweden. The cabinet accepted his recommendation in September, 1948. But further delays occurred; Canadian immigration regulations required that each immigrant family have $2,000 on arrival at a Canadian port of entry whereas Sweden prohibited taking from Sweden more than $500 per person. Thus, single persons and families of less than four could not demonstrate their "independent means" and had to find a sponsor in Canada, as did immigrants from Germany. By February, 1949, only fifteen visas had been issued, yet as time went on more and more Estonians emigrated from Sweden. Those who came to Canada after 1949 did so mainly for economic considerations. Though they had already found gainful employment in Sweden and had the opportunity to integrate into Swedish society, they expected their chances to be better in Canada because of the bigger and more immigrant-oriented society. Also, they did not view Canada in isolation but as part of the whole English-speaking North American continent.

Of course we have again to point out that Estonians formed a small group among Canada's post-war immigrants. Of 165,697 refugees who were resettled in Canada by the IRO between 1947 and 1953, only 9,159 or 5.5 per cent were Estonians.[45] The total number of immigrants who

27

came to Canada in the period from 1947 to 1953 was 717,559, of whom Estonians represented less than 1.7 per cent, or one Estonian in every 57 immigrants. The total of Estonian immigration is further dwarfed when it is realized that approximately 1.4 million immigrants came to Canada during both the 1950's and the 1960's, and that more than 260,000 Italians, 150,000 Germans, and 80,000 Portuguese, to mention only the larger ethnic groups of immigrants from continental Europe, came to Canada between 1956 and 1968.[46]

The immigration of Estonians to Canada has its unique pattern, comparable to similar patterns of Latvian and Lithuanian immigration. It was a "one-shot" immigration that took place within a few years. In addition, considering the use of any opportunity to emigrate from Germany and the unauthorized landings of the "Vikings" from Sweden in Canada, it may be said that the earliest of these Estonian immigrants almost forced themselves upon a cautious Canada.

In general, the post-war Estonian immigrants were mostly young people in their twenties or thirties, although there were also older people in their fifties or sixties. Many were single men or women who had been separated from their spouses by the events of war or when leaving Estonia. The families as a rule were small, with one or two children per family. They were mostly well educated: the overwhelming majority had secondary education or vocational training, and many had university degrees. The high educational level of the immigrants was not only due to the high educational standards in pre-war Estonia, but also because the people who left Estonia in 1944 were in general better educated than the average and many had continued their education or training in Germany or Sweden. Many had made their professional careers in Estonia before the war, but there were as many young men and women who had been conscripted into military or civic duties during the war with no chance to start any profession. Perhaps one of the most important features of this immigrant group was that it included an unusual number of educational, social, civic, youth, cultural, and political leaders of Estonia, people who in normal times never would have left their homeland.

Their personal experiences ranged from those of people who had lived in Czarist Russia before the First World War to those of the young people who had reached adulthood during the war. Despite all the social and other differences they felt themselves united as Estonians, particularly as a result of their experience during the war. They hated the Soviets and communism. But though many of them had fought or worked with the Germans, they did not like the Germans any more than the Russians.

The vast majority, throughout the war, had placed their sympathies with the Western Allies and their values of democracy and freedom, the more so since they personally had experienced totalitarian philosophies of both the left and the right.

NOTES

1. Immigration of Estonians to Canada from 1922 to 1965, as reported in Royal Commission on Bilingualism and Biculturalism, Book IV, *The Cultural Contributions of Other Ethnic Groups* (Ottawa, October 23, 1969), pp. 243-5, was as follows:

1922	12	1937	2	1952	934
1923	33	1938	9	1953	451
1924	65	1939	6	1954	290
1925	27	1940	1	1955	186
1926	77	1941	1	1956	162
1927	110	1942	1	1957	221
1928	107	1943	2	1958	122
1929	98	1944	1	1959	88
1930	83	1945	7	1960	134
1931	8	1946	8	1961	52
1932	0	1947	282	1962	51
1933	1	1948	1,903	1963	63
1934	2	1949	2,945	1964	44
1935	3	1950	1,949	1965	59
1936	5	1951	4,573		

2. Since the late 1950's a few Estonians from Estonia – parents, spouses, and children – have been able to join their family members in Canada; from 1958 to 1980 a total of 132 persons have come to Canada, as indicated in the following data, from *Quarterly Immigration Bulletin* (1958-71) and *Quarterly Statistics: Immigration* (1972-80), Department of Citizenship and Immigration (1958-66) and Department of Manpower and Immigration (1957-80).

1958	4	1966	4	1974	25
1959	6	1967	2	1975	2
1960	41	1968	5	1976	7
1961	7	1969	5	1977	6
1962	3	1970	2	1978	2
1963	6	1971	1	1979	1
1964	none	1972	2	1980	none
1965	none	1973	2		

3. For 1961 and 1971, see Appendix, Table 8. For 1981, see Statistics Canada, *1981 Census of Canada, Population, Ethnic Origin* (Ottawa, February, 1984), Cat. 92-911, Table 1. However, the 1981 figure is misleading because, as it states, it is not comparable with the 1961 and 1971 figures: "As 1971 (and 1961) census processing reduced all multiple (ethnic origin) responses to single responses, it is not possible to compare 1971 (and 1961) data to 1981 for single (origin) responses." XII (4).

Data on multiple ethnic origin of Estonians in 1981 have not been available. But since there is no reason to believe that a substantial decrease, or increase, of Estonians took place in the 1970's, a reasonable estimate of Canadians of Estonian ethnic origin in 1981 (including multiple origin data) would be about 19,000.

4. The basic information for the discussion of Estonian immigration to Canada before the First World War and between the two world wars has been retrieved from O. Laaman and R. Piirvee in A. Kurlents *et al.* (eds.), *Eestlased Kanadas* (Estonians in Canada) (Toronto: KEAK [Canadian Estonian History Commission], 1975). pp. 19-62, 63-100.

5. *Ibid.*, p. 57, also p. 644; cf. A. Hint, "Oma saar: Paadelaid" (Our Island 'Paadelaid'), in *Looming* (Tallinn: Perioodika, No. 8, 1976), pp. 1244ff.

6. J. Pennar *et al.*, *The Estonians in America 1627-1975* (Dobbs Ferry: Oceana Publications, 1975). More than 100 Estonians could be found both in New York and in Los Angeles already in the 1890's; in New York the Estonian congregation was founded in 1896, and an Estonian bimonthly was published in 1898.

7. Kurlents *et al.* (eds.), *Eestlased Kanadas*, especially pp. 26, 48.

8. Estimate based on O. Laamann's data. The year 1916 was chosen because the most complete data were available for this year.

9. Gustav Kulp, taped interview in KEAK (Canadian Estonian History Commission) Archives. In 1926 an Estonian writer, wife of the Estonian ambassador in London, England, at the invitation of an American women's organization, made a lecture tour of North America that included Montreal and Toronto. She complained that nobody in Canada knew anything of Estonia. A. Kallas, *Suurlinnade udus ja säras* (In the Fog and Glitter of Big Cities) (Lund: EKK, 1958), p. 246.

10. I.W. Hutchison, *Arctic Nights' Entertainment* (London: Blackie & Sons, 1935); cf. L. Meri, *Virmaliste väraval* (At the Gate of the Northern Lights) (Tallinn: Eesti Raamat, 1974), pp. 264-74, 325-6.

11. The estimate is made by a projection from various available sources and can be in error up to a couple of hundred either way.

12. A. Nigol, *Eesti asundused ja asupaigad Venemaal* (Estonian settlements and locations in Russia) (Tartu: Postimees, 1918); A. Vassar, *Uut maad otsimas* (In Search of the New Land) (Tallinn: Eesti Raamat, 1975); V. Maamägi, *Estonskie posselentsy v SSSR* (Estonian Settlements in the USSR) (Tallinn: Eesti Raamat, 1977).

13. See above, note 1. But it must be noted that these figures of emigrants *from* Estonia may include those who were ethnically not Estonians, and it excludes Estonians who immigrated to Canada from countries other than Estonia.

14. Emigration from Estonia, 1924-31:

1924	1,222	1928	1,293
1925	2,676	1929	1,293
1926	2,426	1930	1,005
1927	2,322	1931	644

From 1932 to 1940 about 300 to 600 emigrated annually. K. Inno and F.

Oinas (eds.), *Eesti Teatemeteos* (Reference Book on Estonia), vol. II (Geislingen/Steige, Germany: ERS & EUKS, 1949), p. 10.

15. Nine Estonians have been verified as having university education: Dr. J. Sillak, Professor E. Aksim, Dr. E. Kuitunen-Eckbaum, E. Lasn, J. Waimel, V. Kerson, Dr. J. Kask, M. Gerhardt-Olley, and E. Silverton. The list is incomplete.

16. See above, note 14.

17. The Estonian Indpendence Day was celebrated in Canada for the first time in Eckville in 1926, and next in Winnipeg in 1928.

18. Colin S. Macdonald (comp.), *Dictionary of Canadian Artists,* vol. II (Ottawa, 1967), p. 174; *The Who's Who in Canada,* vol. IX, 1961-1963, p. 275. Also Oral History Project, taped interview with E. and V. Voitk; H. Höövel in *Vaba Eestlane,* September 20, 25, 1984.

19. Adele Adfeldt-Grunau in Kurlents *et al.* (eds.), *Eestlased Kanadas,* p. 121; and KEAK Archives, doc. no. 24.

20. Kurlents *et al.* (eds.), *Eestlased Kanadas,* pp. 71-8; *Eesti Biograafiline Leksikon* (Estonian Biographical Lexicon) (Tartu, 1936).

21. R. Piirvee in Kurlents *et al.* (eds.), *Eestlased Kanadas,* p. 77.

22. L.W. Holborn, *The I.R.O.: A Specialized Agency of the United Nations* (New York: Oxford University Press, 1956); L.W. Holborn, *Refugee: A Problem of Our Time* (Metuchen, N.J.: The Scarecrow Press, 1975), pp. 24-36; J. Vernant, *The Refugee in the Post-War World* (New Haven: Yale University Press, 1953), pp. 67-9, 542-78; U.S. Department of State, *Foreign Affairs Background: Displaced Persons* (Washington, D.C.: G.P.O., 1948). There were some displaced persons from the Western countries also who refused to be repatriated, but their numbers were very small; the great mass of those who refused repatriation were from eastern Europe.

23. This was definitely confirmed by the Oral History Project interviews of 1976-1979. Less than a dozen later emigrated from Canada to the United States.

24. Quoted from Gerald E. Dirks, *Canada's Refugee Policy: Indifference or Opportunism?* (Montreal: McGill-Queen's University Press, 1977), p. 147.

25. *Ibid.,* p. 148.

26. *Ibid.,* pp. 126ff.

27. Warren E. Kalbach, *The Impact of Immigration on Canada's Population* (Ottawa: Dominion Bureau of Statistics, 1970), p. 20.

28. J.J., Oral History Project, taped interview of September 13, 1979.

29. Kurlents *et al.* (eds.), *Eestlased Kanadas,* p. 109; L. Turbo, "Eesti naine Kanada metsades" (Estonian Women in Canada's Lumber Camp), manuscript, 1966, in KEAK Archives.

30. Kurlents *et al.* (eds.), *Eestlased Kanadas,* pp. 105-16; A. Aasma, "Kanadasse asumine ja Rolphton" (Arrival in Canada and Rolphton), manuscript, in KEAK Archives: J. Tohver, "Lahkumine Saksamaalt ja

asumine Kanadasse'' (Departure from Germany and Arrival in Canada), manuscript, in KEAK Archives. Also, Arvi Kork (pseudonym for A. Tinits), *Tammiraiujad* (The Dam Builders) (Lund: EKK, 1966), a novel in which people and life at the Rolphton Hydro construction site are described by the author, who was a member of one of the work teams; later he became a captain in the Metropolitan Toronto police force.

31. Two of the Estonian domestic servants were medical doctors by profession.

32. John W. Holmes, *The Shaping of Peace: Canada and the Search for World Order 1943-1957*, vol. I (Toronto: University of Toronto Press, 1979), p. 101. The statement of Holmes concerns the acceptance to Canada of 3,000 men selected from 4,500 veterans of General Anders' Second Polish Army in 1946, but Canada's policies in admitting other displaced persons did not change much in the next year or two.

33. Also, relative to its population, Canada, with 123,000, took many more refugees from Europe than the United States, which during the same period until December 31, 1951, took 329,000. Vernant, *The Refugee in the Post-War World*, p. 38.

34. Dr. Elmar Jaska, Oral History Project, taped interview of February, 1976.

35. Kalbach, *The Impact of Immigration*, p. 20.

36. Kurlents *et al.* (eds.), *Eestlased Kanadas*, p. 107.

37. *Ibid.*, p. 106; J. Saarniit in *Meie Elu*, September 21, 1978. Compare Voldemar Veedam*, Sailing to Freedom* (London: Hutchinson, 1961), a diary of an Estonian journalist who was on board one of these boats, which landed at Miami, Florida.

38. Kurlents *et al.* (eds.), *Eestlased Kanadas*, p. 107.

39. *Ibid.*, pp. 107, 193-4; and Oral History Project interviews.

40. *Ibid.*, pp. 106, 107. The exact figures differ from figures in other sources, but the other sources do not count those who landed in the United States and then immigrated to Canada. Cf. Dirks, *Canada's Refugee Policy*, p. 166.

41. Dirks, *Canada's Refugee Policy*, p. 166.

42. The following discussion is based mainly on the Oral History Project interviews, but also on information from Kurlents *et al.* (eds.), *Eestlased Kanadas*.

43. *Ibid.*, pp. 104-5; Edgar V. Saks, ''Märkmeid Kanada eesti koloniist 1947-1950'' (Notes on Estonian Colony in Canada 1947-1950), manuscript, in KEAK Archives; and Oral History Project interviews.

44. Dirks, *Canada's Refugee Policy*, p. 165, on this and other information on emigration from Sweden.

45. *Ibid.*, pp. 272-3.

46. In the late 1950's Canada's immigration policy changed substantially; not only were larger numbers of immigrants from continental Europe allowed, but preference shifted from unskilled manual labour to semi-skilled and skilled occupations. However, that was when Canada's econ-

omy already showed an unprecedented growth. On these almost diametrical changes of policy, see Freda Hawkins, *Canada and Immigration: Public Policy and Public Concern* (Montreal: McGill-Queen's University Press, 1972), pp. 89ff; and Alan G. Green, *Immigration and the Postwar Canadian Economy* (Toronto: Macmillan of Canada, 1976), especially pp. 34ff.

THREE

Adjustment to Canada

IMMIGRANTS BEFORE THE SECOND WORLD WAR

Although the Estonian immigrants before the First World War had very little in common with one another they tended to come from small rural communities. However, they were not typical of the destitute peasants or members of the landless proletariat who emigrated en masse from their home countries because of unbearable economic conditions, as was the case with the Irish, the Ukrainians, the Poles, and other immigrants from Europe. In fact, many of the Estonians who arrived in Canada did not come directly from Estonia. In any case those who did emigrate directly from Estonia formed not a mass exodus to the New World but rather the fringe of those who emigrated east to the rich farmlands and growing cities of Russia.

Because immigration to such a faraway, little known, and socially and culturally different country as Canada took exceptional initiative and courage, those who came to Canada were, almost without exception, people of enterprising spirit, and more often than not, of wider than usual experience and know-how.[1] Their immediate aim was the personal economic satisfaction that Canada appeared to offer, but they did not seem to suffer from illusions of easy riches. They were people used to hard work and limited rewards who expected the hard work in this country to bring greater rewards. They came to Canada with meagre means and had to start their careers at the very bottom. Some of the earliest Estonian settlers cleared bush and established homesteads while others obtained neglected farms or those on poor land. Nevertheless, step by step they moved on to better lands and larger farms. As time went on, in the 1920's there were already some quite wealthy Estonian farmers in Alberta and elsewhere in Canada.[2] Some Estonian farmers also supplemented their income by seasonal work and subsequently many moved on to various skilled or semi-skilled jobs elsewhere and left their farms altogether. Others started in unskilled work in the lumber, construction, or

34

mining industries, even if they possessed some previous skills or training. Gradually, they also invariably moved on to more demanding semi-skilled work and some established themselves as independent tradesmen after accumulating the needed capital for equipment and tools. All in all, the early Estonian settlers were very mobile people who frequently changed their living places and jobs and occupations.

This mobility was not unique to the Estonian immigrants of the time, for North American society as a whole was marked by a high degree of mobility as a result of both the westward movement and massive waves of immigration. The Estonians simply adapted themselves to the environment of their new country, with a considerable degree of success. Looking back, most of them express satisfaction with their resettlement, and they always attribute their success to hard work. There are no references to any "new-found paradise."[3] The general characteristics of this successful economic adjustment process are personal initiative, occupational adaptation, capital accumulation, acquisition of new knowledge, and a trend toward urbanization. Again, it must be emphasized that these factors were not unique to the Estonians but marked the successful immigrant in all of North American society at the time.

Those who came to Alberta and established Estonian farming settlements enjoyed several advantages over Estonians who simply disappeared among the many other immigrants elsewhere. For example, they were able to communicate with each other in their mother tongue and carry on traditional social intercourse, which left them free to pursue economic opportunities without the usual language and social pressures. Surrounded by non-Estonians, they formed communities of self-help and co-operated in finding jobs and in jointly improving their farming techniques. These Estonian communities established some of the earliest economic co-operative enterprises in Canada and provided mutual security in cases of need in the form of mutual assurance societies. In addition, some Estonians established family-owned local enterprises such as saw and flour mills and hydroelectric power stations.[4]

None of these Alberta Estonian communities, however, was organized with the objective of preserving ethnicity; instead, ethnicity was a means of providing for economic adaptation to the New World. In fact, to some extent these communities were actively encouraging their own demise. For example, children were urged to attend school and learn English so that they could prepare themselves for skilled jobs requiring educational preparation. The result was that despite a vigorous ethnocultural life in these communities as late as the 1930's, in the 1940's they were already disintegrating as the younger people left the settlements.

During the 1920's and the 1930's conscious efforts were made to maintain ethnic traditions, celebrate ethnic holidays, and promote the reading of books and periodicals in Estonian. But these efforts were neither sufficient nor in time: the young people were moving to the cities, leaving behind only the old and those few who could make local careers, such as some exceptionally successful farmers and local small entrepreneurs. It is interesting to note that those who remained on the farms in the Alberta Estonian settlements in the 1950's deplored the demise of their ethnic communities, yet they were inordinately proud of the careers their off-spring had made in the cities. Some of the latter could still speak Estonian but many had no interest in their ethnic background.[5]

The Estonian immigrants outside the Alberta settlements were widely scattered across Canada, mostly in urban industrial areas. They had almost no contact with other Estonians and relied mainly on other recent immigrants for their social activities, since they had many common interests and shared difficulties and were thus able to relate to each other better than to the host population. Moreover, they could communicate more easily with other new immigrants than with English-speaking Canadians because most of the Estonians, as well as many European immigrants, could speak Russian or German besides their mother tongue. The result was a rapid and complete cultural assimilation of the Estonians into the larger northern and eastern European immigrant community. If any particular pattern can be discerned, it seems that Estonians mixed most easily with the Finns. Certainly it was not only because of the geographic similarities of their northern European home countries, but because they felt closer to each other ethnically, linguistically, and culturally.[6]

It was simply not possible for the early Estonian first-generation immigrants to establish social and cultural contacts with English-speaking Canadians, or immigrants from the British Isles, because of the profoundly different cultural and social patterns and attitudes of the Estonians and the Anglo-Saxon Canadians. Naturally, language formed the most important barrier. Another barrier was that English-speaking Canadians held the better, and especially the white-collar, jobs. To break into these circles gradually became the aim of the second- and third-generation Estonians.

The Estonians who immigrated to Canada during the interwar years were few in number and scattered across Canada but were found mainly in the cities. There were proportionately more among them with better education and vocational training than among the earlier Estonian immigrants, but like the latter, they, too, had to start their careers in Canada mostly as labourers or semi-skilled workers.[7] But they, too, provided a number of entrepreneurs.[8] And, as in the case of the earlier immigrants, their social contacts were mainly with the other continental European immigrants, although more intermarriage took place with Canadians of British descent. Nevertheless, the better jobs and those requiring more education were felt to be the preserve of Canadians of British descent.

Although social and cultural assimilation was rapid there were also a number of conscientious efforts to preserve Estonian culture in Canada, especially by establishing the first Estonian associations in the Canadian cities of Winnipeg, Montreal, and Toronto, in 1929, 1933, and 1939, respectively. Their main functions were social and cultural, but the objective of seeking contacts with other Estonians was also socio-economic, in order to learn how other Estonians were doing and to exchange information. It should also be pointed out that these Estonian associations were established in economically difficult times. However, the depression of the 1930's did not hit very hard those Estonians who had immigrated earlier and who had already firmly settled in their occupations, but some of those who had recently arrived encountered hard times. One of the latter relates in an article in an Estonian periodical how he travelled coast-to-coast together with many other unemployed Canadians looking for any job – and in vain. [9]

Ethnic awareness was primarily created by the fact that Estonia had become an independent state and the Estonians who immigrated during the 1920's had personal experiences of independent Estonia, including participation in the War of Independence (1918-1920) and in public life. [10] Moreover, the Estonians who settled in Canada during the interwar years visited Estonia more frequently than in the case of earlier immigrants. Some Estonian men even went to Estonia to find a wife to bring back to Canada. More information became available about Estonia and also about the Estonians in the United States with the increase in communications, and thus Estonian-language newspapers published either in Estonia or in New York became relatively easily available, as did Estonian books. [11] Large numbers of periodicals and books published in the 1920's and the 1930's were subscribed to and collected by the Estonian association in Alberta and elsewhere, and substantial collections have survived the settlements and associations themselves. In the 1930's it was the official policy of the Estonian government to promote awareness among Estonians abroad of similar Estonian communities in other countries and of current events in Estonia.

On one occasion, during the 1938 national song festival in Tallinn, the capital of Estonia, a group of expatriate Estonians from the United States, Canada, and elsewhere was officially received by the president of the republic and extensively interviewed by the media. [12] This, of course, had an important psychological effect on the Estonians abroad.

Because of extensive diversity, rapid occupational mobility, and their geographic dispersion, it would be an arduous task to try to find the typical occupations of Estonians in Canada before the Second World War. Nevertheless, a listing of known occupations shows a wide variety of economic activity. Thus, in addition to the farmers (in Alberta, the other Prairie Provinces, British Columbia, southern Quebec, western Ontario, and the Niagara Peninsula), there were lumber and construction workers (in northern Ontario, Alberta, and British Columbia), tradesmen of various kinds (carpenters, locksmiths, surveyors, technicians, tool makers, etc.), entrepreneurs (sawmill owners, contractors in the lumber and construction industries in Alberta, British Columbia, and northern Ontario), office workers and domestic servants in the cities, fishermen on the west coast and in the Maritimes, and miners in northern Ontario. The absence of storekeepers and restaurateurs, enterprises that have always been profitable and attractive, is notable. The reason, it may be speculated, is that Estonian immigrants were more conditioned to working with their hands and with things rather than dealing with people. Insufficient knowledge of English and a lack of investment capital certainly also help to explain the absence of Estonians in these economic categories.

Hence the socio-economic profile of Estonians in Canada, including the second generation, before the Second World War shows a range from the upper-lower to the upper-middle class: the lower level consisting of semi-skilled and skilled workers in lumbering, construction, and mining and the upper level including a few entrepreneurs, professionals, and some comparatively wealthy and enterprising farmers.

THE REFUGEES OF THE SECOND WORLD WAR

The story of adaptation of the post-war Estonian immigrant to his new home of Canada may seem perplexing, and even bizarre, especially to readers who have never been forced to flee the society they grew up in and cherished. It should be remembered that these Estonian immigrants left their home country as a result of fear and force and not because they wanted to leave. Due to the foreign forces of which they became victims they had lost all they had: material possessions, social and professional standing, and many close friends and relatives, often including parents, spouses, sons, and daughters. Moreover, families, relatives, and friends had been not only separated, but most had not heard of each other since their separation during the war. In the light of strong attachment to their home country and to the people there, it is understandable why they could not even contemplate making any other country their permanent home. Certainly, they preferred Canada to staying in Sweden or Germany, but even this was not from voluntary choice. Although in Sweden economic conditions were acceptable, political uncertainties forced many to emigrate; in Germany, on the other hand, the economic situation was unacceptable, the camps were to be liquidated, and resettlement – preferably across the Atlantic to the safest place politically – was a necessity.

Professor G.E. Dirks has aptly differentiated the predicament of the refugee from that of the migrant: ". . . the refugee flees *involuntarily* because he feels *compelled* to do so while the economic migrant *voluntarily seeks greater personal satisfaction*, usually based on improved material well-being."[13] This political refugee was not so much immigrating as still fleeing when he came to Canada. Indeed, there is abundant evidence to demonstrate that the majority of Estonian refugee-immigrants in the late 1940's and early 1950's hoped sooner or later to return to Estonia, after settlement of the Big-Power struggle and the freeing of Estonia.[14] Hence, they refused to call themselves immigrants, but rather refugees or exiles, and continued doing so even after they had established their personal lives in this country. This is a crucial point to be remembered when we probe into the psychological aspects of their adjustment in Canada.

From today's vantage point this hope to return to Estonia seems illusory and even ridiculous. Certainly it was a self-delusion, but nevertheless, it was widely shared by Estonian and other post-war refugees. And, though it was illusory, it did not seem so far-fetched at the time: the Cold War was approaching its peak and anticipations of a "hot war" were not uniquely Estonian. In any case, the aftermath of the Second World War had not yet stabilized and a return to Estonia seemed not entirely impossible. It is questionable how much of this was firm conviction and how much merely wishful thinking, but it had strong repercussions on the behavioural and organizational patterns of the Estonian ethnic group. Consequently, it was not until the late 1950's and the early 1960's that these hopes were finally shaken, though not yet fully abandoned. The Hungarian revolution of 1956, which the West failed to support, may perhaps be described as the watershed.[15] However, the realization of the futility of these hopes came gradually and without any public debate or public statement reversing the previous stand. And, even when the hope of return to Estonia faded, the hope that Estonia once again would be freed of Soviet domination remained, and is still solemnly reaffirmed at most Estonian formal gatherings today. Viewed from this perspective the adaptation of the post-war Estonian immigrant in Canada was a dual process: on the one hand, the typical immigrant's adjustment to the cultural, social, and economic environment of his chosen host country; and on the other, an adjustment to the changing attitudes and beliefs among the refugees themselves, not as much a deliberate process as one reluctantly succumbing to fate.

The four years between 1949 and 1953 saw widespread migration of Estonian immigrants within Canada as they changed jobs and moved from their initial places of employment to urban industrial centres. Thus, all who came to Canada in the late 1940's from Germany as contract labour for farms, lumber camps, or hydro construction sites left their jobs once the contract year was up and moved on to cities such as Toronto, Montreal, Hamilton, and Vancouver. Many Estonians who originally arrived in the Maritimes or the Prairie Provinces in the first years of the 1950's also moved on to Toronto or other southern Ontario centres. The bulk of those who came to Canada from Sweden or later from Germany or England had already immigrated directly to Montreal or Toronto.

Thus, during these migratory years Estonian communities formed in urban industrial centres in Canada, the largest, in Toronto, containing almost half of all Estonians in Canada, between 9,000 and 10,000. Smaller Estonian communities formed in Montreal (about 3,000) and

Vancouver (about 1,500), followed by Hamilton, Ottawa, Sault Ste. Marie, Thunder Bay, Kitchener, and other cities. While it is easy to see the attraction of the cities with their employment opportunities and job variety, it must also be noted that the larger Estonian communities had equal power of attraction. Information about jobs and living conditions in these places was obtained from the Estonians who had already settled there, and more often than not the newcomers were invited by Estonian residents and were provided temporary accommodation and assistance in finding jobs. Moreover, the ethnic community offered mutual advice and assistance in adjusting to the new Canadian environment, while providing an emotional framework with stable cultural referents.

Given these attitudes it is understandable that the emphasis among Estonians was on remaining distinguishably Estonian, which meant primarily the preservation of the Estonian language and Estonian culture. In addition to maintaining one's own participation in Estonian cultural matters, remaining Estonian also meant socializing the next generation to Estonian language and culture. This was the root from which the elaborate ethnic organizational structure and many-faceted cultural activities of Estonians in Canada emerged during the 1950's. However, the "explosion" of organizations and activities in Canada originated from the dynamics that had already been generated among the Estonians before they immigrated to Canada.

In Germany, in the refugee camps, promotion of ethnic culture among refugees was not only an activity to pass the time but for many became a way of life, for language, post-war confusion, and enforced inactivity produced ethnic enclaves in the multinational refugee camps. The organization of the camps assisted in establishing the enclaves, in that refugees lived together on a nationality basis. In the Estonian camp at Geislingen, Bavaria, for instance, there were more than 4,000 Estonians who organized Estonian theatre, opera, choirs and orchestras, various civic associations and clubs, and self-government. The camps in Lübeck near Hamburg at one time contained more than 4,000 Estonians. Estonian schools, including high schools, for the children of the refugees were the first organizations to be established in these camps, run by the professional teachers among the refugees. Although the camp atmosphere was not conducive to creative work, there was ample time for social and cultural activities, such as scouting, folk dancing, choir singing, theatre, athletics, and study groups, and there were large numbers of professional people to organize all these activities.

In Sweden the Estonian refugees quickly formed a large cultural community of more than 20,000 in Stockholm and naturally established theatre groups, concert series, and even a certain type of limited cultural self-government. Moreover, the Swedish governmental and administrative structures assisted the establishment of full-time publicly supported Estonian-language elementary schools in Stockholm and other bigger cities and a high school in the town of Sigtuna near Stockholm.

Among Estonians during the early decades after the war there was a strong feeling that while the Soviets occupied Estonia and suppressed Estonian cultural activities, only the Estonians abroad had the freedom, and therefore the obligation, to carry on fostering the development of Estonian culture. Consequently, wherever Estonians went, whether to the United States, Australia, Canada, or elsewhere, they formed Estonian associations and promptly established ethnic cultural activities as soon as an adequate number of Estonians arrived. Eventually Toronto emerged as the Estonian cultural centre in this country.

The determination to remain Estonian had a messianic element to it. The way of life, value systems, and standards specifically of pre-war Estonia were idealized and became the measurement of the way of life, values, and standards of the refugee immigrants everywhere. Such ethnocentrism could only sharpen the cultural shock that anyone immigrating to a different culture experiences. And so the Estonian immigrants to Canada expressed their criticism of Canadian society in no uncertain terms. For many Estonians who landed in Halifax and took the train to their destination in northern Ontario or the Prairies the first impression of Canada was negative. To them Canada was a vast but undeveloped country of sparsely inhabited countryside with unkempt farms without orchards, dirty railway stations, sloppily dressed people, and so on. Of the Canadian cities, only Montreal was found to be "pretty European." The initial negative impression was often reinforced by the primitive living conditions of the interim immigrant camps (Oshawa, for example) or at the lumbering and mining towns where they found their first jobs. Although these negative impressions became overlaid with positive images as time did its work, the image of the "primitiveness" of Canada continued to linger for a long time. It should be noted that it was not only the people of the theatre, professional musicians, youth leaders, and former social workers – the "cultural elite" – who found much to criticize, but even engineers, architects, and accountants continued to find many professional shortcomings in Canada. At the level of popular culture the professional sports of football and baseball were abhorred and the lack of facilities for amateur sports was strongly criticized. What was called "American materialism," the measuring of everything in dollar terms, was unacceptable; and social etiquette was found to be either clumsy or artificially refined and self-consciously snobbish. A major complaint was that Canadians were interested in a very limited range of subjects on which they could converse: professional sports, neighbourhood gossip, cars, and the economic aspects of life. The limitation was especially noticeable because the main predilection of the Estonians themselves was to discuss world and European politics and their own plight as political refugees, matters that Canadians either were not interested in or were uninformed and naive about. Therefore, social relationships were slow in developing with native Canadians and relationships developed more easily with other recent immigrants from Europe. This was the case especially with the older generation, who could also use a language besides English – German or Russian – as the language of conversation. And naturally the foods habitually eaten by Canadians were different and whole rye bread especially was missed.

In contrast to their habits, Canadians themselves were found, almost without exception, to be very friendly and always ready to help. Nor were there any complaints of discrimination against Estonians, whether in living accommodation, in the neighbourhood, or at work. Of course, the odd incident of jealousy was noted when an Estonian immigrant passed a Canadian old-timer on the occupational ladder, but this was the exception.[16] Also, some complaints were made by women who immigrated as domestics, who thought that they were overworked, but it also must be noted that none of them had worked as domestics before. It was also the impression of many Estonian immigrants during their early years in this country that they were not fairly paid for the work that they did, but this was usually explained away as a result of one's own shortcomings, such as inadequate knowledge of English or lack of professional experience and/or licences required by Canadian professional bodies. We must also remember that most of them started in their new professions first in Canada. There are no incidents recorded where Estonians felt that old-time Canadians were given job preference over Estonian immigrants.

The cultural differences, whether real or imaginary, reinforced Estonian ethnocentrism, especially among those to whom the workplace could not afford full satisfaction. Nearly all adult professional immigrants had to start with non-professional jobs first, which established at the very beginning of Canadian work experience a barrier to personal identification with co-workers. As a result, in many cases Estonian immigrants developed a pattern whereby they lived one life at the workplace in English, conforming to Canadian social customs, and another in their leisure time in their own Estonian society and organizations. Such dualism was especially noticeable in Toronto and other cities with substantial Estonian communities. However, the phenomenon was neither a deliberate action nor a well-defined and uniform experience among Estonian immigrants. Rather, it was the inevitable result of active members of the Estonian social, political, and economic elites abruptly being cut short in mid-career. Moreover, although many post-war Estonian immigrants led dual lives during the 1950's and even later, the dualism was one of degree and was dependent on a number of factors. The older the immigrant and the less proficient in English that he was, the more he separated his "Canadian" economic life at work from his social, cultural, "Estonian" life after work and on weekends. Other factors that played a role in the degree of commitment to, and importance of, the Estonian cultural and social life were profession, special interests, temperament, and, of course, whether or not one lived in a place where there was an Estonian community.

Dualism, however, did not lead to isolationism. A survey by the Canadian Estonian History Commission in 1965, for example, showed that about half of those surveyed had friends among both Estonians and non-Estonians, and about a third participated regularly in both Estonian and non-Estonian community organizations; a majority reported that they habitually read both Estonian and non-Estonian books, magazines, and newspapers, and one-quarter replied that they had more non-Estonian than Estonian books in their libraries.[17] Ninety per cent of those who answered the questionnaire were Canadian citizens. Although the survey did not specifically address the question, there are good reasons to believe that the vast majority of the Estonian immigrants, already during their initial years in Canada, regularly read English-language Canadian and American newspapers, magazines, and books. It also must be noted that Estonians, though they preferred to live in certain areas of the cities – the Eglinton-Yonge area, Humber Valley, and later Don Mills in Toronto – lived scattered among the non-Estonians and no Estonian ghettos developed.

Although the phenomenon of dualism was largely psychological, the sociological impact was very important, since the time and energy expended by the most committed "dualists" in building the Estonian organizations in Canada are incalculable. Nevertheless, the phenomenon was one that permitted those generally over age forty-five who had lost their social and professional status as a result of the war to preserve the image of this in the Estonian communities in Canada. Their heavy participation in the Estonian communities also acted as a counterweight to the cultural shock of moving to a culture that in many ways was diametrically opposed to their own. Hence, all those who had socially and professionally performed the functions of leading the building of the Estonian state and nurturing its culture, such as former cabinet ministers, county governors, members of parliament, civil servants, teachers, and lawyers, could overcome the cultural shock and rediscover the meaningfulness of life in immersing themselves in the activity of continuing to build the Estonian community abroad along Estonian cultural lines.[18] To many this provided a safety valve, for without it many undoubtedly would have suffered nervous breakdowns. As one older prominent Estonian activist, whose professional career in Estonia had been replaced by routine factory work in Canada, put it: "What prevented the boring routine of my work from driving me crazy was the energy I expended mentally in calculating the meaningful and useful work that I could do for the Estonian community after my boring day of routine."[19] Thus, both status and mental balance were preserved by dualism: for example, a former member of parliament in Estonia, now a maintenance man, was still treated as a member of parliament in the Estonian community and could humorously refer to himself as a "broom engineer"; similarly, a former lawyer was still treated as a lawyer, a former teacher could continue to teach in the Estonian supplementary school, and so on.

Dualism was also practised by those slightly younger immigrants who, professionally, had landed on their feet in Canadian society. Though less committed to a dualist life and more concerned with their newly re-established, or initiated careers, the engineers, economists, construction company owners, and industrialists found a great psycho-cultural outlet in performing voluntary professional services and acting as liaison with Canadian society for the Estonian community.

Paradoxical though it may seem the strong ethnocentrism in the Estonian community also led to a drive for economic and professional success in Canadian society. Thus, the Estonian community created the myth, and operated on the assumption, that an Estonian was successful in Canadian society mainly because he was an Estonian. The Estonian community demanded that the children of Estonians remain Estonian, but they must be outstanding in the Canadian schools simply because they were Estonian. Community awards, distinctions, and activities that Estonians were engaged in in Canadian society were routinely and lavishly reported in the Estonian press.

And, although "catching up with the Joneses" in its standard materialistic sense was openly sneered at, catching up with other Estonians in the materialistic sense became normal, and catching up with other Canadians in status became almost a moral imperative. It was the odd Estonian indeed who did not aspire to career advancement, through upgrading courses or new professions, or, at the very least, outstanding performance at the workplace. In addition to all this, all Estonian immigrants – including those who because of age and language difficulties did not enter the race for career improvement – exhibited parsimony and thrift in their economic lifestyles in order to buy houses, cars, and summer cottages, or even businesses. Indeed, it was the less-educated Estonian immigrants from the coastal population, who in Estonia had been simple fishermen-subsistence farmers (living in conditions akin to those of the Newfoundland outports), who had the most rapid economic success in Canada. On coming here, for example, they kept their family budget to a minimum with the whole family working, often at several jobs, including the children, who sold newspapers or ran errands, and put all proceeds into the family chest. Soon the family was able to buy a house with several apartments, with the help of a loan from the Estonian Credit Union. All apartments were rented out and the family lived in the basement until a second apartment house was bought, when the family moved into the best apartment. Inevitably, the children were sent to university and acquired a profession.[20]

The 1965 survey by the Estonian History Commission shows that by then the Estonians in Canada had surpassed the average economic level in Canada, partly by parsimony, but mostly by advancement in professions and occupations.[21] Two sets of factors are responsible for the adjustment that led to this economic success, the one endogenous to the Estonian ethnic group, and the other exogenous and environmental.

Among the former, the most important was the relatively large number of adult Estonian immigrants who, before coming to Canada, had completed or enrolled at institutions of higher learning in Estonia and abroad since 1930. These people, in contrast to those who had completed higher education before 1930, were both young enough and had a learning orientation that permitted them to learn the language of the country, to upgrade professional qualifications, or to learn new professions. Second, a large number of this group had already learned new skills or occupations during their initial refugee years in Sweden or Germany; hence, adaptation to Canadian conditions was but a continuation of the process. Third, the immigrant group as a whole was relatively youthful, by and large under age forty-five, and thus still mentally oriented to growth and development rather than maintenance of status. Fourth, the Estonians' economic success in Canada was assisted to no mean degree by the fostering of the Estonian ethnic culture of collective mutual support by the elaborate organizational structure established mainly by the older Estonian immigrant leaders. Hence, the co-operative culture so deeply rooted in Estonia (as it is in the other Nordic countries, but particularly in Finland today) encouraged the exchange of information, the establishment of joint enterprises in the fields of construction, co-operative housing, and manufacturing businesses, but most importantly in the establishment of the Estonian Credit Union, the financial powerhouse of the Estonian community in Toronto, providing loans for both real estate purchases and commercial investments.[22]

Four principal environmental factors assisted the Estonian immigrants to adjust rapidly to Canadian economic conditions. First was the growth of the Canadian economy during the 1950's, which led to an extensive construction boom in Toronto, London, Vancouver, and Sault Ste. Marie, in each of which Estonian enterprises flourished. Estonians were also quick to take advantage of manufacturing opportunities, particularly in plastics and textile industries. Those without entrepreneurial skills but with organizational abilities found work plentiful in managerial, clerical, and research facilities. Many former civil servants and physical education teachers took advantage of the initial take-off of recreational and amateur sporting activities during the 1950's and found employment with the YMCA-YWCA or city recreational staffs and schools. Also, the rapid post-war urbanization of Canada permitted some Estonian agronomists to establish specialist truck-farming enterprises and nursery businesses to serve the expanding numbers of suburban amateur gardeners. The second most important environmental factor in assisting Estonian economic adjustment was the huge influx of immigrants from Europe during the 1950's. Because the Estonians, along with Latvian and other refugees, came here first, they were able to establish consumer, particularly food-oriented, businesses serving the new European consumption patterns. Hence, specialist bakeries, meat products firms, food retail stores, and other retail businesses did very well in producing wealth

45

for the Estonian community. Because many Estonians spoke German and/or Russian, the retail businesses, and some professionals, were able to increase their clientele among newcomers greatly beyond the small Estonian community. The third environmental factor was the drain of professionals from Canada to the United States during the 1950's. Hence, there were many openings for engineers, physicians, chemists, librarians, and professors at Canadian universities, and Estonians were not slow to take advantage of these. This was assisted particularly by the fourth factor, the facilities in Canada for upgrading professional qualifications by part-time study. Large numbers of Estonians with European professional qualifications took advantage of these courses and were able quickly to replace those Canadian professionals who moved to the United States.

Because of the variety of experiences of professional and occupational adjustment in Canada of the immigrant group during the 1950's and early 1960's, a brief review of different categories will give a better understanding of the adjustment processes. These may be divided into four: (1) those having professions not transferable to Canadian society; (2) those with professions that after licensing could be transferred to Canadian requirements; (3) those with apparently easily transferable occupations; and (4) those without professions or occupational skills.

The first group included judges, lawyers, school teachers, journalists, civil servants, policemen, army officers, writers, actors, musicians, and most businessmen. Most of these adjusted to economic demands in Canada by getting clerical jobs or by becoming skilled workers (masons, carpenters, house painters) or lab technicians (school teachers especially found employment in this field). Former lawyers tended to become interpreters, tax experts, title searchers, real estate agents, insurance agents, or insurance company employees in various capacities. A large number of those whose professions were not transferable to Canada also ended up in the various kinds of accounting – from bookkeeping to chartered accountancy. Many former professionals ended up in technical fields, whether through ingenuity in adaptation, accident, or deliberate relearning, because of the economic-technological demands of the boom times of the 1950's.

Three examples will suffice to demonstrate the variety of successful adjustments in this group.[23] An Estonian journalist in his early forties, who had been an amateur gardener back home and had fled to Sweden after the war, sent an ad to a Toronto newspaper from Sweden offering himself as a gardener. He was hired, sight unseen, came to Canada, and worked as a gardener in southern Ontario for a year, then moved to Toronto as an office worker, became an accountant, and retired as secretary-treasurer of a mid-sized Canadian firm in Toronto. A former director (department head) of the (State) Bank of Estonia who could not get a job in banking because he was over forty-five years of age and thus considered too old to start a banking career in Canada (although his wife got a clerical job in a bank) became a bookkeeper. However, in the Estonian society he was one of the founders of the Estonian Credit Union in Toronto and became its president at the age of seventy-five! Finally, a still young lecturer in law in Estonia came to Canada as a lumberjack from Germany, moved to Toronto within a year, became a welder, attended Osgoode Hall simultaneously, passed his bar exams, and built up a large clientele of immigrants with his knowledge of several languages.[24] Needless to say, however, a large number of this group, particularly the older people who did not acquire English or learn new skills, ended up permanently in maintenance or other unskilled work.

The second group, those whose professions could be transferred to Canadian society, usually after licensing exams or other upgrading, included medicine, engineering, architecture, agronomy, dentistry, pharmacology, and nursing. Most of these had to upgrade their professional qualifications by courses at universities and/or pass licensing exams. Certain teachers in subjects such as physics, mathematics, and music also found jobs without much upgrading, as did some businessmen who had continued their international business contacts throughout the war years. Also, sea captains and merchant officers found jobs in Canada after passing their exams and receiving their licences. It should be pointed out that, by and large, this group was composed largely of people under forty-five who already had good knowledge of English or were able to acquire it rapidly, and who were "learning-oriented." Older professionals, even in this group, who would have been able to pass the licensing examinations with little difficulty, such as engineers, but who did not have an ability to learn English rapidly ended up as draftsmen and lab technicians.

The third group, those whose occupations were more easily transferable, such as electricians, mechanics and other tradesmen, and women as office workers, could resume their old occupations usually without much difficulty. But among this group, of those whose occupations at first glance also appeared to be fully transferable, such as farmers and fishermen, many did not continue their former occupations. They landed mainly in construction work or in factories because they lacked the initial capital to purchase their own farms or fishing equipment while industrial jobs were easily available. However, some former farmers later returned to the land after they had accumulated sufficient capital to purchase their own farms. Incidentally, a few former teachers, seamen, and some lifelong urbanites also purchased farms and became farmers, but many years later.

The fourth group, mainly the younger people who did not have any profession, consisted of those just over or under eighteen. At least half of the over-eighteen age group ended up at various vocational schools (such as Ryerson Polytechnical Institute) or universities and rapidly found positions in Canadian professions and technical occupations during the boom times of the 1950's. Of those who came to Canada under the age of eighteen, most went on to university during the 1950's, with the majority ending up in technical fields. The number of those who entered the social sciences, humanities, or law during the 1950's can be counted on the fingers of two hands. The reason for the popularity of technical education was mainly because at the time there was a great economic demand for personnel with higher technical skills, but the disappointing experience of the older generation, educated in the social sciences and humanities, who could not continue their former professions in Canada, also played an important role in the younger generation's choice of profession.

NOTES

1. For instance, Fritz Kinna, who had learned engineering in Norway before he came to Canada, built a hydro station in Eckville, Alberta. There were other Estonians who had new ideas and past experience that they tried to implement in Canada, especially in Canadian agriculture.

2. For example, Gustav Erdman, an exceptionally wealthy wheat farmer and riding-horse breeder in Barons, Alberta. Another wealthy Estonian farmer, by name of Sarapuu, had been reported near Winnipeg. Kurlents *et al.* (eds.), *Eestlased Kanadas,* pp. 48-50, 58. Also, *Wheat Heart of the West: A History of Barons and District* (Barons, Alberta: Barons History Committee, 1972), pp. 236-9, 244-5.

3. The reference here is to G. Leibhardt, *Little Paradise: Geschichte und Leben der Deutschkanadier in der County Waterloo, Ontario* (Kitchener, Ontario: Allprint Company Ltd., n.d.), pp. 43ff.

4. For instance, Karl, Oskar, and August Moro, a father and his two sons, owned mills and hydro stations in Eckville and Peace River, Alberta.

5. Information from Kurlents *et al.* (eds.), *Eestlased Kanadas;* taped and written reports in the KEAK Archives; and author's conversations with Helene Johani and Robert Kreem, who, as representatives of the Estonian Federation in Canada, visited and interviewed the Alberta Estonians several times in the early 1960's.

6. The immigration pattern of the Finns was different from that of Estonians. Their earlier pattern was similar to the Swedish one, with the poor, landless rural dwellers immigrating to North America in search of free farmland; in the early 1920's many Finns immigrated to Canada for political reasons. These were primarily members of the rural and urban proletariat or the "Reds," the losing side in the Finnish Civil War; they concentrated in the Sudbury and Thunder Bay areas.

7. Dr. J. Sillak, who as a missionary pastor served small Estonian, Latvian, and German communities both in the United States and Canada, and Professor Eduard F. Aksim, who in 1924 came from Estonia to teach at Waterloo Lutheran Seminary in Ontario, were exceptions. Kurlents *et al.* (eds.), *Eestlased Kanadas*, pp. 241-2; and author's interview with Mrs. Aksim in Waterloo, Ontario, 1971. Pastor Aksim had previously worked

in Canada from 1900 to 1906 as a travelling minister serving mainly German congregations, then he was pastor in the Caucasus, Russia, before the First World War, and in Estonia after the war. E. Aksim died in 1927.

8. For instance, Eugen Lasn, owner of a pulp and paper company in Port Arthur, and Villem M. Kerson, furniture manufacturer in Montreal.

9. Aguraiuja (Agur), in *Meie Tee* (New York); and Kurlents *et al.* (eds.), *Eestlased Kanadas*, p. 84. Some Estonian farmers in Alberta lost their farms during the depression, but most were able to recover them later.

10. Among these immigrants at least five veterans of the War of Independence are known: J. Pitka, J. Waimel, E. Lasn, R. Jürine, and Hühne.

11. A new monthly, *Meie Tee* (Our Road), started publication in New York in 1931 and was aimed at Estonians in all foreign countries; at the same time also a tradition to celebrate the "Day of Estonians Abroad," on November 30, was started. Oral History Project, interviews with Eduard Riisna, September 10, 1975, May 2, 1977. Mr. Riisna, now in Toronto, visited Estonian organizations and lived abroad – in the United States, Canada, Australia, and other countries – in the early 1930's, and had specifically the task to promote communications among Estonians abroad and with Estonia; previously he had been a youth leader in Estonia and in the late 1930's he was a member of the parliament of Estonia.

12. According to one report about 300 Estonians from foreign countries came to Tallinn for this occasion, but only two from Canada are known, although there must have been some others. The Congress of Estonians Abroad, which was held in Tallinn, endorsed a concert tour of North America by the Academic Male Choir of the University of Tartu, which, however, never took place because of the oncoming war. R. Ritsing *et al.* (eds.), *Eesti laul Ameerikasse* (With Estonian Song to America) (Tartu: Academic Male Choir, 1939), esp. p. 55.

13. G.E. Dirks, "The Plight of the Homeless: The Refugee Phenomenon Behind the Headlines," *Canadian Institute of International Affairs*, XXXVIII, 3 (August, 1980), p. 3. (Italics are mine.)

14. Oral History Project interviewees unanimously confirmed that, when they came to Canada, they believed that Estonia would soon be freed from Soviet occupation; many said they were convinced that this was to happen in two or three years; only about a fifth said they already had doubts whether they would be able to return to Estonia; the rest stated that they believed they were going to return.

15. Oral History Project interviewees who were asked the question why they believed in the liberation of Estonia gave mainly one or both of the following answers: (a) inevitability of a war between the United States and the Soviet Union, and (b) internal disintegration of the Soviet Union because of its inability to absorb the many nations it had conquered after the Second World War. The Hungarian revolution of 1956 was the first serious uprising of this kind, where direct American support was also ex-

pected. See B. Kovrig, *The Myth of Liberation; East-Central Europe in U.S. Diplomacy and Politics since 1941* (Baltimore: The Johns Hopkins University Press, 1973).

16. Oral History Project, Mrs. V., interviewed in September, 1976. Well-versed in several languages and in editorial work, after coming from Sweden in 1951 she got a job as an editor of an English publication. Later she was promoted to the position of chief editor, over an English woman who had been employed earlier and expected the job herself. The intrigues that followed forced her to leave the publication. Thereafter she was employed as the secretary of a lawyer in Toronto and was a member of the editorial staff of an Estonian newspaper. Many Estonians, however, reported that they were advised in a friendly manner by their Canadian co-workers not to work too hard and thereby disrupt the solidarity of the workers.

17. The mail survey was carried out by the Canadian Estonian History Commission in 1965. Of about 10,000 questionnaires, 1,600 were returned. On the detailed results of the survey, see Kurlents *et al.* (eds.), *Eestlased Kanadas,* pp. 123, 124, 176.

18. Among this immigrant group to Canada were three former members of the government of Estonia, ten members of the parliament of Estonia, many dozens of higher civil servants, about a dozen principals (directors) of secondary or vocational schools, over 150 "jurists" – judges, practising lawyers and bankers, journalists, and others who had a formal university law degree. Never before had so many highly positioned Estonians emigrated from Estonia.

19. Oral History Project, A.V., interviewed in December, 1975, January, 1976.

20. This description is based partly on articles and reports in Toronto Estonian newspapers, but mainly on the author's own conversations with Estonians in Toronto. For the analysis of the adaptation of the post-war Estonian immigrants in Canada, many sources have been used, such as *Eestlased Kanadas*, Oral History Project interviews, Estonian newspapers, and the author's own experience as a member of the Estonian community in Canada.

21. Kurlents *et al.* (eds.), *Eestlased Kanadas*, p. 124. Of those who returned the questionnaires, 14.1 per cent reported themselves as professionals, 26.6 per cent were "office workers," 10.6 per cent "tradesmen," and only 1.7 per cent were farmers or fishermen; 20.3 per cent reported themselves as "workers," but the questionnaire did not specify whether skilled or unskilled. Almost 30 per cent did not answer this question.

22. See Chapter Nine.

23. Oral History Project, three interviews selected more or less at random from among the interviewees of this group.

24. Added may be J., who was quoted in Chapter Two above (see page 23 there) as an immigrant from Germany to Canada. After his contract in Manitoba expired he moved to Kitchener, Ontario, because there was al-

ready an Estonian community in Kitchener. For a short while he worked in a factory as an unskilled labourer, then answered an ad in the local newspaper and got a job as an accountant. He ended up as secretary-treasurer and shareholder of a specialized shoe factory in Kitchener and was also one of those Estonians who divided his time and talent equally between his workplace and Estonian community activities.

FOUR

Estonians in Canadian Society

THE ESTONIANS – AN URBAN ETHNIC GROUP

The Estonians in Canada are overwhelmingly urban residents: according to the 1971 census 85 per cent of Estonians lived in the metropolitan areas of Canada.[1] Moreover, they are concentrated in the four industrial centres of Toronto, Hamilton, Montreal, and Vancouver. In 1971 Toronto accounted for 49.79 per cent of all Estonians in Canada. This settlement pattern is similar to that of the two other Baltic ethnic groups, the Latvians and the Lithuanians, although the urban concentration of Estonians and their concentration in Toronto are greater than for the other two groups: 44 per cent and 31 per cent of Latvians and Lithuanians respectively were settled in Toronto in 1971. Needless to say, the urban concentration of all three ethnic groups came about as a result of the concentration of immigration into a few years after the Second World War.

In contrast, the first Estonian immigrants to Canada at the beginning of this century were mainly farmers and even if they came from cities they tended to settle on farms in western Canada. However, the farming life did not hold much of an attraction for the Estonians – already during the 1920's more Estonians in Canada lived in towns and cities than in rural areas. The Estonian immigrants of that period were mainly skilled labourers, craftsmen, construction workers, technicians, clerks, and a few professionals, and they preferred the industrial centres of Canada and the accompanying urban lifestyle. At the same time the rural Estonian settlements in Alberta began to break up when the younger people left the settlements for the towns and urban centres in Alberta, as well as elsewhere in Canada. The trend established by the pre-war immigrants was continued by those who came to Canada after the Second World War. Even most of those who immigrated as farmers, miners, or lumbermen soon moved to the major cities, primarily Toronto.

Although the heavy urban concentration of Estonians in Canada is incongruent when compared to the fact that two-thirds of the population of Estonia during the late 1930's was still rural, the reasons for the urban orientation of the immigrants are quite clear. Among the most important of these was the urban and industrial expansion that took place in Canada during the 1940's and 1950's and which entailed the availability of better-paying jobs in the cities. Thus, even former farmers were attracted to the large cities and settled there. But there are two other reasons. Although most Estonian immigrants had been born in the countryside the majority had occupations, training, and education that fitted them better for an urban-industrial environment than for a rural one. In fact, urbanization and industrialization had already begun in Estonia and continued apace after the war to the extent that more than two-thirds of Estonia's current population is urban-based. Moreover Estonians, both new immigrants and those already settled in Canada, were attracted to the larger Estonian ethnic communities, which could only be found in the bigger cities. Hence, one of the main attractions of Toronto, in addition to the economic opportunities, was the size of the Estonian community. The attraction of Toronto has continued, along with that of Vancouver, in both of which the Estonian communities have grown, particularly since the 1960's, whereas the community in Montreal and all small Estonian communities in Canada have declined in size.

Nevertheless, despite their spatial concentration in a few cities the Estonians everywhere, including Toronto, have formed only a tiny fraction of the local populations. And, since Estonians do not have any physically distinguishing traits, they easily intermingle with other Canadians of European origin. Moreover, whether because of their small numbers or because of their individualistic habits, the Estonians have never formed even the beginnings of an Estonian "ghetto" in any sector of any Canadian city. Although certain sections of a city seem to be preferred, very rarely have Estonians ever had Estonian neighbours. In the early years after immigration many Estonians in Toronto lived in the central area north of Bloor Street; now, however, as many live in the western suburbs and Don Mills. In fact, scattered among other Canadians, the Estonian presence has lacked the visibility of an ethnic group in Canadian society.

Educationally, Estonians number among the better-educated ethnic groups in Canada. The 1971 census shows that 52 per cent of Estonians over the age of twenty-five had completed secondary education, 8 per cent had some university training, 11 per cent had completed first degrees, and 3 per cent had earned post-graduate degrees. Clearly, since more than three-quarters of the total ethnic group consisted of post-war immigrants and their children, these census data primarily represent them. Although data are not available on whether the education was obtained in Canada or before immigration, the breakdown into age groups permits certain conclusions to be drawn. In common with the increase in education in modern societies, the younger age cohorts show a higher educational level than the older age groups. This is especially true of the age group 25-34 of whom 27 per cent had first university degrees and 8 per cent had post-graduate degrees. This group represents mainly those who came to Canada as children aged between five and fourteen. Most of their education took place in Canada although the older ones had completed elementary school and had a few years of secondary school before immigration. The majority of the next age cohort, 35-44, must have completed secondary school before immigration, and a few would have had some higher education, since at immigration they would have ranged in age from fifteen to twenty-four years. Hence, much of their university education would have been obtained in Canada and nearly all post-graduate degrees would be Canadian. Of those twenty-five years or older at immigration, that is, forty-five and over in the 1971 census, some would have continued their education in Canada, mainly by upgrading through evening or correspondence courses. Much of this upgrading was heavily oriented toward the acquisition of new technical skills usually unrelated to former educational attainments. The age group over sixty-five in the 1971 census, that is, forty-five and over at immigration, for all practical purposes acquired its education before immigration to Canada. It is interesting to note that this oldest age cohort and the age cohorts twenty-five years and older at immigration consistently demonstrate higher educational achievements than the Canadian average, meaning that the Estonian immigrants to this country brought along with them substantial educational levels. This fact needs additional explanation.

There are three main reasons for the prominence of education among the Estonians in Canada: first, the average level of education in Estonia; second, the level of education of the emigrant group; and third, the social values attributed to education among Estonians. Historically, education in Estonia has been regarded as the one means for Estonian ethnic emancipation from the cultural and economic domination of the Germanic and Germanized minority. At the end of the nineteenth century an Estonian educated elite emerged and at about the same time compulsory elementary education was introduced. This led to a rapid growth of education, with the result that during the years of independence in the 1920's and 1930's the average level of schooling rose so high that by the late 1930's there was an overproduction of university graduates, which in turn led to competitive examinations and quotas being introduced for university admissions. Second, the education level of the escapees from Estonia in 1944 was higher than average, since a large part of the political, economic, and social leadership fled the country. At the same time the education of younger refugees was interrupted under the two foreign occupations of Estonia during the war, but many of them made up the lost years and continued their education during the first years of exile in Germany or Sweden. Third, education, and especially education in technical subjects, rapidly became accepted as the means for successful adjustment in Canada. Estonian parents everywhere urged their children to go to university in order to be able to cope better than their parents with the social and economic competition of their new homeland. This explains the relatively high number of university graduates among both the children of Estonian immigrants and the younger immigrants themselves. It may be concluded that the educational level of the Estonians in Canada has played a significant part in the adjustment process of the ethnic group to its new country.

Normally, in modern industrial society there is a correlation among level of educational attainment, type of employment, work force participation, and income level. The 1971 census data show that there is a positive correlation among all these factors for the Estonian ethnic group in Canada. Labour force participation, for example, both for males and females, was considerably higher than the Canadian average. The female participation rate was particularly high, 42 per cent in comparison to the Canadian average of 27.5 per cent. This can be explained in various ways, including the higher percentage of professional training, greater experience, and the fact that a larger percentage of Estonian married women worked. It appears that Estonian women were both better qualified and that, especially among married post-war immigrants, wives normally sought employment to supplement family income. In fact, in the early post-war years women were often more employable than men, whose former professional training and experience were often not immediately applicable in Canada. In contrast, in certain fields, such as office work, women found work easily, provided that they had a minimum knowledge of the language and some office experience. Later, the same women continued to work because of the addition to the family income as well as the amenities associated with long service. It also seems to be common among Estonian young couples that both spouses work, apparently for the same reasons – family income and the employability of wives. Interestingly enough, although the rate of self-employment among Estonians is only slightly higher than the Canadian average, the women's self-employment rate is 3.7 per cent versus the Canadian average of 2.8 per cent.

The average earned income of Estonians according to the 1971 census was $6,477 against the Canadian average of $5,033, that is, it exceeded the Canadian average by almost one third. Estonians, in fact, ranked third after the Jews and the Latvians among the ethnic groups with the highest average incomes. The women's average income was substantially lower than that of the men, $4,362 against $7,866, but the average income of Estonian women was half again higher than the average income of women in Canada. It may also be assumed that the younger age groups of Estonians play a significant role in the high income levels of the Estonian group as a whole because of their high educational attainments, but the assumption does not explain why the income of the Estonians was already above the Canadian average in the early 1960's when the younger groups were still attending school.

A survey conducted in 1962 by the Estonian Credit Union shows that the Estonians in Toronto then owned over 300 enterprises of various kinds and sizes and that the Estonians in Toronto, in addition to about 2,200 family homes, owned over 1,500 summer cottages and about sixty farms purchased for both recreational and investment purposes. The total of Estonian households at the time in Toronto was estimated at 3,300.[2] The corresponding data for Hamilton, a considerably smaller Estonian community, included forty-five businesses, 200 family homes, and fifty-five summer cottages and farms. The combined market value of the private property of the Estonians in the Toronto area was estimated at $42 million, including $12 million in unpaid loans.[3] It should be reckoned that most of the summer cottages and many of the family homes had been built by the owners themselves during weekends, at substantial savings in labour costs, and that the income provided by the working wives was a considerable help in acquiring all this property.

The breakdown into major occupational groups reveals some peculiar characteristics of the Estonian group in Canada. In the major group classified "Natural Sciences" in the 1971 census the Estonians are strongly overrepresented and rank along with Latvians at the top of the list of ethnic groups in Canada. The rate of representation of Estonians is over three times the Canadian average at 13 per cent, compared to the national average of 4 per cent. In the occupational group, "Construction," Estonians exceed the national average by two percentage points, but place far below other groups, for example the Italians, who top the list. Since, however, the Estonian absolute figure is small, only 700 compared to the Italian 47,000, and it is known that many Estonians are building entrepreneurs and civil engineers, it must also be assumed that the total is inflated by the latter and that the actual number of construction workers among Estonians is relatively low. The Estonians are also slightly overrepresented in the major group listed as "Managerial, Medicine, Social Sciences, Technical and Clerical, Art and Recreation, Forestry, Machining, Product Fabrication, and Crafts." On the other hand, Estonians are substantially underrepresented in the occupations listed in the major group "Sales, Services, Farming and Transportation," in which their percentage is about half the national average. In the major occupational grouping "Processing, Materials Handling and Mining," the Estonians place slightly below the Canadian national average. However, as we are dealing with such small absolute numbers, a shift of very few individuals may cause a statistical but unrepresentative percentage difference. It may thus be more informative to collapse the major occupation groups in the census into larger categories, in which case we find that Estonians are substantially overrepresented in the category of "Professionals" and substantially underrepresented in "Sales and Services." They are also underrepresented in "Primary Industry," but the Estonian percentage of the industrial blue-collar workers is about the national average.

Despite the wealth of statistical data, many questions concerning the role of Estonians in Canadian society and economy remain unanswered. At least two of these, the role of Estonians as entrepreneurs in the Canadian economy and Estonians as professionals in Canadian society, may be dealt with descriptively.

ESTONIANS AS ENTREPRENEURS

Although only between 3 and 4 per cent of the Estonian post-war immigrants became entrepreneurs, they played an inordinately important role in the Estonian ethnic group as well as a significant role in the Canadian economy. They responded to the market demands and contributed to the growth of the economy, and for the ethnic group they provided jobs, lifted the status of Estonians as a whole, and assisted greatly in the social adjustment of many of their fellow immigrants. This was especially important for the older educated Estonians who otherwise would have had difficulty in finding acceptable jobs and integrating into Canadian society. The linkage role of Estonian enterprise, that of providing a cushion that facilitated the immigrant adjustment process, was particularly important during the 1950's and early 1960's in the metropolitan Toronto area, where over three-quarters of all Estonian enterprises in Canada were located.

Estonian entrepreneurs are found mainly in product creation and manufacturing, and to a much lesser extent in sales and services. While there have been few Estonian store owners or restaurateurs in Toronto or anywhere else in Canada, there have been many Estonian builders, craftsmen, and manufacturers. The new Estonian stores that opened in Toronto sold specialty products primarily to Estonian customers. Service agencies opened by Estonians were also almost exclusively patronized by an Estonian clientele, with the exception of the Estonian ski resorts and a few other recreational enterprises whose Estonian clientele was in the minority. In contrast, although many Estonians were employed in services and retail sales industries as sales personnel, in clerical work, or in management, they seldom showed the initiative for independent entrepreneurship that those Estonians employed in the construction or manufacturing industries did. It is impossible to determine the causes for this orientation, but three possible reasons may be advanced: a general inclination toward technological problem-solving, particularly among the post-war adult immigrants; the general unwillingness to take the greater risks in a new society that the sales and service industries pose; and the general value system prevalent in an ethnic society – Estonians have never been known for their trading skills.

Historically, the first Estonian entrepreneurs in Canada were the owners of rural saw and flour mills in the first part of the century in the Canadian West, particularly in Alberta. Moreover, as agricultural enterprise in Canada became specialized, Estonian farmers also specialized, in wheat farming and horsebreeding in Alberta and fruit farming in the

Niagara Peninsula in Ontario. The first Estonian industrial entrepreneurs in Canada did not emerge until the Second World War when Canada experienced the first rapid industrial take-off: V. Kerson and E. Lasn, both of whom had immigrated during the 1920's, established furniture manufacturing in Montreal and a lumber industry in Port Arthur, respectively. But it was in the 1950's that Estonian industrial enterprise really began, as a result of both the new wave of Estonian immigrants and the favourable economic conditions of the first war-free decade, in which the pent-up demands of war and European reconstruction, combined with the stimulation of demand by large-scale immigration, created a sustained period of economic boom. Thus, the rapid growth of the industrial cities of Canada created a housing shortage that led to a flourishing construction industry, and the influx of continental European immigrants created new market demands, especially in the food products industries. Without the special conditions of the post-war boom it would have been next to impossible for a newcomer with little investment capital and no experience of the traditional markets of a foreign country to start a successful new enterprise.

A striking example of the economic opportunities presented by the social and economic conditions of the 1950's is the Estonian bakeries in Toronto and in Hamilton. The influx of new continental European immigrants to these cities created demands for European-type foods, particularly for dark whole rye and whole wheat breads – something that Canadian bakeries were not able to supply – so a number of Estonian immigrants established small bakeries. None of these entrepreneurs had any investment capital or even any previous experience of bakeries, but they had a guaranteed market in the Estonian communities and a growing market among the other continental European communities they were able to penetrate because they understood the importance of different types of breads to European diets better than Canadian bakeries, which were either uninterested or unaware of this new market. Thus, in short order the small bakeries were built into sizable enterprises. At first they hired Estonians and then other continental European immigrants in their manufacturing and marketing and expanded their bakeries rapidly by catering to the various tastes of their customers. The products of four of these bakeries have now been established on the southern Ontario food markets for three decades: Annette Bakery (F. Krabi), Viking Bakery (A. Tralla), and Rooneem's Bakery in Toronto, and Baltic Bread in Hamilton. Of course, all bakeries were not as successful as these four; some ventures failed because of competition not only among the Estonians but with other ethnic bakeries. And, during the 1960's, competition increased when many new German bakeries were established and began to cater to the same market. A few years later, during the 1970's, all the Estonian bakers, except for Rooneem, sold their businesses and retired on the proceeds. Rooneem and his sons, however, rose to the competition and extended the variety of their products to include a wide range of pastries.

The case of Amjärv Sweets in Toronto differs sufficiently from the other bakeries to merit brief description. Although Amjärv also began as a baker of breads he had some previous experience in pastry-making. He soon limited his product to high-quality central European-type pastries and opened a store on Yonge Street, where he also sold imported delicatessen products. Because of the exceptionally high quality of his products, including handmade chocolates, he attracted a select clientele and had almost no competition, at least not during the 1950's and the 1960's. But he, too, sold his business in the early 1970's, to a Swiss Canadian who has continued Amjärv's high-quality production.

Four other food product firms must be mentioned. Poko's Meat Products and Central Meat were two meat-producing and retail chains that offered foods, especially cooked and smoked meats and fish, produced to European tastes, mainly to Estonians and other Baltic and north European customers in metropolitan Toronto. Both were subsequently sold to new, non-Estonian owners who have, however, continued to serve their established customers. Northrand Foods and Viking Foods and Imports, special food products (fish and meat) wholesale and retail firms in Toronto, were purchased during the 1960's by an Estonian immigrant who had been manager of the two firms (L. Jänes). He subsequently expanded these operations to serve the growing specialty food markets, including the restaurants in metropolitan Toronto.

In addition to these entrepreneurs in the food business, a number of other less well-known ones have been active in Toronto, Vancouver, and Montreal. In general, they were most successful during the 1950's and 1960's when they had the specialty market largely to themselves, but in the 1970's when food tastes in general began to change in the metropolitan areas in Canada aggressive competition forced many of the now elderly proprietors to sell out.

In addition to the food stores, a number of other small businesses catering largely to Estonian and other European immigrant customers have been established by Estonians, such as souvenir stores, jewellers, watchmakers, insurance agencies, and realtors; other businesses, such as garages, repair shops, pharmacies, and furriers, although welcoming Estonian customers, have not been dependent on them and have catered to a wider clientele. It has also been usual that an Estonian manager or employee of a firm has been used as a means to advertise for Estonian customers, especially in Toronto. Ads for stores and services in the Estonian newspapers note that "Estonian is spoken" or insert the name of an Estonian representative in the advertisement. Oddly enough, sometimes an ad specifies that the store is "Latvian," "Finnish," "Lithuanian," or "German," which testifies to the interrelationships of ethnic enterprises.

It is clear that Estonian construction firms and manufacturers assisted the Estonian community considerably by employing a number of them, and that many food product stores greatly assisted in the adjustment of Estonians to their new country. However, it is equally clear that for any of these, or indeed for any business to become successful, the ability to attract customers and clients beyond the Estonian ethnic and other immigrant groups was necessary. And this is precisely what the large construction firms did, some even expanding their operations into the United States.

In 1962 there were seventy-eight construction firms, seventy-four industrial enterprises, and twenty-four commercial establishments in Toronto owned by Estonians.[4] Although there were also Estonian building firms in Vancouver, London, Calgary, Sault Ste. Marie, and other cities, Toronto was the centre of the Estonian construction industry with about 180 firms between 1955 and 1957.[5] Most of these were small one-man firms, and most were sub-contractors who built less than a dozen family homes a year. Virtually none of these entrepreneurs had any experience in the building industry before coming to Canada; they were led into it by beginning as construction workers during their first years here. It was the building boom of the 1950's that led many of the former lawyers, civil servants, farmers, teachers, army officers into construction work and provided the opportunity for them to establish their own businesses. For example, in Victoria, B.C., during the late 1950's every second Estonian male was a builder.[6] When the sustained building boom led to the mass production of housing, the large number of small builders could not compete with the large construction firms and only a few survived into the 1970's as independent entrepreneurs. The rest either remained as sub-contractors or moved on to other activities. In Toronto, many bought apartment buildings or managed them for others.

A couple of large construction firms deserve mention. J. Aloe, formerly a farmer in Estonia, became a small builder in Canada but quickly adopted techniques of mass production and subdivision development in the early 1960's, with his son (a Canadian engineering graduate) established a construction and building supplies conglomerate, and became a large builder of subdivisions and shopping centres in Canada and the United States. In Vancouver, Lepik Brothers, besides family housing, from 1960 to 1971 built high-rise apartment and office buildings at English Bay, changing the skyline of that city considerably. It is estimated that between 1952 and 1972 over 1,400 family homes to a value of $29 million were built in Vancouver and Victoria by Estonian builders.[7]

The best-known Estonian manufacturers have been located in Toronto and have been active mainly in the plastics, chemicals, textile, and wood industries. Among these, several picture-frame companies, including Artistic Woodworks, Multiframe, and Victorian Picture Frames, a maker of tents and camping equipment, Anglo Trader, and a manufacturer of beach and recreational equipment, Scepter Manufacturing Company

(E. Torokvei), bear mentioning. The last one, perhaps the largest Estonian enterprise in Canada, has plants in and sells its products mostly in the United States.

Although some of these firms were sold in the 1970's, a number of new ones have been established, particularly in the high-technology chemical engineering and related industries. In summary, it may be said that despite the relatively small size of the ethnic group, Estonian entrepreneurship in Canada has been noteworthy and has been a net contributor, not only to the ethnic group itself, but to the Canadian economy as a whole.

ESTONIANS AS PROFESSIONALS IN CANADA

Undoubtedly one of the significant factors that has placed the Estonians in a high income group is their high percentage of professional people. The occupations included here as "professional" are engineering, architecture, law, medicine, secondary school and post-secondary school teaching, professional library work, chemistry, mathematics, accounting, economics, nursing, social work, scientific research, and management and admininstration normally requiring a university education or specialist training.

In the early 1940's there were a few Estonian professionals in Canada. In origin they were mixed: some were descendants of the Alberta Estonians and others were more recent immigrants. However, as has already been pointed out, the post-war Estonian refugee-immigrants included a disproportionately large number of professionals, both those who had completed their professional training in Estonia and those who had acquired their professions in Germany or Sweden after the war. Unfortunately, it is impossible to ascertain their exact numbers from immigration statistics. Either the last occupation is listed or the immigrant simply listed an occupation that facilitated immigration. But the last real occupation the immigrant worked in, either in Sweden or Germany, often varied from his original occupation in Estonia. However, it is possible to determine the approximate number of these refugee professionals and break them down into component professions by surveying the current Canadian Estonian professional and academic organizations, as well as individual senior and knowledgeable active professionals. According to these surveys the post-war immigrants included thirty-one physicians, three dentists, ten pharmacologists with university degrees, eight architects, almost fifty graduate agronomists, almost thirty ministers of various denominations, over thirty economists and accountants, at least fifteen natural scientists and mathematicians, about 100 engineers, ten chemists, over 100 primary and secondary school teachers, between 120 and 140 lawyers, including judges and university-trained civil servants, about thirty army officers, close to thirty professional performing and fine artists, about 100 nurses, as well as other specialists. Although most

61

of these figures are approximations it should be noted that they understate the significant proportion of professionals among Estonian postwar immigrants. It should also be noted that, although in the Canadian context the absolute numbers are not large, as a proportion of the Estonian immigrant group they are remarkable.

All these professionals, of course, could not resume their former professions in Canada; for example, of the lawyers, only three resumed legal practice in Canada, and among the army officers none continued his professional career here. Nevertheless, about a third of all professionals, including all physicians, dentists, and architects, and almost all ministers, chemists, and engineers, were able to continue their former professions in this country, although in many cases they had to take qualifying examinations and some further training. Surprisingly, the agriculturalists as a rule did not regain their previous professional specialist occupations, but all remained in the professional category: in federal and provincial agricultural services, as teachers or researchers at universities and research institutions, or as chemists in the food industry. More important, however, is the finding that in the long run, after a period of manual or other non-professional work, about another third rejoined the ranks of professionals or semi-professionals by upgrading their qualifications or by learning new professions. This group includes some army officers who had previously had technical training and were able to become engineers in this country. In addition, we have already indicated that many lawyers became taxation specialists, office managers, and so forth; some also became industrial designers or draftsmen through learning new skills. Similarly, many former teachers became librarians, researchers in government institutions, industrial chemists, or draftsmen or designers. A number of former painters were employed by commercial firms as commercial artists. A few journalists found employment with the Estonian newspapers and the former economists with Estonian enterprises. Actors and musicians found part-time employment in the Estonian community, as church organists, for example, and a few established themselves professionally in Canadian society. Thus, in the long run only about a third dropped permanently out of the ranks of professionals or semi-professionals after their arrival in Canada.

The analysis leads to three conclusions. First, it tends to suggest that education and specialist training more often than not pay off even under adverse circumstances. Also, an orientation to learning, once acquired, tends to be retained for long periods and leads to the interchangeability of knowledge. Second, there is little question that these former professionals provided a reservoir of trained manpower in Canada from which specialists could be drawn as required by the economic growth of the country. This pool also provided the work force with broader experience and a higher quality than the immediate jobs required, for instance, lawyers working as title searchers or as real estate agents. Third, this reservoir of professionals, though small in number, probably saved

Canada large sums of money that otherwise would have been needed for education and training of professionals.

Nevertheless, the overwhelming majority of Estonian professionals currently in Canada are Canadian graduates. A study by Professor Träss of the University of Toronto in 1975 shows that between 1950 and 1972 a minimum of 1,200 Estonians graduated from Canadian universities, 143 received Master's degrees, and twenty-seven earned doctoral degrees.[8] Unfortunately, this study does not show how many of these graduates already had degrees before they immigrated to Canada, nor does it show how many of them took second degrees or whether some already had partial university education prior to immigration. Clearly, however, the numbers in these categories cannot be very large. The study shows a heavy concentration in engineering (more than 200 graduates), but it also shows fifty-nine graduates in education, thirty-six in medicine, fifty-eight in physical education, and 528 in the humanities and natural sciences. It may be assumed that the graduates in natural sciences total a far larger number than that for the social sciences and humanities together. What is interesting in the above figures is the fairly significant proportion of graduates in education and physical education, especially if one were able to add to this the number of Estonian graduates in the humanities and natural sciences who acquired post-graduate teaching certificates. Clearly, a large number of Estonians have chosen teaching careers.

Although the Träss study only takes us up to 1972, our earlier demonstration of the rapid trend of increase among Estonian university graduates permits us to assume that between 1972 and 1982, proportionately, an even larger number graduated, thus bringing the total number of Estonians with professional and university degrees in Canada well above 2,000. This projection is corroborated by information from the Estonian professional and academic organizations in Canada, which also show a total of "2,000 plus." These estimates include only those currently active and exclude those who have died or have retired. Hence, according to current sources, there are over 500 Estonian engineers, over eighty physicians, about fifty architects, thirty agriculturalists, fifteen journalists, fifty chemists, fifty-five natural scientists, over 260 teachers, about 130 nurses, five Canadian army officers, about twenty lawyers, and over forty Estonian professors at Canadian universities.

It can be concluded, then, that entrepreneurship and professionalism have been the two characteristic features of the Estonian ethnic group in Canada during the past thirty years.

NOTES

1. The statistics on which this chapter is based will be found in Tables 1-7 in the Appendix.
2. E. Kareda, in *Eestlaste paiknevusest ja majandus likust ettevõtlikkusest*

(Localization and Economic Entrepreneurship of Estonians) (Toronto: Toronto Eesti Ühispank [Toronto Estonian Credit Union], n.d.), p. 8.
3. A. Peel, *ibid.*, p. 10.
4. E. Kareda, *ibid.*, p. 8.
5. A. Ekbaum, in Kurlents *et al.* (eds.), *Eestlased Kanadas*, p. 302.
6. A. Joasalu, *ibid.*, p. 228.
7. *Ibid.*
8. O. Träss, *ibid.*, pp. 482, 484.

PART TWO

Organizations and Activities

FIVE

Network of Estonian Organizations

More than 200 Estonian organizations are now active in Canada. Historically, the Estonian Association in Montreal is the only one that has existed uninterrupted from the period before the Second World War; all the rest are newer creations. By 1955, a complex network of Estonian organizations had been built up all over the country. These organizations either were brought over in fragmentary form from Estonia or were new ones set up to assist Estonian immigrants in adjusting to the new environment. Many even today continue the structural patterns and the functional aims that they had when they were initially established in this country. Since the 1950's about a third of the original organizations have succumbed to the exigencies of time, but their place has been taken by new organizations created during the 1960's and 1970's that reflect the demands and circumstances of the times when they were created. Thus, because of the different aims and origins there is considerable diversity in both structure and function among the Estonian organizations in Canada.[1]

STRUCTURAL DECENTRALIZATION

No serious attempts to centralize Estonian organizations in Canada have been made. The Estonian Federation and the Estonian Central Council have claimed to represent the Estonians in Canada, but neither has effective control over other organizations, nor do they represent all Estonian organizations in Canada. A number of organizations with common purpose and function, such as congregations of the same church, Boy Scouts, and war veterans, have joined in effective Canada-wide federations. Nevertheless, a large number of Estonian organizations have no structural link with any other Estonian organization in Canada. Among these may particularly be counted the professional, special interest, academic, and some youth organizations.

The Estonian Association and the Estonian Lutheran congregation are the typical local organizations in Estonian communities of 100 or more Estonians. Where the number of Estonians is too small to run a formal organization only occasional gatherings take place, usually to commemorate Estonian Independence Day and to attend a church service conducted by a visiting pastor. In larger Estonian communities, such as those in Montreal and Vancouver where there are 1,000 or more Estonians, a variety of organizations exist, including choirs and special interest and social clubs, and ethnic activities are frequent and elaborate. Nowhere, however, is there any single umbrella organization, although the Estonian Association usually assumes the role of co-ordinator of the main ethnic activities. During the 1950's the Toronto Estonian Association also performed the role of co-ordinator within the Toronto Estonian community.

The only effective regional organization, Seedrioru, in southern Ontario, is a joint enterprise of the Estonian Associations of St. Catharines, Hamilton, Kitchener, and London. Attempts to create similar regional federations in northern Ontario and on the Prairies have failed, mainly because the Estonian communities in those areas have been too small and scattered and because there has been no common focus.

Toronto is the the de facto "capital" of Estonians in Canada. It has the largest Estonian organizations, the ethnic events are far more frequent, and the ethnic activities pursued in Toronto are far more varied than anywhere else in Canada. About half of all the Estonian organizations in Canada are actually Toronto organizations, including a score with no counterparts elsewhere in Canada, for example, the Estonian (Toronto) Credit Union, the Society of Estonian Artists, the Estonian National Theatre in Canada, and Tartu Institute. A number of these are in principle all-Canadian organizations, although their activities hardly reach beyond the Toronto area. The fact that not a single Canada-wide Estonian federation has its headquarters outside Toronto adds to the organizational focus and weight, as well as self-centredness, of the Toronto Estonian community.

The consequence of this concentration is that the Toronto Estonian community is over-organized. Memberships and leadership of organizations overlap and there is some parallelism in functions and activities among the organizations. At certain times of the year some ethnic events take place simultaneously, or follow very closely, thus straining the support capacity of what is, after all, one of the smallest ethnic communities in Canada. Vacant leadership positions are frequently difficult to fill because the obvious candidates are already involved as executives of other organizations and are reluctant to accept them.

Leadership, however, has become a problem only recently and is not limited to Toronto. It has become a problem because of the aging of both the leadership and of the organizations of the 1948-1955 vintage. Many organizations have failed to recruit sufficient numbers of younger people into their membership and to groom them for leadership. In organizations founded during the 1960's and 1970's by predominantly younger people, and those among the original post-war organizations that have always been led by young people, both membership and leadership rejuvenation seem to have taken place normally.

The diversity and versatility of Estonian organizations in Toronto have defied structural centralization. Although ready to co-operate to attain specific goals, each organization is determined to maintain its independence. Consequently, it can be argued that it is not the geographic distance between Estonian communities but rather the diversity and independence of organizations, particularly in Toronto, that has militated against any centralization of Estonian organizations in Canada.

FUNCTIONAL CO-OPERATION

Despite the organizational diversity and desire for autonomy, there is a surprisingly high degree of functional co-operation. Many ethnic events are organized jointly by several clubs, associations, or congregations. Indeed, none of the major festivals has ever been run by only a single organization, except for celebration of the Estonian Independence Day, which by tradition is the responsibility of the local Estonian Association. Even this is run in collaboration with other local organizations.

Toronto has reached the point where, in order to rationalize the plethora of events and to maximize the possibilities of mobilizing support for the major events, an annual calendar has been adopted for the main events of the major Toronto organizations.[2] Despite this, some events and meetings inevitably collide, but audiences also often differ: an academic lecture, for example, hardly interferes with a sports event or a social evening.

Functional co-operation is also aided by the fact that it is in the nature of several organizations to support each other. Thus, choirs usually have associations or congregations as their parent bodies and the larger organizations have various special purpose clubs as their subsidiary branches. The location of the bureaus of the major organizations in Toronto either in Estonia House or in Tartu College also facilitates inter-organization communication, as does the overlapping of both membership and leadership among the organizations. The main reason, however, for the high degree of co-operation among the Estonian organizations in Canada is their concentration in Toronto. It is easy to keep up inter-organizational communications by local telephone calls, ad hoc committee meetings called at short notice, and frequent contacts at the events and meetings taking place in Toronto.

Toronto has also assisted in the establishment of a synchronized calendar for regional and all-Canadian events. Hence, Boy Scout jamborees, special jubilees, congresses, and seminars with large attendance are co-ordinated with other major ethnic festivals in Canada as well as with similar major festivals in the United States and even in Europe. Thus the conflicting claims for the same weekends for events that arose in the 1950's have been taken care of.

The vehicle of co-operation in the case of a major event has always been a joint ad hoc committee created by the organizations that are primarily concerned and interested in the event. The committee organizes and runs the festival, reports back to the congress of delegates after the festival, and then ceases to exist. For the next festival a new committee is created. Thus, for instance, all the summer festivals of the Toronto Estonian community have been run by ad hoc committees consisting of representatives from a dozen or more Toronto organizations. Similarly, the Estonian festivals on the American west coast have been organized by joint ad hoc committees of the organizations concerned even though a League of Estonian Organizations exists on the west coast. Ad hoc committees are also used for major music festivals and even for cultural seminars. This system has become so entrenched among the Estonians in North America that, for instance, the Killamängud, a new type of summer festival initiated by the Estonian Federation in Canada and first held in 1978, is also run by an ad hoc committee created by the delegates representing the provinces of Estonia from which they or their parents had come. The experience of the Estonian communities in Canada for over thirty years seems to prove that this method is able to bring about functional co-operation by harnessing the energies of many organizations without, however, bringing about any structural centralization.

The system is also used for the festivals of Estonian communities of several countries. For such festivals each country establishes its festival committee. The committee of the country in which the festival takes place becomes the main committee. Thus, the Canadian Committee of the Estonian World Festivals (in Toronto), even though a permanent and incorporated body since 1972, is nevertheless always reorganized as the main committee before the festival is held in Canada. In March, 1981, more than 100 Canadian Estonian organizations sent the delegates to the organizing meeting of the Estonian World Festival held in Canada in 1984.[3] The main committee makes the arrangements for the festival, decides the main points of the program, and solicits the support of organizations in Canada and other countries. A complex network of committees and sub-committees is established and a very large number of leaders from many organizations is involved. In preparation for the World Festival the chairman of the main committee and the chairmen of the sub-committees usually make several trips to other countries to develop programs, solicit support, and iron out problems.

LINKAGE WITH CANADIAN ORGANIZATIONS

Most Estonian organizations in Canada have links either with English-Canadian organizations or with the organizations of other ethnic groups in Canada. In some cases the link takes the form of a dual allegiance;

that is, affiliation of an Estonian federation with a Canadian organization. Estonian Lutheran congregations in Canada, for example, belong to the Estonian Lutheran Synod in Canada, which is a branch of the Estonian Lutheran Church in Exile headquartered in Stockholm, and they are also member-congregations of the Canadian branches of either the Lutheran Church in America or the Missouri Synod. Similarly, local Estonian Boy Scout troops belong to the local Canadian Boy Scout organizations, but at the same time they are members of the Estonian Boy Scouts in Canada headquartered in Toronto. Moreover, in both these cases informal but close co-operation is also pursued with the counterpart organizations of some other ethnic groups. For example, an Estonian and a Latvian congregation in Toronto jointly own St. Andrew's church buildings, and representatives of the Boy Scouts of other ethnic groups are invited to participate in Estonian Boy Scout jamborees.

A type of linkage more common than the dual allegiance is the co-operation for specific purposes among organizations. For example, the Ontario Loppet (Ski Festival) was initiated and is still largely run by the leading members of the Estonian ski clubs in Toronto; the Estonian athletic clubs usually belong to Canadian sports federations, and athletes from Estonian clubs compete in Canadian competitions. Similarly, members of Estonian professional, youth, academic, and student clubs are also usually members of the Canadian English-language counterpart organizations. In some organizations the inter-organizational contacts between the Estonian and the Canadian English-language organizations are very informal, as in the case of Estonian veterans' contacts with Canadian veterans' organizations, which are usually conducted through those Estonians who belong to both organizations. These casual relations are normal in any society where free association is encouraged by the culture, and will increase infinitely in the future as the Estonians move into the third and subsequent generations in Canada.

Another type of link is the formal ethnic federation. Estonian organizations have joined together with the other Baltic, Latvian, and Lithuanian ethnic groups, as in the case of the League of the Baltic Veterans and the Baltic Officer Corps. Moreover, the main organizations of the Estonian, Latvian, and Lithuanian communities in Toronto have formed the Baltic League and the Baltic Women's League. The Baltic League has been active in furthering direct links with the Canadian political centre by annually holding the Baltic Evening on Parliament Hill, in collaboration with senators and members of the House of Commons.

From the above examples it follows that practically every Estonian organization has some kind of contact with Canadian organizations and/ or with other ethnic group organizations in Canada. Clearly, Estonians are not introverted organizationally, as sometimes has been asserted by others. However, Estonian participation in Canadian national, usually English-language, activities often escapes visibility because of the very small size of the Estonian ethnic group, which, furthermore, is scattered across Canada. The visibility of Estonian active participation in national Canadian activities is also obscured by the fact that the Estonian organizational structure in Canada is diverse and decentralized and hence it is up to individual Estonian organizations to decide when, where, and how to participate.

LINKS WITH OTHER COUNTRIES

The links that Estonian organizations in Canada have with Estonian organizations in other countries cannot be over-emphasized. Indeed, for some Estonian organizations in Canada contact and co-operation with the same type of Estonian organization in other countries, especially in United States, is more important than any relationships they have with other Estonian organizations in Canada. These international relationships are of two kinds: close occasional and/or informal co-operation, and a highly structured co-operation by means of formal federations.

The Estonian Central Council of Canada is a member of the Estonian World Council located in New York, with the other members being the main Estonian organizations in the United States, Sweden, England, Germany, and Australia. The World Council has convened congresses of delegates from all Estonian organizations in these and other countries. The congresses discuss problems of common concern to Estonian communities in the different countries.

The Estonian churches, Boy Scout and Girl Guide movements, professionals, war veterans, and interest group associations and clubs in the several countries are similarly federated. The structures, strength of membership, and effectiveness of the co-ordination of their activities vary, depending on many factors such as tradition, initiative of leadership, and immediate purposes. Nevertheless, one of the characteristics of these special purpose groups and their federations is that they invariably hold their conferences, seminars, and meetings in connection with the Estonian World Festivals. In the summer of 1980, for example, during the World Festival in Sweden, more than twenty such meetings, conferences, and seminars were held by the various federations. For example, the Teachers' Conference, attended by more than 150 teachers from various countries, dealt basically with a question of retention of the Estonian language. Similarly, about forty agriculturalists held a two-day seminar at the Agricultural Institute of the University of Uppsala; and the social evening of the war veterans attracted more than 1,000 people. All these events attracted participants from six or seven countries.[4]

Some federations also publish magazines or bulletins of information, such as *Eesti kirik*, put out by the Lutheran churches, *Triinu*, a magazine for women, *Võitleja*, a periodical of the veterans, *Tulehoidja*, the bulletin for the Boy Scouts and Girl Guides, and yearbooks published by the Estonian academic organizations. The editorial boards of these bulletins, magazines, and yearbooks either rotate from country to country or consist of co-editors from the different countries of domicile.

There are also links among Estonian communities in different countries when no formal structure exists. For example, the Metsaülikool, an annual one-week seminar of about 100 Estonian graduates and scholars held since 1967 at a Muskoka recreational retreat, is organized each year by a group of young Estonian intellectuals in Toronto on a completely ad hoc basis. It attracts about an equal number of students and lecturers from Canada and the United States and always a few from Europe, as well as an occasional Australian.

Among such global links, the academic organizations and alumni and student clubs have a unique place. Their main aim is to promote mutual friendship and to propagate the values of Estonian intellectual elites. There are about twenty such academic organizations, all originating from the Estonian homeland, that were transplanted to Canada and the rest of the Western world by the refugees of the Second World War. All of them have chapters in several countries. The largest, for example, in 1980 had 726 members located in twelve chapters in six countries.[5]

The above examples demonstrate that Estonian organizations in Canada to a very large extent are oriented toward Estonian organizations and activities in other countries. The global nature of Estonian organizations, however, is limited to the Estonian diaspora outside Estonia. There is no formal contact between the organizations in Soviet Estonia and the Estonian organizations outside Estonia. The Soviet authorities have not permitted any contact with émigré organizations, nor do the organizations of Estonians abroad seek contact with Soviet organizations in Soviet Estonia. But there are limited personal contacts between Estonians in Estonia and those abroad.

The main objectives of the organizations of the Estonian diaspora are to maintain Estonian culture and to link together Estonian communities abroad. The results go beyond the original objectives. Professional and special interest groups, scholars and students, folk dancers and choir singers, artists and writers, though organizationally based within the ethnic group, disseminate the influences of their different environments, thus promoting international contact and enriching the environments they move in. Canada as a whole thus also gains through the organizational network links that Estonians have in many countries and cultures.

NOTES

1. The Estonian newspapers in Toronto, *Meie Elu* and *Vaba Eestlane*, both publish annual calendars in which Estonian organizations in Canada and major Estonian organizations in other countries are listed along with their addresses. It is a useful reference source from year to year, but it also

should be noted that not all organizations are listed. For the last ten years about 180 organizations, including the congregations, have been listed in Canada. About half of them have their addresses in Toronto.

2. The schedule of events is published a year in advance by the same calendars that publish the list of Estonian organizations.

3. *Meie Elu*, March 12, 1981; *Vaba Eestlane*, March 10, 1981.

4. *Teataja* (Stockholm), August 23, September 20, 1980; *Vaba Eestlane*, August 26, 1980.

5. *EÜS Paguluses: Liikmete Nimekiri* (EÜS in Exile: Membership List) (Toronto, 1980). This booklet of eighty-five pages lists the members by chapter and country. Three chapters were in Sweden, four in the United States, two in Canada, and one in each of England, Australia, and Argentina. Of the total of 726 members, 184 belong to the Toronto or Montreal chapters in Canada.

SIX

Principal Organizations

LOCAL ORGANIZATIONS

The Estonian Association

The local Estonian Association is the hub of the smaller Estonian community. Other Estonian activity groups and clubs, such as a choir, the supplementary school, the folk dance group, the scout troops, and the drama and athletic clubs, cluster around the association and form either subsidiary sections of it or are affiliated with it in some fashion. In addition, there is close co-operation between the Estonian Association and the local Estonian Lutheran congregation.

In Estonian communities of a larger size, such as Montreal, Hamilton, and Vancouver, the local Estonian Association plays a relatively small role because there are usually a number of independently viable Estonian clubs that do not need the support of the association. Thus, the folk dancers and the scouting troops usually have their own supporting organizations and actually compete with the local Estonian Association both in ethnic activities and for income sources.

In contrast to both the small and the larger Estonian communities, in Toronto the Estonian Association has been completely overshadowed by the plethora of other Estonian organizations and other activities, although the Estonian Association in Toronto is the oldest Estonian organization there. Indeed, many of the new independent organizations were created by it and others originated as its sections. Nevertheless, two central functions still remain with the Toronto Estonian Association – the celebration of the Estonian Independence Day and the running of the supplementary school. Until recently it also organized an annual series of public lectures on popular topics, and it still maintains some special purpose clubs.

Over the years the Estonian Associations in Canada have developed a routine calendar of events. The highlight of the year is the commemoration of Estonian Independence Day on February 24, and by custom it is the local association that organizes this event and mobilizes the support of other community organizations. There are also a Mothers' Day celebration in May, a party at Christmas in connection with the supplementary school, and two or three strictly social dinner-dances, one in the spring, another in the autumn, and often a New Year's Eve party.[1]

Historically, the earliest Estonian Associations of Canada were established in Alberta, in Stettler, Eckville, and Barons. In Stettler an Estonian community hall was built in 1911 and was rebuilt in 1931 after a fire. However, by the time that the immigrant wave arrived in Canada after the Second World War the Estonian settlements in Alberta had lost most of their members. With increasing industrialization in the West, the younger Estonians moved to the city, as did the few newcomers who went first to the settlements. Thus, the Estonian communities in southern Alberta along with their local Estonian Associations were doomed already before the new wave of Estonian immigrants, and only one, the Eckville Estonian Association, has nominally survived to the 1980's. Recently it sold its community hall and donated $20,000 from the proceeds to the Eckville Community Centre.[2]

The Estonian Associations had also been established in Winnipeg, Montreal, and Toronto but they, like those in the Alberta rural settlements, had become inactive or had virtually ceased to exist when they were reactivated and/or refounded by the new Estonian immigrants to the cities in 1948-49.[3] The post-war Estonian immigrants also established Estonian Associations in Ottawa, Port Arthur, and Vancouver in 1948, and in 1949 founded no fewer than eight new Estonian Associations – in Kirkland Lake, Kitchener, St. Catharines, London, Hamilton, Sault Ste. Marie, Edmonton, and Calgary. The last Estonian Association to be founded was the one in Sudbury, in 1952. All of these associations, refounded or newly established between 1948 and 1952, are still active in the 1980's, with the exception of the one in Kirkland Lake, which was liquidated in the early 1960's. The association at Kirkland Lake actually ceased to exist years before its formal dissolution because the Estonians who had come under one- or two-year work contracts in mining or in the lumber industry moved on to Toronto and Montreal after the expiry of their contracts.

During the 1950's each of the then sixteen Estonian Associations had a choir, a folk dance group, a Boy Scout troop, a drama club, and various other activity clubs. Hence, the ethnocultural activities even of the smaller communities were diverse and intense. During the 1970's these activities declined noticeably, especially in the smaller Estonian communities. At the beginning of the 1980's most of the communities still run supplementary schools for the children and support Boy Scout and Girl Guide troops, but there are no choirs or drama or literary clubs. As a result the programs presented to the local ethnic gatherings have changed. Instead of plays being presented by drama groups and choirs singing, soloists are brought in from outside; the emphasis has shifted from communal cultural content to providing imported entertainment. In the larger communities the old choirs still continue, and even new choirs composed of young singers with their own leaders sporadically appear.

It has always been difficult to ascertain the exact membership of the various Estonian Associations because paid-up membership in voluntary associations fluctuates widely. However, it is clear that the membership of associations in smaller Estonian communities has always been more stable and has formed a higher percentage of the total community than in the larger centres. For example, during the 1970's the membership of the Toronto Estonian Association fluctuated between 300 and 600 members (from among approximately 10,000 Estonians in the Toronto community), whereas the membership of the Kitchener Estonian Association remained stable at about 100 (out of a community of 200-250 Estonians). Clearly, many viable Estonian organizations in Toronto are competing for membership and activities, whereas in Kitchener there is only the Kitchener Estonian Association. The total membership of the fifteen Estonian Associations in Canada at the beginning of the 1980's may be conservatively estimated at 2,000 to 2,500.

THE ESTONIAN CONGREGATION

Although most Estonian congregations in Canada are Lutheran there are also Orthodox, Baptist, Pentecostal, and Seventh Day Adventist congregations in Toronto, Montreal, and Vancouver. All of these were founded by the post-war wave of immigrants, most within the 1948-52 period. The only earlier attempt to establish an Estonian congregation in Canada was made by the Estonian community in Stettler, which established a Lutheran congregation and built a small chapel. Unfortunately, it disintegrated into factions and ceased to exist long before the parallel Estonian Association in Stettler declined. In any case, the reason for the formation of the congregation was questionable: it was hoped that the Alberta government would grant a large tract of land free of taxes for the support of the church. This, however, proved to be wishful thinking. Moreover, the congregation never acquired the services of a regular pastor.

Some of the early Estonian settlers in Canada were atheists and hence opposed the establishment of churches in principle. Furthermore, the majority had been brought up in the northern European Christian tradition, where the church performs a strictly religious function only and does not play any significant social or cultural role. The spiritual function was further emphasized in the Estonian case since the Lutheran church, historically, had been dominated by a hierarchy of "foreign" German clergy; thus, even when the popular Estonian national church

75

was established during the period of independence in this century the church followed tradition and continued to confine itself mainly to the spiritual and moral guidance of its members.

Hence, even in Alberta, there was a separation between the church and the secular organizations, associations, and co-operative enterprises. Although no further attempts were made to establish congregations beyond the abortive one in Stettler, the Alberta Estonians were nevertheless served by visiting ministers who performed the usual church functions of baptizing children, confirming the teen-agers, burying the dead, and sometimes also officiating at weddings. In particular, three visiting Lutheran pastors performed yeoman service during the early decades in Alberta: Hans Rebane from the New York Estonian Lutheran congregation, Dr. Jaan Sillak, a travelling missionary pastor, and Eduard Aksim, who was also professor at the Lutheran seminary in Waterloo, Ontario.

A number of factors were responsible for increasing the role of the church among the post-war Estonian immigrants and raising it to a virtually parallel position with that of the Estonian Association. The first factor was the continuation of the part that church had played in Estonia in opposition to Communist rule during the takeover in 1940-41; second, the deprivations and sufferings of wartime and the loss of family members and friends kindled and renewed spiritual and religious attitudes; third, the American and Canadian churches played a significant role in the immigration processes; and finally, the Estonian clergy formed the direct channel between the American and Canadian congregations and the immigrants, both in sponsoring them and in assisting them in their new country.[4] But none of these factors could have had the effect they did had it not been for the increased number of immigrants, who were now capable of supporting viable congregations.

The process of building the strong and viable network of the Estonian Lutheran Church in Canada began in 1946 when the Missouri Synod of the Lutheran Church in America called Pastor Rudolf Kiviranna from Sweden to serve the Estonian congregation in New York. Pastor Kiviranna was an activist and immediately began to lobby American congregations to assist the immigration of Estonian refugees from Europe. He also travelled widely and visited the scattered Estonian communities on the continent, including the nascent Estonian community in Toronto. The first post-war Estonian congregation in Canada, the St. Peter congregation, was founded in Toronto in August, 1948, and acquired its pastor a few months later when Oskar Puhm emigrated from Sweden. Pastor Puhm also served Estonians in St. Catharines and London, Ontario, and helped to found Estonian congregations in these cities.

In December, 1948, Pastor Karl Raudsepp came from Germany to Kitchener, Ontario, the seat of the Eastern Canada Synod of the Lutheran Church in America, at the invitation of the Canadian committee of the Lutheran World Federation, to organize and serve Estonian congregations in Canada. His mission was endorsed by the Archbishop of the

Estonian Lutheran Church, Johan Kõpp, who resided in Stockholm.[5] During the next two years Pastor Raudsepp travelled Canada from coast to coast serving Estonians and laying the foundations for congregations, which then acquired immigrating pastors quickly after their formation. Pastor Raudsepp himself settled in Montreal as minister of the St. John Estonian congregation he had founded in January, 1949.

In the short period of six years, 1948-54, fourteen Estonian Lutheran congregations were founded in Canada: St. Peter, Toronto (1948); St. John, Montreal (1949); St. Andrew, Toronto (1949); St. Paul, St. Catharines (1949); St. Paul, London (1950); St. Peter, Vancouver (1950); St. Paul, Ottawa (1950); the First Estonian Lutheran Church, Hamilton (1951); St. Jacob, Toronto (1951); Estonian Lutheran Church, Sault Ste. Marie (1951); Estonian Lutheran Church, Port Arthur (1952); Estonian Lutheran Church, Sudbury (1952); Trinity, Toronto (1952); Estonian Lutheran Church, Winnipeg (1952); and St. Paul, Montreal (1954). The founding of Estonian Associations and Estonian Lutheran congregations followed a parallel pattern, with the associations in general being founded first. However, in a few cases the church provided the first meeting place for the new immigrants and it was there that the idea of forming an Estonian Association was initiated.

The Estonian Lutheran congregations became members of either the Canada Synod of the Lutheran Church in America or the competing Missouri Synod. This split in membership between two competing church bodies in North America delayed the establishment of a united Estonian Lutheran Church in Canada;[6] it was not until the 1960's that the Estonian Evangelical Lutheran Synod in Canada was created with Pastor Karl Raudsepp as provost of the synod.[7] When in 1977 Pastor Raudsepp was appointed Bishop of the Estonian Lutheran Church in North America, he was succeeded by Pastor Oskar Puhm. Raudsepp belonged to the Lutheran Church in America and Puhm to the Missouri Synod. This kind of duality of membership continues among the Estonian Lutheran congregations in Canada with about two-thirds belonging to the Lutheran Church in America and the remainder to the Missouri Synod. But the primary allegiance is to the Estonian organization structure, which is global. Hence, the Estonian Canadian Synod is a member of the Estonian Evangelical Lutheran Church in exile, which has its consistorium (the governing body) and the archbishop located in Sweden. The parent global body is supported by five other Estonian synods in addition to the Canadian synod, in Sweden, the United States, England, Germany, and Australia.

The relationship between the Estonian congregations and the English-language congregations in the Lutheran fold in Canada displays no consistent pattern. Where Estonian churches have their own buildings there is little contact with the indigenous Canadian Lutheran congregations, but where the Estonian congregations share churches with English-language congregations there are varying degrees of interrelationships, especially in small communities where the host congregations have continued to make available premises and facilities for such non-spiritual cultural activities as choir singing, folk dancing, and scouting. These linkages have led many smaller Estonian congregations to assume social and cultural functions that had been foreign to the church in Estonia, and the character of the church has changed somewhat from the original Estonian-Nordic model of an austere, strictly spiritual leader to a mixture of the spiritual and the socio-cultural, along the North American model.

The formal linkages of Estonian Lutheran congregations in Canada can be shown by the following:

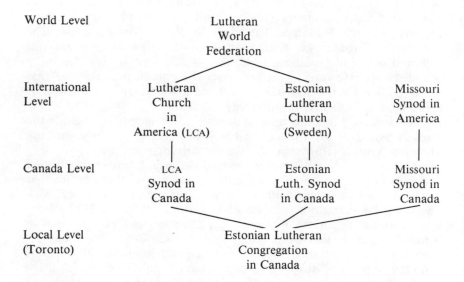

World Level	Lutheran World Federation		
International Level	Lutheran Church in America (LCA)	Estonian Lutheran Church (Sweden)	Missouri Synod in America
Canada Level	LCA Synod in Canada	Estonian Luth. Synod in Canada	Missouri Synod in Canada
Local Level (Toronto)		Estonian Lutheran Congregation in Canada	

Both the Lutheran Church in America and the Estonian Lutheran Church headquartered in Sweden are members of the Lutheran World Federation. The Missouri Synod is not a member of the Lutheran World Federation.

By the 1950's virtually all congregations, even the very small ones, had either a resident pastor or regular visiting pastors, with some pastors also holding other jobs or serving Canadian congregations as well. But since the 1960's many older pastors have died and not enough young Estonians in Canada have chosen to enter the ministry, and not all of these have chosen to serve the Estonian churches. In fact, there is such a dearth of Estonian Lutheran pastors that more recently three congregations have had to call their new pastors from abroad, two from England and one from Sweden.

The sizes of the Estonian congregations in Canada vary considerably.

The largest is St. Peter in Toronto with about 4,000 members; the next largest are St. John in Montreal and St. Andrew in Toronto with over 1,000 members each. The congregations in Hamilton and Vancouver and St. Jacob in Toronto number between 400 and 500 each. All the rest of the Lutheran congregations in Canada have fewer than 200 members. Four Lutheran congregations own their own churches and have built facilities for social and cultural activities. St. Andrew in Toronto and St. John in Montreal both purchased their churches; St. Peter in Toronto and St. Peter in Vancouver erected new buildings, the latter together with the Estonian Association of Vancouver.

In addition to the Lutheran congregations there are also other denominational congregations in Estonian communities in Canada. Toronto, Montreal, and Vancouver have Estonian Orthodox congregations with the Toronto congregation numbering about 400 members. It holds its services in the St. Peter Lutheran Church.

The Estonian Baptist congregation in Toronto was founded in June, 1949, and has over 500 members currently. It is perhaps the most active Estonian congregation in Canada, has a newly built modern church, several choirs and ensembles, and often holds church concerts, fellowship meetings, and seminars on a variety of topics. It also broadcasts services regularly and produces these in its own radio studio.

There are also a number of smaller Protestant "free churches" in Toronto and Vancouver, such as the Adventists, Pentecostals, and others. Although in Toronto they hold separate services in premises shared with Canadian congregations, in Vancouver they formed an Estonian Evangelical Alliance and built a new church. One of the Toronto congregations and the Vancouver one broadcast services regularly.

Summing up the Estonian church congregational activities in Canada we note that the Estonians own six churches in Canada, of which four are Lutheran; three are in Toronto, two in Vancouver, and one in Montreal. The Estonian congregations number over 10,000 members altogether, with about 90 per cent belonging to the Lutheran denomination.[7] All services are held in the Estonian language only. In addition, many Estonians, especially in smaller cities and rural areas, belong to various Canadian congregations and churches.

CENTRAL ORGANIZATIONS

If we define "central organization" as any council, committee, or board that claims a representative or co-ordinative role in one of the activity fields organized by Estonians in Canada, then by definition there are several dozen such central organizations. Virtually any and every activity attempts some kind of organizing or representative role. Unfortunately, and almost without exception, they are all located in Toronto with input from minor Estonian communities in Canada usually nominal or nonexistent.

Nevertheless, it is possible to distinguish organizations that provide some kind of umbrella function to all the Estonian communities in Canada, and not only to the Toronto community. Two organizations – the Estonian Federation in Canada and the Estonian Central Council in Canada – have attempted to bring organized Estonian activities in Canada together, in either a representative or an umbrella organization. In addition, a number of single-function organizations also attempt to serve Estonians on an all-Canada basis and actively solicit support from across the country. Among these are the Estonian Relief Committee, the Estonian National Foundation, the Estonian Arts Centre, and the Canadian Estonian History Commission. All of these are located in Toronto and hence may be confused by a casual observer as being Toronto community organizations.

Estonian Federation in Canada (Eesti Liit Kanadas)

The federation was founded in 1949 to assist and co-ordinate the activities of various local Estonian Associations and to promote and protect the interests of Estonians in Canada.[8] Although membership is open to all Estonian ethnic organizations, the primary objective of the federation has been to gather all the Estonian organizations into its membership. As a result, membership has fluctuated between a low of a little over two dozen to as many as sixty member organizations. Financially, the federation has been severely restricted since its main income has been in the form of membership fees, which have remained very low. It meets annually in a congress of delegates from member organizations to elect the executive board, which serves for two years.

The activities of the federation have leaned more toward information dissemination and initiation of activities than to action by the federation itself, although during its early years it was very active, particularly during the period of Estonian immigration to Canada. It assisted the Estonians who arrived by the Viking boats from Sweden and promoted emigration from Europe by providing information on Canada and lobbying the Canadian government for Estonian immigration.

Since the disappearance of the need to act on immigration questions the federation has initiated a number of activities, organizations, and projects. It established the Estonian Relief Committee and the Estonian Central Council in Canada and later set up a sub-committee that became the Estonian History Commission. During the 1970's the federation also initiated an extensive oral history project in which 200 interviews with older Estonians were taped. In addition, in the 1970's the federation twice ran a leadership seminar for younger Estonians on the campus of Trent University.

The federation's seminal role in initiating and co-ordinating cultural activities is due in no small measure to its ability to attract prominent public personalities to its executive.[9] It has also been successful in combining the older and younger generations. To promote its all-Canadian reach and to increase input from Estonian communities outside Toronto, one vice-president normally has come from Montreal and a second from Vancouver. Its bulletin, *Sillas*, has formed a link among Estonian communities in Canada and is the federation's primary disseminator of information.

The Estonian Central Council in Canada
(Eesti Kesknõukogu Kanadas)

The Estonian Central Council in Canada originated as the political action committee of the Estonian Federation in Canada. It became an independent organization in 1954 under the name Estonian Council for Political Action and changed its name to the present one in 1974. The members of the council are elected at large for three-year terms by Canadians of Estonian descent by means of a mail-in ballot. Originally only twenty councillors were elected, but the number was increased to thirty-five and subsequently to fifty-five to increase participation from outside Toronto and among younger Estonians. Of the elected councillors usually a little over 10 per cent come from outside Toronto – from Montreal, Vancouver, and southern and northern Ontario. Traditionally, one vice-presidency goes to either a Montreal or Vancouver councillor and another to an Ottawa councillor or a representative from southern or northern Ontario. The council numbers among its past presidents two former Estonian cabinet ministers and two former members of parliament.[10]

The council claims to be the parliament "of the Estonian community in Canada." Hence, it assumes the right to make decisions on all matters concerning the public and communal affairs of the Estonian ethnic group in Canada. It has established an elaborate system of standing committees, including committees on ethnocultural and ethnopolitical affairs, finance, information, legal matters, and so forth. Since the council's ultimate stated objective is the eventual restoration of Estonia as an independent sovereign state, its main function is the dissemination of information about Estonia and Estonians and about the Soviet occupation in Estonia to Canadians, including political parties and members of Parliament and legislatures. In addition, the council has attempted to govern Canadian Estonians' attitudes toward, and relations with, Soviet-occupied Estonia. In fact, the main impact of the council is the influence that its deliberations and guidelines have within the Estonian ethnic community in Canada.

The council's most successful external activity has been the institution, together with Latvian and Lithuanian organizations, of the annual Baltic Evening at the Parliament Buildings in Ottawa. These programs consist of discussions and presentations about the Baltic nations and their ethnic groups in Canada to members of both the houses of Parliament. A second political event is an annual reception in Toronto during the Estonian Independence celebration on February 24 to which federal politicians in the Toronto area, members of the Ontario legislature, and Toronto-based diplomatic representatives are invited. The council's efforts at building links between the Estonian community in Canada and the Canadian public at large take up a considerable amount of time of the councillors and must be judged very successful.

Part of the reason for the success is the increasing number of younger Estonians who have become members of the council.[11] They have brought with them a greater understanding of the political and social processes in Canada, as well as an entrée into social, political, and economic institutions of Canada that the older generation lacked. Nevertheless, although its leadership appears to be passing into the hands of the younger generation, the council still has not become fully representative of the Estonians in Canada since input from outside the Toronto community remains limited.

The council is also responsible for maintaining archival material generated by Estonians in Canada and established the Estonian Archives in Toronto. These currently consist of about 4,000 volumes of books, most issues of Estonian newspapers and magazines published since the Second World War outside Estonia, and collections of photographs, films, sound recordings, maps, music scores, documents, manuscripts, and papers deposited by private individuals.

The Estonian Relief Committee (Eesti Abistamiskomitee)

The Estonian Relief Committee was established in Toronto in August, 1950, to assist Estonians immigrating to Canada and to aid in their adjustment to Canadian conditions by soliciting sponsorships, arranging for employment, and finding housing. The plan to make the committee a nationwide organization did not materialize because a number of other Estonian organizations and congregations already existed across the country that were fully capable of carrying out these functions. Hence, the committee remained a Toronto-based organization.

Increasingly, after the end of the period of immigration, a second aim of the committee became the assistance of the Estonians who had remained in Germany. Most of these were the old, the sick, and Estonian war invalids who were not accepted for immigration by other countries. From 1951 to 1971 the Estonian Relief Committee spent over $150,000 on this activity. When the government of the Federal Republic of Germany undertook the care of these people the burden on the committee eased.

From the late 1960's on, the attention of the Estonian Relief Committee has focused on helping the older Estonians in Canada. In 1977 it built a condominium complex for senior citizens named *Eesti Kodu* (Estonian Home) in West Hill, a suburb of Toronto. Four years later a nursing home, *Ehatare*, was added to the complex. Although it is the first such project in Toronto, a similar complex in Sault Ste. Marie was built jointly by the Finns and Estonians.

The main income of the Estonian Relief Committee has come from donations solicited annually from individual Estonians and, to a lesser extent, from its store in the Estonian House in Toronto, which sells Estonian ethnic handicrafts and souvenirs.

The Estonian National Foundation of Canada
(Eesti Rahvuslik Sihtkapital Kanadas)

The Estonian National Foundation of Canada, headquartered in Toronto, was established in 1974 to secure a financial base for the future of the Estonian cultural and communal activities in Canada. Many of those Estonian immigrants who had come to this country as adults were aging and reaching the end of their lives, and the aim is for the foundation to provide an outlet for the estates of those who do not have close relatives in Canada. In addition to bequests, the foundation actively solicits donations and gifts. To date it has raised over $300,000 and has been bequeathed a well-known gardening and nursery enterprise in southern Ontario.

The foundation is governed by a board of directors, all of whom have so far come from the Toronto Estonian community, as have most donations, although some gifts have come from other Estonian communities in Canada.

The Canadian Estonian History Commission
(Kanada Eestlaste Ajaloo Komisjon)

The Canadian Estonian History Commission originated as a committee of the Estonian Federation of Canada, but when the commission established its own sub-commissions in all the Estonian communities in Canada it broke off from its parent body and became an independent organization. Its original aim was to collect material for a history of the Estonians in Canada. As a result of the co-operative efforts of its network of contributors from all over Canada, a 670-page folio-sized volume under the title *Eestlased Kanadas* (The Estonians in Canada) was published in 1975.

In the 1980's the commission is planning to publish a second volume updating the 1975 edition to the end of 1982 and to issue a 60-page summary of the book in English. It still has a network of contributors throughout the Estonian communities in Canada but the system of local sub-commissions disappeared after 1975.

The Estonian Arts Centre (Eesti Kunstide Keskus)

The Estonian Arts Centre originated as a branch of the now defunct Estonian Arts Council and became an independent operation in 1971. Located in Toronto, its aim is to promote and foster Estonian ethnic art in all its various forms, from folk art to customs, visual art, music, and drama, throughout Canada. Until now its main efforts have been confined largely to music and fine art. It has arranged series of concerts by

Estonian singers and soloists from Canada and Europe and exhibitions of Estonian paintings. The centre has actively encouraged new generations of artists by means of lectures, conferences, seminars, and competitions, especially for young musicians. It has also provided stipends for young Estonian artists and musicians and has arranged concerts and exhibitions specifically for them.

A second major objective of the centre is to establish collections of Estonian art. Currently it is pursuing a project to catalogue and photograph all works of fine art by Estonian artists in Canada, now mainly in the possession of private collectors. The centre already owns some paintings by Estonian artists and is in the process of acquiring more.

The centre is governed by a board of trustees elected annually from among the members of the centre. Its income derives mainly from donations, concert and conference fees, and commissions on art sales. The long-term aim of the centre is to establish a permanent collection and a gallery of Estonian fine art in Canada.

VETERANS' ORGANIZATIONS

Veterans' Associations (Võitlejate Ühingud)

One in every two Estonian adult males who came to Canada immediately after the Second World War was a war veteran, and some were veterans of more than one war.[12] A few had been officers and soldiers in the Czarist Russian army in the First World War and many were veterans of the Estonian War of Independence that lasted from 1918 to 1920. The overwhelming majority of veterans, however, had been soldiers and officers in the Second World War, fighting under various colours and on various fronts. Most had been drafted either into the German army (or, more correctly, into the various German armies, both the regular and the Waffen-SS) or into volunteer Estonian units attached to the German army; others had served in the Finnish army or navy.[13] Hence, it is not surprising that Estonian war veterans formed very active organizations in Canada soon after their arrival in this country. The Toronto Estonian Veterans' Association was founded by fifty charter members in November, 1952.[14] Other associations were founded at about the same time in Montreal, Hamilton, Ottawa, and Vancouver. In 1954 the local associations joined together to found the League of Estonian Veterans in Canada; the league in turn joined the International Centre of Estonian Veterans headquartered in the United States.

The Estonian Veterans' Associations are parallelled by Latvian, Lithuanian, Polish, Hungarian, and other foreign veterans' organizations; three co-operative organizations have been established among these in which the Estonians have participated. The earliest was the Mutual Cooperation League of émigré war veterans' associations that united in their anti-Communist and anti-Soviet fervour. A cover organization, the Baltic Veterans' League in Canada, was formed by the Estonian, Latvian, and Lithuanian veterans' organizations and in 1966 the Baltic Veterans' Corps, consisting of former officers from the three Baltic countries, was established. All of these are Toronto-centred organizations.

Among the Estonian veterans' organizations three interrelated functions are predominant. The first, of course, is the standard one of renewing comradeship, reminiscing about past glories and/or miseries, and remembering fallen comrades. Second, since wars are fought for ideas for which great sacrifices are often made, the memory of these ideas and sacrifices is a powerful bond that unites the comrades-at-arms. The Estonian units attached to the German army did not fight for Germany but for Estonia and against the Soviets in the firm conviction that this would lead to the re-establishment of a free Estonia. Had the Germans been the suppressors of independent Estonia, as the Russians were, the Estonians would have been just as anti-German as they were anti-Soviet. In other words, the Estonian Veterans' Associations have as one of their important goals the restoration of an independent Estonian state. The third aim of the veterans' associations has been pragmatic, involving matters such as looking after their common welfare and supporting members in need. Among the welfare functions, one keenly felt duty has been the moral and financial support of Estonian war invalids in Germany. The associations have raised considerable sums of money for building several communal homes for the war invalids. They have also assisted their members in successfully making claims for veterans' benefits as officers in the Russian Czarist and German armies.

In addition to their frequent comradeship meetings and social get-togethers, dances, and balls, the Estonian Veterans' Associations have also held public meetings to air various issues. One of their concerns has been the lack of attention paid by the Estonian communities to other Estonian national events besides the Independence Day, such as the beginning of the Estonian War of Independence against the Soviets and the Victory Day (June 23) when the Estonian armed forces defeated the German mercenary Landeswehr in 1919.

The largest gatherings of former soldiers have taken place at the larger Estonian festivals. For example, many hundreds of veterans from several countries, including Canada, attended the 1980 World Festival in Stockholm. Smaller local, Canadian, or North American meetings take place every summer and have in recent years been held at Seedrioru, an Estonian summer camp near Elora in southwestern Ontario. The Estonian Veterans' Association published a quarterly, *Võitleja* (the Warrior), in Germany until 1979. In 1980 the editorial office was transferred to Toronto. In 1959 a monument commemorating those who had given their lives fighting for Estonian independence was erected at Seedrioru. The money was raised and the monument commissioned and built by a special committee created for this purpose, composed of the delegates from both veterans' and non-veterans' organizations in Canada.

In the 1960's a new association, the Estonian Patriots Club *(Eesti Rahvulaste Klubi)*, was formed in Toronto by a group of Estonian nationalists who felt that the veterans' organizations had become too lax in their loyalty to the ideals of an independent Estonian republic. Hence, the club, formed to emphasize Estonian patriotism, welcomed as its members not only veterans but anyone who supported its aims. The club has taken strong patriotic stands on some Estonian community issues and has published a news bulletin, *Rahvuslane* (The Patriot).

Soomepoisid (Men of Finland/Les Gens de la Finlande)

The Finnish Army's Infantry Regiment No. 200 was made up solely of Estonian officers and men. The regiment's 3,000 men had fled German-occupied Estonia mostly to avoid being conscripted into the German army; some, however, were deserters from the German armed forces and yet others had fled to avoid arrest by the German police for political reasons. In Finland these men had voluntarily joined the Finnish army or navy and the Finnish high command had established Regiment No. 200 as an independent Estonian unit. The regiment fought valiantly with heavy losses in the most heated battles in Finnish Karelia in 1943 and 1944. When the Finnish-Soviet armistice talks started during the summer of 1944 the regiment was disbanded and the officers and most of the men, given amnesty by the Germans, returned to Estonia to fight the Soviet invaders at home. In Estonia the regiment again suffered heavy losses and was among the last of the Estonian forces defending the country against the Soviet invasion. When Estonia finally fell under the onslaught of the Soviet forces only a few of the original *Soomepoisid*, as they were commonly called by other Estonians, succeeded in escaping to either Germany or Sweden. About 200 eventually immigrated to Canada and founded the *Soomepoiste Klubi* (The Club of the Men of Finland) in Toronto.

The club has confined its activities largely to comradeship and to cultural activities. Its members have remained largely aloof from the Estonian Veterans' Associations and have co-operated with them only occasionally and selectively. The various clubs of the Men of Finland in Sweden, Canada, and the United States have kept contact with each other but have not formed a cover organization. Along with other Estonian organizations they also tend to hold major meetings at the World Festivals of Estonians. Hence, a meeting of more than 200 took place at the Estonian World Festival in 1980 at Stockholm, which included a substantial attendance from Canada. The Men of Finland have also published a serial, *Põhjala Tähistel* (The Outposts of the North), alternately in Sweden and in Canada, and a history of the regiment titled *Soomepoisid*, which appeared in 1973 in Toronto. The latter has also been issued in abbreviated version in English under the title *For Freedom Only*. [15] The Men of Finland who immigrated to Canada from Germany came here as lumberjacks under contract to the lumber industries in

"Estonian" School in Medicine Valley, Alberta, 1908. (Courtesy Estonian Central Archives in Canada)

Opening of "Linda Hall" in Eckville, Alberta, 1911. (Courtesy Estonian Central Archives in Canada)

Winnipeg Estonian Association "Side" outing in 1929. (Courtesy Estonian Central Archives in Canada)

Estonian Association in Montreal, 1933. (Courtesy Estonian Central Archives in Canada)

Time magazine of December 27, 1948, reporting on Walnut *arrival at Halifax, N.S. (Courtesy Estonian Central Archives in Canada)*

New Canadians?

Into Halifax harbor last week slipped a rusty, tubby naval trawler that had once been H.M.S. *Walnut*. Instead of a navy complement of 80, she was jampacked with 347 Baltic refugees. As she tied up at pier 21, men & women crowded up on deck, cheered, wept, and sang their national anthems. After a rough 30-day voyage from Sweden, the refugees hoped they had come to journey's end.

For four years they had waited in Sweden, where they had fled from their homelands ahead of the Russian invasion. They had hoped vainly for visas and transportation out of Europe. Finally they pooled their funds, for $63,000 bought the aging *Walnut*, manned her with their own members who had been fishermen and sailors. They crammed into triple-deck bunks, rigged hammocks where they could. Last month, the biggest group of Balts to try the North Atlantic crossing slipped out of Göteborg harbor and headed for Canada.

"We fled," said chunky, Estonian-born Captain August Linde, 47, "because we were afraid of the Russians. They had their specialists everywhere in Sweden. Many of our people who had fled to Stockholm were kidnaped in broad daylight. We never knew when our turn would come."

In Halifax, Chief Immigration Inspector Harry Wade listened sympathetically to Captain Linde's story. "O.K., bring them ashore," he said. Only 15 had visas. The rest had to go through a routine health and immigration check. Cots were put up in detention quarters and the waiting room and the long-vacant Rockhead Detention Hospital was opened for the overflow.

Since last December, when Canada admitted 24 Baltic refugees whom the U.S. did not want, four tiny refugee-laden Baltic craft had pulled into eastern Canadian ports. Canada had checked and admitted all 198 of those aboard. The fact that this time the refugees came in a bigger group and a bigger boat did not bother immigration officials. Said Inspector Wade: "They have proven themselves fine people to date . . . We hope all of them can become Canadian citizens."

TIME, DECEMBER 27, 1948

An Ontario Hydro crew of Estonian men in Burlington, Ontario, 1949.
(Courtesy Estonian Central Archives in Canada)

Estonian Volleyball team of Toronto Central Y, Canadian
champions, 1956. (Courtesy Ilmar Kasekamp)

Memorial at the Estonian summer camp, Seedrioru, near Elora, Ontario, erected in 1959, design by Vello Hubel. "Remember what was lost, and which remains." (M. Under) (Courtesy Estonian Central Archives in Canada)

Eaton's window decoration in Montreal on the occasion of Estonian Independence Day, February 24, 1955. (Photo Viktor Rein, courtesy Estonian Central Archives in Canada)

Estonian built and owned ski resort, Horseshoe Valley, near Barrie, Ontario, 1960. Architect E. Tampōld. (Courtesy Estonian Central Archives in Canada)

The Third Estonian Song Festival in Canada, at Seedrioru, 1962. (Courtesy Seedrioru Archives)

Estonian Lutheran Church and Estonia House "Meie Kodu" in Vancouver, B.C.
(Courtesy Väino Veemees)

Altar woodcarvings in the Estonian Lutheran Church in Vancouver, B.C.
(Courtesy Väino Veemees)

Inset: Estonia House in Toronto, side view after renovation and addition, 1964.
(Courtesy Estonia House, Toronto)
Above: Tartu College, Madison Avenue and Bloor Street, Toronto.
(Courtesy Endel Aruja, Tartu Institute)

Estonian Female Choir concert in Toronto, 1958.
(Photo H. Roomeri, courtesy Estonian Central Archives in Canada)

Toronto Estonian Mixed Choir in 1960.
(Courtesy Estonian Central Archives in Canada)

Estonian Male Choirs, concert at Massey Hall, Toronto, 1972.
(Photo Uno Kabal, courtesy Estonian Central Archives in Canada)

*Part of the cast of Shakespeare's "Hamlet," Seedrioru, 1963. In the front row from left:
A. Vabamäe (Polonius), L. Vohu (Ophelia), K. Söödor (the King), R. Reinik (the Queen),
R. Lipp (Hamlet), E. Silm (set design), T. Lipp (costumes). (Courtesy Estonian Central
Archives in Canada)*

*A scene from A. Kallas's "Reigi õpetaja" (Pastor of Reigi) by Toronto Estonian National
Theatre, 1968. (Photo Tommy Thompson, courtesy Lydia Vohu)*

Scenes from folk dance club Kungla. (Courtesy Estonian Central Archives in Canada)

Kalev-Estienne gymnasts. (Courtesy Estonian Central Archives in Canada)

Toronto Estonian Supplementary School in 1954. (Courtesy Estonian Central Archives in Canada)

An Estonian Senior Girl Guides' choir, Toronto. (Courtesy Estonian Central Archives in Canada)

Signing the agreement between Boy Scouts of Canada and Estonian Boy Scouts in Canada in Estonia House, Toronto, September 8, 1983. (Photo Vaba Eestlane)

A panel discussion in Metsaülikool, 1968. Left to right: professors O. Arens (modern history), I. Ivask (comparative literature), T. Parming (sociology), I. Lipping (Estonian history), O. Millert (psychology), and O. Träss (chemical engineering). (Courtesy Ants Toi [ed.], Näod (Faces): Metsaülikool 1967, 1968 [Toronto, 1968].)

*Scenes from the
Fourth Estonian World
Festival, Toronto, 1984.*

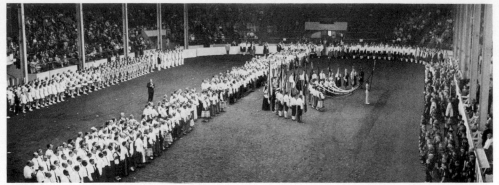

Opening ceremony of North American Estonian Festival in the Coliseum, CNE, Toronto, 1968. (Photo Uno Kabal, courtesy Estonian Central Archives in Canada)

Estonian Independence Day in Massey Hall, Toronto, February, 1973. (Courtesy Estonian Central Archives in Canada)

northern Ontario. None, however, remained there after the contract ended, and most moved to Toronto. Those who came from Sweden were free to choose their employment but because of language difficulties most began their new lives in Canada as unskilled labourers. Since their average age at immigration was about twenty-five, nearly all had secondary education, many had partial college training, and some had completed university degrees. Subsequently, quite a few upgraded their education in their chosen fields in Canada and others acquired new professions, predominantly in technical fields.[16]

Lennuväeabiteenistuslased (Air Force Auxiliaries)
In 1944, in the concluding phases of the war, many thousands of Estonian schoolboys aged sixteen to eighteen were drafted into the German air force auxiliary services. In fact, this was conscription to front-line service in disguise and the draftees were given battle training in Germany. Only the rapid end of war saved them from front-line duty. After the war these teen-aged draftees ended up first in prisoner-of-war camps and then in refugee camps in West Germany, where they completed their education and learned additional skills or went on to either the Baltic University in Hamburg or the German universities. None, however, completed university training before emigration from Germany. The majority immigrated to the United States, Australia, and England and about 150 came to Canada. In 1960 they founded the Club of Estonian (former) Air Force Auxiliaries in Toronto. The club's activities have been restricted to comradeship and social activities.

Almost all these men came to Canada as lumberjacks. Nearly all had secondary education and some had one or two years of university or additional training in technical skills though they were without any actual experience. Almost all moved to Toronto, where they found various kinds of employment, initially mostly in the unskilled and semi-skilled categories. Like the Men of Finland, almost none missed any opportunity to upgrade his technical training, to learn new professions, or to continue studying at university. Also like the Men of Finland, the auxiliaries are proud that many of them have had outstandingly successful careers in Canada.[17]

NOTES

1. E. Lootsma *et al.* (eds.), *Eestlased Londonis* (Estonians in London) (London, Ontario, 1979), is a review of a typical Estonian small community in Canada from the early 1950's to the late 1970's. Also, E. Rebane (comp.), "Kitcheneri Eesti Seltsi Kroonika" (Chronicle of Estonian Association in Kitchener), 1979, manuscript in Estonian Central Archives, which is less descriptive but has much statistical detail.
2. *Meie Elu*, November 17, 1979, September 4, 1980. *Meie Elu* of August 2, 1984, however, reported that the "74 years old Medicine Valley (Eck-

ville) Estonian Association was liquidated on March 16, 1984." See also, *Vaba Eestlane*, August 2, 1984.

3. There were in Toronto and the Niagara Peninsula in 1948 actually two Estonian clubs, Edu and Sõprus, but both ceased to exist and merged into the Toronto Estonian Association after the new immigrants arrived.

4. P. Wukasch, "Baltic Immigration in Canada, 1947-1955," *Concordia Historical Institute Quarterly*, 1 (1977), pp. 4-22, gives some detail on assistance by the Canadian Missouri Synod. See also C.R. Cronmiller, *A History of the Lutheran Church in Canada* (Toronto: Ev. Lutheran Synod of Canada, 1961).

5. Archbishop of Estonian Ev. Lutheran Church (Stockholm), Johan Kõpp, February 14, 1948, and President of Ev. Lutheran Synod of Canada, Dr. J.H. Reble, July 14, 1948, to Pastor Karl Raudsepp. Letters in Bishop Raudsepp's archives.

6. P. Wukasch, in "Baltic Immigration," is mistaken when he assumes that there was a split among the Estonian pastors that caused animosities. The animosities between the two church bodies in Canada, the Lutheran Church in America and the Missouri Synod, caused the split among Estonian pastors in Canada. See Cronmiller, *A History of the Lutheran Church in Canada*.

7. According to Kurlents *et al.* (eds.), *Eestlased Kanadas*, p. 437, there were 9,400 Estonian Lutherans in Canada in 1967. According to a letter from Bishop K. Raudsepp of September 26, 1979, to the author there were 8,711 members of the Estonian Lutheran Church in Canada. Membership includes all baptized members, children, and minors.

8. Founding date of the federation has been debated. E. Soomet in *Sillas*, no. 4/5 (1979), states that a provisional executive was elected on June 26, 1949, at the Estonian summer festival near St. Catharines, by representatives of various Estonian organizations, including some organizations from the Prairies and Alberta.

9. For instance, the following members of the parliament of Estonia have served as presidents of the federation: A. Weiler (1949-50), M. Hansen (1950-51 and 1953-56), K. Kurg (1956), and E. Riisna (1956-58 and 1972-76).

10. Former cabinet members in Estonia, J. Holberg (1952-53) and J. Müller (1954-56), and former members of the parliament of Estonia, M. Hansen (1958-59) and E. Riisna (1953-54 and 1957-58).

11. The average age of the councillors elected in May, 1981, was forty-eight. Nine councillors were under thirty and eight were in their thirties. *Vaba Eestlane*, May 14, 1981.

12. Typically, Major B. Leeman, who celebrated his eighty-fifth birthday in 1979 in Toronto, was an officer in the First World War, the Estonian War of Independence, and the Second World War. A.J. Kala (ed.), *Toronto Eesti Võitlejate Ühing* (Toronto Estonian Veterans Association), (Toronto, 1979), p. 31.

13. To make the picture more confused, Captain Endel Susi, a World War II

combat pilot in the British Air Force, may be mentioned. As a member of the Estonian air force in 1940 he was transferred to the Soviet air force, which he deserted in 1941. Oral History Project sources.

14. Kala (ed.), *Toronto Eesti Võitlejate Ühing*, p. 19.
15. E. Uustalu and R. Moora (eds.), *Soomepoisid* (Toronto, 1973); Uustalu, *For Freedom Only* (Toronto, 1977).
16. Among them are some Estonian writers, lawyers, architects, successful businessmen, and university professors in Canada.
17. Some have made outstanding careers in university research and university teaching or in fields of public life in Canada.

SEVEN

Cultural Activities

CHOIRS AND MUSIC

It has become conventional wisdom among non-Estonians that when Estonians get together they like to sing. And it is true. Traditionally among Estonians any social gathering or family reunion with a dozen or more people has been unimaginable without group singing, sometimes for hours on end. For Estonians such group singing both provides entertainment and functions as a psychosocial release that uplifts and unites them.

The singing tradition naturally formed the base for formal choir singing. Music, drama, and literature in general, but choir singing in particular, were a hallmark of the Estonian national awakening during the nineteenth century. Every small community established its own choir that learned songs for presentation at concerts and song festivals. The national song festivals became occasions where hundreds of choirs and orchestras joined into one mighty choir and orchestra.

In present-day Soviet Estonia even larger national song festivals continue to be held. After the war, choirs were immediately organized among the refugees and concerts and song festivals were held in Sweden and in the refugee camps in Germany. In Canada, Estonian choirs were established first in Southern Alberta during the 1920's and 1930's and sang at Estonian gatherings as well as at other ethnic and English-Canadian events. It is interesting to note that some who were anti-church in the Estonian communities at the time were enthusiastic promoters of choir singing.

After the Second World War the first Estonian choirs, formed as early as 1948, were the female choir in Montreal and the male choirs in Kirkland Lake and Rolphton, Ontario, and in some of the lumber camps in northern Ontario. The latter were formed by the young unmarried men and family heads who had left their families in Germany and were working either as miners, Ontario Hydro construction labourers, or lumberjacks. Some of the male choirs in the northland were formed jointly with Canadian Finns working and living up there. None of the northern choirs, however, lasted more than a year or two, because after the original work contract under which these men had come to Canada expired they moved on to the south, mainly to the cities. The only one of the original 1948 choirs still in existence is the female choir in Montreal.

The early 1950's saw between thirty and forty Estonian mixed, male, and female choirs of various sizes established. The larger and the more specialized choirs were naturally established in the larger Estonian communities, in Toronto, Montreal, Hamilton, and Vancouver, but all Estonian Associations had at least one choir. If in other matters Estonians have been reluctant to appear before non-Estonian audiences, the choirs have not; they missed no opportunity to sing to Canadian audiences. The prime reason was to acquaint the Canadian public with the Estonian ethnic group and to present Estonia's case as enjoyably and effectively as possible. Indeed, Estonian choirs in the 1950's, and even into the 1960's, appeared before non-Estonian audiences as often as before Estonian audiences.

The 1960's, however, produced a considerable change. Many of the smaller choirs disappeared as the core members aged and not enough replacements among the younger people were forthcoming. In the smaller communities choir singing has become a sporadic activity usually revived only before the main festivals. Viable choirs are limited to Toronto, Montreal, Hamilton, and Vancouver; and even among them, although their singing has improved technically, their members have been aging. The past decade and a half has also seen a considerable decline in the number of choir appearances before non-Estonian audiences.

On the other hand, a few new choirs, made up of young singers, have emerged. The most significant of these have been "Vikerlased" in Montreal, its successor, "Leelo," which is still in existence, and the choir of the Estonian Girl Guides in Toronto. There have been few Estonian church choirs, but "Cantate Domino," a contemporary church choir in Toronto, may be counted among the best Estonian choirs in Canada. Also, St. Andrew's Church in Toronto has both male and female choirs, and the Estonian Baptist Church in Toronto has several choirs and smaller local ensembles as well.

The two strongest male choirs have been in Toronto and Montreal. Both have given concerts all over Canada and the United States to both Estonian and non-Estonian audiences. Of the two, the Toronto Estonian Male Choir once had over 100 singers, including large numbers of soloists. This choir has regularly sung at Massey Hall and the O'Keefe Centre in Toronto, at university auditoriums, and also at Lincoln Centre in New York. It has performed at the 100th anniversary celebrations of the Canadian Lutheran Synod in Kitchener, at the Stratford music festivals, and at summer concerts of the Toronto Symphony Orchestra. In 1970 the choir was selected by the Ontario government to represent

Ontario in the 100th anniversary celebrations of Manitoba in Winnipeg. It has also given joint concerts with the Rochester University Symphony Orchestra in Toronto, Rochester, and New York City. From 1964 on it has made a number of European tours. Moreover, its conductor-directors have established reputations beyond the Estonian community; the director of the choir, for example, was invited in 1962 to direct the Finnish North American Men's Song festival. There is little question that the Toronto Estonian Male Choir once was one of the best choirs in Toronto.

Toronto and Montreal have also maintained female choirs, but their range of concerts has not been nearly as wide as that of the male choirs. Usually the female choirs have limited themselves to one concert annually, performed mainly before Estonian audiences, plus participation at the various Estonian festivals.

Most of the choirs, however, are mixed choirs; the best known of these is the Toronto Mixed Choir. Naturally, there is a certain degree of overlap in the membership of the different choirs in Toronto, and the conductor-directors have also often interchanged podiums. The primary problem of the adult choirs, even in Toronto, during the 1970's was rejuvenation of singers, although there has been no problem of finding new conductor-directors.

Youth choirs have invariably consisted of those who really love to sing for the sake of singing, and thus they invariably run into the problem of finding enough enthusiastic members, although some have managed at times to reach a membership of thirty to forty. But their main problem has been the lack of a core of experienced and accomplished singers. This lack of experience has limited their repertoire severely, usually to the easier songs and those more widely known and entertaining. As in the case of the adult choirs, the youth choirs also regularly perform at ethnic festivals in addition to the concerts they give at other occasions.

The children's choirs are almost exclusively choirs formed in the supplementary schools, although various churches have sporadically formed children's choirs. Supplementary schools include singing as part of their curriculum. Public presentations of singing by the supplementary school choirs are usually limited to school festivals, at Christmas, and at the end of the school year in the spring. Despite the limitations of children's singing, some of the choirs formed are relatively large, for example, the Toronto Estonian Supplementary School has had over 100 children in its school choir. And there have been children's concerts at the ethnic festivals at which between 400 and 500 children have formed a joint choir.

In repertoire the Estonian choirs in Canada have not only carried on the old traditions but have contributed to the development of Estonian choir singing, and quite a number of new songs have been composed since the Second World War. Some of the best known of these composers live in Canada, with the result that many of their new songs have had their first presentation by a choir here. The best known of the Estonian composers in Canada are Roman Toi, Kaljo Raid, Lembit Avesson, Udo Kasemets, and Uno Kook. Their production, and that of their colleagues in other countries, has been such that in recent years often half of the concert program has been made up of songs composed by them since the Second World War. The choirs have been active in soliciting and in encouraging new compositions, usually through competitions in which Estonian composers from different countries participate.

On an organizational basis the Estonian choirs are very loosely federated into the League of Estonian Singers in North America. Although the league has given some initiative to choir singing, all concerts and festivals have been organized either by the choirs themselves or by ad hoc committees established by them or by the principal conductor chosen for the particular occasion.

ORCHESTRAS AND INSTRUMENTAL MUSIC

Although the tradition of establishing community orchestras began almost at the same time as the choirs, the amateur orchestra was always less popular than amateur singing in Estonia. Nevertheless, at song festivals in Estonia, both before and since the war, as well as among Estonian communities abroad, orchestral concerts are also given at song festivals. Orchestras and bands have been created for specific purposes – symphony orchestras to accompany operatic productions and broadcasting, bands established for parades, and small ensembles to provide accompaniment for dancing. In Estonia before the war each professional theatre, as well as the broadcasting system, had its own semi-professional or professional orchestra. But in Canada the Estonian ethnic group has been too small to afford the development of orchestras. The only attempt to establish a symphony orchestra was made in the 1950's by the Estonian theatre in Montreal, which formed a temporary ensemble to accompany an operetta.

Brass bands, however, are another story, with the earliest Estonian amateur brass band being formed in southern Alberta before the Second World War and others, mainly in Toronto, since that period. The best known of the latter has been the "Estonia" orchestra formed in 1957 in Toronto. "Estonia" performs for its own concert public as well as at various Estonian ethnocultural events, such as the Estonian Independence Day celebrations in Toronto and at the various song festivals. It has maintained a successful recruiting program and has ranged up to fifty brass and percussion players.

THEATRE

The theatre has formed the second most important sector of Estonian ethnic culture in Canada. Estonian theatre in Canada is rooted in the traditions of the home country, where amateur theatre was as popular as the professional theatre and was pursued actively on a wide scale, not only in the cities but even in small rural communities. Amateur theatre formed an integral part of the Estonian national awakening during the latter part of the nineteenth century. Like choir singing, drama is a collective art and as such performs a multiplicity of social and cultural functions. Even rehearsals emphasize community involvement, and performances – particularly amateur ones – serve as program items at local social events. Public appreciation of the performance becomes a form of community award. Hence, a theatrical performance not only entertains but promotes social-cultural values and becomes an effective agent of socialization.

The first Estonian play was performed in Canada at the 1907 Summer Festival in Barons in southern Alberta, in a community that comprised fewer than twenty families. Later, during the 1920's and 1930's, plays were frequently performed at various ethnic festivals in southern Alberta and in Toronto and Montreal. During the 1950's almost every Estonian Association had its theatre troupe and plays were produced and presented several times a year. Difficulties encountered with the limited choice of texts available in Estonian – because they could not be acquired from Soviet Estonia – were overcome by translation, new writing, and copying. Considerable expertise was available with actors who continued to play or develop roles that they had already played in Estonia or in refugee camps in Germany. Although most presentations were local, occasionally troupes would also tour neighbouring Estonian communities.

A distinction must be made between amateur acting, performed mainly for leisuretime social objectives, and the theatre of the trained and experienced professional actor, which is primarily aimed at cultivating the art of the theatre for its own sake.[1] Since the Estonian immigrant post-war population contained a number of professional actors, actresses, and producers, the Estonian theatre in Toronto, and also the theatre in Montreal for a few years, rose above the amateur level. The immigrant professional theatrical group included a number with substantial experience, both in stage plays and in the Estonian National Opera, and many had received accolades for their outstanding talent. Most of the immigrant theatrical group, including their outstanding members, were still in their professional prime and thus able to rise to new heights of accomplishment under normal circumstances. None, however, was able to pursue his or her former theatrical profession in Canada: they simply did not have the linguistic skills even if otherwise they would have been an asset to the very rare professional theatres in Canada.

Hence, the Estonian theatre became the "second life" of these former professionals, into which they poured all their abilities, energies, and time after the work day and at weekends. This second life became even more real to these theatre professionals than it was to many of the other community leaders because they hoped that they could return to the professional full-time theatre eventually, either in Estonia or elsewhere.[2] With these hopes and aspirations the former professionals established the Estonian theatre in Toronto and in Montreal. They also attracted new and young talent and, as early as 1949, conducted a seminar in Toronto for young people interested in acting. A decade later, in 1958, a more diversified seminar was held with instruction in selected fields of the theatrical arts.

The Estonian National Theatre in Canada was founded in November, 1951, in Toronto by eight actors and actresses, who formerly had been professionals in Estonia and who had established the Estonian Theatre in Geislingen, Germany, during the initial post-war refugee years. In fact, the new theatre in Toronto was the direct successor of the latter, which had ceased to exist because of the exodus of Estonians from Germany between 1948 and 1951. However, the theatre in Geislingen, a small Bavarian town with a population of about 4,000 Estonian refugees, had established, in its very brief existence, recognition for its standards in drama and musicals. Fourteen years later, in 1965, the Estonian National Theatre in Canada consisted of a permanent repertoire company of twenty-three members, with dozens co-opted to play minor roles and fill in as extras.

That the theatre has been eminently successful is demonstrated by the statistics. Throughout its three decades of existence it has presented three to six plays annually. Of the seventy-eight productions during the twenty-year period from 1952 to 1972, sixty-six were performed only once, while six productions were repeated in Toronto and eighteen performances were given outside Toronto in Canada (Montreal, St. Catharines, Hamilton) or in the United States (New York, Chicago, Lakewood, New Jersey). The average audience per performance has ranged from 600 to 800. Open-air performances at Seedrioru festivals have had larger audiences, with an all-time record of an estimated 8,000 in 1972, the result of the Estonian World Festival being held simultaneously in Toronto. In 1968 it was estimated that the theatre had performed before a total of 50,000 theatre-goers.[3]

Although the theatre laboured under the severe handicap of an audience limited to one of the smallest ethnic groups in Canada, it nevertheless reached out across linguistic and cultural borders and kept up with developments in theatre in the Western world. Between 1952 and 1972 about half its productions were written by Estonian authors, six of them first performances of newly written plays, and the list of non-Estonian authors has ranged widely over Italian, American, British, German, and Hungarian dramatists, such as M. Pagnoli, Eugene O'Neill, Noel Coward, D. Molnar, Oscar Wilde, L. Verneuil, Tennessee Williams, W. Somerset Maugham, Eugene Ionesco, and William Shakespeare. It is only because of the small band of former professional actors and actresses that this enormous breadth of theatrical productions has been undertaken. They have co-opted hundreds of Estonians, both young and old, to assist them in playing minor roles, often for the first time. These accomplishments appear even more outstanding when one considers the technical handicaps under which the theatre had been working. Only spare time could be devoted to the planning and production, including casting and rehearsals, of new plays; also, the overwhelming majority of plays were limited to only one performance. Yet, despite the need to produce a new stage setting and new costumes, with the attendant financial costs, the theatre was nevertheless able to produce as many as six new plays in a year!

In 1971 a division occurred within the ranks of the theatre and a group of its members withdrew and established the Canadian Estonian Theatre. The resultant competition, while it added variety, also split up the small resources of the former theatre professionals. Still, during the past decade both theatres have been able to produce between one and three plays annually, but of course frequently they have had to employ the same actors, for the core did not change very much from the 1950's and 1960's.

Montreal is the other site in Canada where an Estonian professional-quality theatre once existed. The Estonian Theatre of Montreal was founded in 1951 by former actors who settled there.[4] Although the group had some outstanding actors and producers, their total number was small and the Estonian community in Montreal itself was less than a quarter of the Estonian population in Toronto. As a result, the theatre lasted only six years. Ten theatrical works were produced, most of them comedies by non-Estonian playwrights. In 1952, one year after its founding, the Estonian Theatre of Montreal produced a popular Estonian operetta[5] that became one of its greatest successes: when presented at the Eaton Auditorium in Toronto the performance was sold out and theatre-goers were turned away for lack of space. The production was also presented in Hamilton and twice in New York. In both 1953 and 1954 the Montreal theatre group presented more than half a dozen performances at Estonian communities in Canada and the United States. In 1956 a comedy with three actors was performed in Montreal, Toronto, and twice in New York; in 1957 they also presented it in Sweden.[6] But this was also the last production of the Estonian Theatre of Montreal. When two key members of the troupe moved to Toronto and joined the Estonian National Theatre, the Montreal theatre ceased to exist for practical purposes.[7]

The Rein Andre Theatre Studio was founded by Rein Andre, an actor and teacher of drama, in Toronto in 1955 with the aim of attracting young talent and training them through practical performance. For six years, from 1955 to 1961, the studio enjoyed great success. It produced fourteen plays and toured extensively. Its "10,000-mile tour" of 1958 included performances in Detroit, Chicago, Los Angeles, San Francisco, Vancouver, Lakewood, N.J., Hamilton, St. Catharines, Sudbury, and Montreal. And in the summer of 1961 the studio toured Europe and gave nine performances in England, the Netherlands, Sweden, and Finland. This tour also constituted the studio's farewell performance, for it disbanded and its members and students joined the Estonian National Theatre in Canada.

There has been a regular and lively exchange of theatre performances between the Canadian and American Estonian communities. The Estonian theatres in New York and Lakewood, New Jersey, have returned the Canadian visits and have played regularly once or twice a year in Toronto. Moreover, Aario Marist, a well-known French actor and producer of Estonian origin who lived and worked in Paris, gave a series of one-man theatre performances in Toronto and Montreal and produced a play for the Estonian National Theatre in Canada in the 1950's. And, on the occasion of the Estonian World Festival in 1972, the Estonian Theatre of Stockholm presented several plays in Toronto.

Unfortunately, the Estonian theatre has largely been limited in its activities to the Estonian communities in Canada and the United States; it has had scant impact beyond Estonians. The only visible external impact has been made by Rein Andre, who in 1963 became one of the founders of the New Canadian Theatre in Toronto and its artistic director. This theatre was established with the aim of bringing together actors from different ethnic origins to produce plays in English for a wider audience. Only one play by an Estonian playwright, *The Kratt*, by Eduard Vilde, was produced by the theatre.

LITERATURE: ORTO IN TORONTO

Although there are a number of well-known Estonian authors in Canada, there are few literary clubs in the Estonian communities. The ones that have existed have been small and nearly always affiliated with the Estonian Associations. A few larger clubs have existed for short periods in Toronto but none of them has succeeded in attracting popular support for any length of time. The Literary Club of the Toronto Estonian Association was originally formed in 1953 and held regular literary evenings and discussions during the 1950's. In the 1960's the Canadian section of the Swedish-based Estonian Literary Association held a number of highly successful literary evenings in Toronto, with audiences ranging from 200 to 300. But it was a short-lived phenomenon and did not survive to the 1970's. In 1966 the Society of Friends of Estonian Literature was formed in Toronto by younger-generation intellectuals and it lasted to the present, although it is not a particularly large organization. In fact, it has limited its activities to literary discussions among its own members and has not tried to approach the larger public. The Estonian Arts Centre, established during the 1970's, has also made some attempt to expand its activities into the field of literature. In general, however, public literary activities among the Estonians in Canada have never achieved the same popularity as theatre and music.

97

Despite the lack of organized activity, Toronto has been one of the publishing centres of Estonian literature outside the Estonian homeland, mainly because Orto, one of the most productive literary publishers of the Estonian diaspora, was headquartered in Toronto. Orto began as an Estonian publisher in Sweden and was transferred to Toronto in 1951 when its owner immigrated to Canada. The publisher had Estonian subscribers across the world and it regularly published a book a month for nearly two decades. Orto published originals, reprints of books originally published in Estonia, and translations from the literatures of many languages. Orto's high level of literary activity was aided by a team of literary critics, editors, and translators located in several countries and by annual literary prizes that promoted interest in original creative writing among Estonians abroad. Orto also published journals and dictionaries, and thus made itself indispensable and familiar to every Estonian home. The two great landmarks of Orto's publishing era were the luxury-edition reprints of the epic saga *Kalevipoeg* and *Great Bible*.[8]

Between 1951 and 1971 Orto published 298 novels, thirty-nine memoirs, twenty-five volumes of poetry, and twenty-four dictionaries and handbooks – altogether over a million copies. Among the total, no fewer than forty-two were written by Estonian authors living in Canada; more than one-third of the total were novels and translations of world classics.[9] Unfortunately, with the death of its director, Andres Laur, in 1973, the Orto publishing enterprise came to an end. Although Orto was a co-operative of literary people and subscribers, its success was entirely due to the financial and management talent of Andres Laur.

JOURNALISM

Estonian journalism came to Canada with the founding of the weekly *Meie Elu* (Our Life) in March, 1950, in Toronto. The paper was established by Aleksander Weiler, an Estonian journalist who had come to Canada in 1948 from Sweden in the first wave of Estonian immigrants. By 1950 there were enough Estonians in Toronto to support a newspaper and there were about a dozen former editors, writers, and reporters in the Estonian community who had immigrated during the previous two years. Within a year the surplus of former journalists led to the establishment of a second Estonian paper in Toronto, published twice a week, *Vaba Eestlane* (Free Estonian). The role of the newspapers in disseminating information among the Estonian community and in interpreting public issues to the Estonian community must not be underestimated. The successful continuation of two competing newspapers in such a small ethnic community is the result of sound editorial policy and interpretive competition between the papers. In fact, the journalistic and editorial levels of the two newspapers have led to subscriptions in the United States and overseas. Despite the ever-increasing costs of publishing, *Meie Elu* has maintained a weekly issue of eight-ten pages in a large format, and *Vaba Eestlane* has continued to issue eight-twelve pages twice a week in a slightly smaller format.

In contrast to the success of the two newspapers, Estonian periodicals have not been markedly successful, although a number have been published in Canada. None, however, has been issued either regularly or for any sustained period. In addition to the large number of information bulletins published by Estonian organizations across Canada, some of the more outstanding periodicals are *Triinu*, a monthly for women edited in Sweden and Canada, *Mana*, an irregularly published journal of literature and culture currently edited in the United States, *Varrak*, a socio-political monthly published between 1970 and 1978, and *Ajakiri*, essentially an information bulletin of a socio-political and literary nature produced by younger intellectuals in Toronto since 1976.

NOTES

1. Estonia had eight well-established professional theatres for a population of one million. Besides the National Opera House, two other theatres produced opera and ballet.
2. Interview with the director of Estonian National Theatre in Canada, Lydia Vohu, November 7, 1979.
3. Data primarily from Kurlents *et al.* (eds.), *Eestlased Kanadas*, pp. 503-09. Computed to the Estonian population in Toronto, almost 2,000 Estonians went to the theatre at least once a year.
4. The Montreal group included the former director of the National Opera House in Tallinn, Hanno Kompus, and his wife, Rahel Olbrei, producer and choreographer of ballet at the National Opera House.
5. *Kaluri neiu* (Fisherman's Maiden) by Priit Ardna.
6. *Sammassäng* (High Bed), a comedy by Jan de Hartog.
7. Rudolf Lipp and Riina Reinik, who both had been with the National Opera House in Estonia.
8. Fr. R. Kreutzwald (ed.), *Kalevipoeg* (Toronto: Orto, 1954), illustrated by Eerik Haamer and Hando Mugasto, 320 pages, large format, numbered collector's edition. J.W. Weski *et al.* (eds.), *Suur Piibel* (Toronto: Orto, 1972), illustrated by 226 drawings of Gustav Dore, 1,297 pages, large format, 1,500 copies, numbered collector's edition.
9. Kurlents *et al.* (eds.), *Eestlased Kanadas*, p. 451.

EIGHT

Youth and Athletic Activities

SUPPLEMENTARY SCHOOLS

In 1909 the Estonians in the settlement of Medicine Valley in Alberta built the first school in that region, the "Estonian school," as it became known in the neighbourhood, to provide education for their children. However, education to the farmer-settlers of Medicine Valley meant the preparation of their children for life in their new environment in Canada, and that meant education in the English language.

Half a century later the aim of the newly established Estonian supplementary schools was exactly the opposite of the Medicine Valley pioneer school: to preserve the Estonian culture and to retain the Estonian language. Now the children's advancement in Canadian schools was taken for granted. Nor did the parents themselves run into serious difficulties with the new language of the country, at least not in everyday matters. The parents wanted their children to remain Estonians as well as become successful members of Canadian society. During the first years after the post-war wave of immigration, children were sometimes even told that one day they would return to Estonia and therefore they should prepare for this return. Hence, in the supplementary schools the old curricula of the schools in Estonia were applied *mutatis mutandis*, and former Estonian professional teachers were used as teachers. At the end of the school year certificates of advancement were issued and graduation diplomas were granted at the end of the school program.

Interestingly enough, the supplementary schools did not take off immediately after the wave of immigration and only reached their largest numbers of students in the late 1960's. In 1949 there were ninety-three Estonian supplementary school pupils in Canada, in 1953, 415, and in 1968 and 1969, 826 and 827 respectively. There are two explanations for this gradual gathering of momentum. First, the organizing of the supplementary schools after immigration naturally took some time; and second, the urgency and need of supplementary schools became greater as the years passed by, the hopes to return to Estonia faded, and the young parents themselves became more fluent in English than in Estonian.

Historically, many Estonian supplementary schools began as church Sunday schools. Soon, however, the Estonian Associations took the lead and established independent Saturday supplementary schools, although some schools have continued to be a combination of church school and supplementary school run jointly by the local association and congregation. The total number of Estonian supplementary schools established in Canada has been thirteen. The school in Toronto operated by the Toronto Estonian Association has been by far the largest and has also formed the model for the others to follow. This, however, has not always been easy since the size and efficiency of the supplementary school have depended on the size and cohesion of the local Estonian community. Hence, in Hamilton the number of pupils has declined from a peak of seventy in 1968 to about thirty in the 1970's; in Montreal and Vancouver it has averaged about thirty and in smaller communities it has ranged from as few as eight to about twenty. The Toronto school in contrast had 332 pupils in 1955, 565 in 1965, 601 in 1970, and 628 in 1980-81.

The Estonian supplementary schools meet either semi-weekly or weekly, mostly on Saturdays or Sundays. In addition, in Toronto some classes are held in the evenings during the week. The curricula of the schools consist mainly of Estonian language, literature, geography, and history as well as singing and sometimes folk dancing, or religious subjects, the latter when the school is also a church school. Teaching in smaller schools is much less structured than in the larger ones. The original insistence on only using teachers who had taught in Estonia had to be forgone, although some of the original teachers have continued to teach the supplementary schools for twenty to thirty years. Currently, among the younger teachers a considerable number are professional teachers in Canadian schools. Textbooks and other study aids are continuously revised and updated and are published either in Toronto or in Sweden. Textbooks published in Soviet Estonia have seldom been used because it has been found that these books, including those intended for the primary grades, have been full of Communist-Marxist indoctrination and propaganda. The teachers in the supplementary schools are not paid and the administrative expenses are carried mostly by the Estonian Associations or congregations, and a small fee is levied on the parents.

The Estonian supplementary school in Toronto has three levels: kindergarten, elementary and secondary, and courses in the Estonian language for adults. This last has included a number of young parents of non-Estonian origin married to Estonians who want to learn Estonian. The kindergarten was started in 1963, the secondary school in 1964, and the language courses in 1966. The elementary includes six grades, just like the elementary schools in Estonia. The secondary consists of three years and restricts admission to elementary-level graduates only. The emphasis here is on advanced teaching of language and literature, but other subjects, including history and politics, are also taught. In 1972 the secondary school had eight classes with 105 students and eight teachers. In the kindergarten there is no structured curriculum, but since the teachers are professionally trained kindergarten or nursery school teachers who are Estonians and interested in Estonian language and culture, the program performs the usual kindergarten role of introducing the language and culture in preparation for the first grade of the elementary school.

Over the thirty-year period of the life of the Estonian supplementary school in Canada three different phases may be discerned. From about 1950 to 1959 there was a period of growth, with the number of pupils continually increasing. This was also a time of organizing and experimentation in most of the schools, with different textbooks and study aids being tested. During the second phase, from 1960 to about 1970, enrolment generally still increased, but not so rapidly, and smaller communities experienced a decline. The standards, routines, and methods of teaching had matured and become standardized. Most of the larger Estonian communities by this time had built or bought their own community halls or churches in which these schools found accommodation. In general it could be said that the 1960's were a period of stabilization. The third decade, since 1970, has been one of incipient decline. All the smaller schools have experienced difficulties in numbers of students and teachers and some schools have disappeared. Even the supplementary school in Toronto is encountering problems, specifically a deficiency in the Estonian language that the elementary school program has not been able to rectify. Thus, graduates of the elementary school are entering the secondary school ill-prepared to learn the complexities of the Estonian language.

Although it is hard to get exact figures of the total number of Estonian youth who have attended Estonian supplementary schools during the thirty years because records have not been kept and teachers have changed with an increasing frequency as time has gone on, it can nevertheless be estimated that in Toronto an average of 100 new pupils has entered each year, and roughly of any four pupils in Estonian supplementary schools in Canada three have attended the Toronto school. The rough figure of 4,000 thus arrived at is not high, even for such a small ethnic group as the Estonians. The one factor that limits the participation rate in the supplementary schools is that the Estonians are dispersed across Canada and also across Metropolitan Toronto. Furthermore, the increasing number of mixed marriages inevitably taking place in the second and subsequent generations of Estonian Canadians will lead to a steady decline of Estonian supplementary school attendance in the future, even in Toronto.

There appears to be an unmistakable link between the supplementary school and scouting, folk dancing, summer camp, youth choirs, rhythmic gymnastics, and even dance bands among the Estonian youth. Participants and graduates of supplementary schools, who have become the select core of Estonian youth, are more likely to succeed in studies in the regular Canadian school system and subsequently in their personal and professional lives. Clearly these extra-curricular activities not only fill the leisure time and absorb the energies of the youth, they also assist them in self-discipline and prepare them for taking the responsibilities of leadership. Thus one might even conclude that those that prepare to be good Estonians also turn out to be better Canadians.

Unlike most of the other Estonian organizations in Canada, the supplementary schools have no structural links to the Estonian schools in other countries, although textbooks are mutually produced and there is consultation through the professional organization of Estonian teachers. Of all the Estonian schools abroad, those in Sweden are the most advanced and are in fact not supplementary schools but private Estonian schools supported by the Swedish state with public funds on an equal basis with all other schools in Sweden. All subjects are taught in Estonian in these schools with the exception of the languages, including Swedish and English. Again, as in the case with the supplementary schools in Canada, the Swedish Estonian schools have educated the core elite of the Estonian younger leadership in Sweden for the past thirty-five years, for the schools were already established in Sweden in 1944.

CHILDREN'S SUMMER CAMPS

It is a moot point whether the aim of the children's summer camps was ethnicity retention, as was the case with supplementary schools, or the health and well-being of the children. Both motives appear equally prominent in the Estonian press of the 1950's. On the one hand it was observed that the Estonians who had come to Canada had settled mainly in industrial centres and therefore summer camps were a necessity to promote the health of the children. A typical argument in support of this view ran as follows: "Contact with nature gives a better understanding of the facts of life and gives strength and helps to sustain an inner balance in later years." On the other hand, arguments that the camps provided an opportunity "to learn the Estonian language and to be a part of the Estonian community" were equally prominent. [1]

Although nearly all the Estonian communities had children's camps in 1951 and 1952, the experience was discouraging for the smaller communities. As long as there were no permanent camp sites, adequate equipment could not be acquired or stored, and because the number of children was small the camp cost per capita was much higher than expected even though the counsellors were unpaid volunteers.

However, success was soon forthcoming when two permanent sites were purchased and long-lasting operations were started. The first was the result of the efforts of the women's section of the Toronto Estonian

Association (later the independent Toronto Estonian Women's Association), which operated a summer camp in 1951 and 1952 on a farm owned by an Estonian about 100 kilometres north of Toronto. The facilities were inadequate and the camp overcrowded and primitive; the second summer was especially difficult when 108 children were squeezed into the camp. At the beginning of 1953 an opportunity arose to purchase a large parcel of land crossed by a river about seventy kilometres north of Toronto near the village of Udora. The women's section negotiated to buy the land without hesitation even though there was no money for the purchase. To raise the capital, part of the land was subdivided and 150 lots were sold as summer cottage property to Estonians in Toronto. The summer camp was ready for occupancy by the early summer of 1953. One hundred and eighty children enrolled in the summer camp that first summer and the number increased to 248 by 1955. The campgrounds were given the name Jõekääru (River Bend).

It was expected that children from other Estonian communities in Ontario would also be sent to Jõekääru but because of the distance and the limited transportation facilities (relatively few Estonians owned cars in the early 1950's) these expectations did not materialize. Instead, four Estonian Associations in southern Ontario, at Hamilton, St. Catharines, Kitchener, and London, decided to pool their resources and to purchase jointly land for a children's summer camp. After a year of search in 1955 a neglected farm of sixty-two acres on the Grand River near Elora was purchased. Because of the stand of cedars in the valley scoured by the river that formed the boundary of the farm the campsite was immediately named Seedrioru (Cedar Valley). The purchase price of $7,200 was financed by loans, and summer festivals at Seedrioru were started to raise money for the buildings and the operating costs of the summer camp. The labour for the construction of the buildings and the draining and landscaping of the swampy riverside was provided free by the members of the four associations. The first camp was held in 1956.[2]

The number of children at the Jõekääru camp has ranged from a high of 333 in 1965 to an average of about 200, mostly from the Toronto area. The size of the Seedrioru summer camp has been about half that of Jõekääru, reaching a peak of 158 children in 1969. Half the children at Seedrioru come from southern Ontario and the other half from Toronto and the Buffalo and Detroit areas in the United States, with a few from as far away as Washington, D.C., Chicago, and Minneapolis. Between 1956 and 1979, 692 children had attended Seedrioru summer camp, and about twice that number had attended Jõekääru. In addition, smaller, irregularly held summer camps have been conducted in Vancouver, Sault Ste. Marie, and Montreal (the Montreal camp ran from 1953 to 1956 with a total attendance of 158 children). It may be estimated that by 1980 about 2,500 Estonian children in Canada had attended Estonian summer camps for an average of two weeks in each of three or four summers.

The camp activities have been overwhelmingly outdoor-oriented and have included swimming, hiking, games, sports, pony riding, canoeing, campfires, singing, and handicrafts. During the first decade there were enough people with past experience in summer camp leadership and counselling or youth work who were willing to spend part of the summer voluntarily working at the camps. In the last decade their places have been taken by the graduates of the Canadian camps. As early as 1972 the camp director at Seedrioru was himself a former camper and counsellor there.

Jõekääru and Seedrioru, the two permanent Estonian children's camps in Canada, have been very competitive and have kept the camp fees far below such low-fee summer camps as those run by the Kiwanis and the YMCA and YWCA.[3] A large amount of unpaid volunteer work in administration and maintenance of the campgrounds has permitted the low fees, and in the case of Seedrioru the income from the summer festivals has carried most of the construction and reconstruction and operating costs of the camp. Moreover, it should be pointed out that Seedrioru and Jõekääru are not only summer campsites but also form Estonian summer communities. At Jõekääru there is a track and field stadium built by the sport club Kalev of Toronto and there are facilities for swimming contests and tennis. Several ethnic events take place there during the summer, including inter-ethnic sports activities and training seminars for folk-dance coaches as well as many other adult group activities. Jõekääru also contains more than 100 summer cottages and in recent years some of the older retired people have lived there year round.

In addition, the summer camp facilities at Seedrioru include four dormitories, a main hall, a man-made swimming pool fed by natural springs, an open-air theatre site, a historical monument, several playgrounds, an outdoor dance and basketball floor, volleyball and track and field facilities, and a rifle range. Moreover, the landscaping done over twenty years ago has now produced mature growths of trees providing both visual pleasure and shade. All these facilities have been built at only the cost of materials, with labour being provided by unpaid volunteers. This enormous amount of voluntary labour made Seedrioru a community enterprise that cemented the four parent Estonian Associations together and made it something much more than a mere summer camp.

THE FOLK DANCE: KUNGLA

As in most west European countries, folk dancing had disappeared in Estonia as a social activity long before it was reintroduced as an art form in the twentieth century. The social dances performed in independent Estonia in the 1920's and 1930's were either west European (the polka, waltz, Rhinelander, pas de pas) or contemporary American, European, or Latin American (tango, foxtrot, English waltz, Charleston, rumba, carioca). Although the dance culture in independent Estonia was rich and popular it was also international, modern, and contemporary.

Hardly anyone was interested in the historical dances of his forefathers.

But interest slowly developed in various aspects of folk art, including ethnic costumes, music, ancient customs, folk dancing, native architecture, and handicrafts, and was fostered by a variety of civic organizations and governmental institutions. Thus, burrowing underneath the veneer of modernization, the Estonians slowly rediscovered their ancient heritage. In this, they were aided by the extensive collections of ethnographic materials gathered during the nineteenth century when there were people still alive who practised some of these arts. The collections were especially rich in folktales, folksongs, and folk music, as well as folk dances of many local varieties and variations. It was from the archival material of museums that the modern revival of folk dance originated. Much archival material was published and popularized and folk dance troupes were formed throughout the country. By the late 1930's folk dancing had become so popular that at national youth festivals mass performances of folk dances took place with performers drawn from all over the country. National song festivals also included folk dance performances in their programs. Moreover, folk dance motifs were incorporated in both ballet and musicals presented in opera houses and theatres. The folk dance had thus rapidly become a performing art and a youth activity.

The enthusiasm for folk dancing generated among large numbers of Estonian youths during the 1930's was brought over to Canada when they came here as immigrants after the war. This is not to say that Estonian folk dancing was entirely absent from Canada prior to the new wave of immigrants, for the southern Alberta Estonian settlements had performed Estonian folk dances and members of the Estonian Associations in Montreal and Toronto had tried to learn the new folk dances. However, it was the influx of new immigrants that brought the folk dance as a youth activity to even the smallest Estonian community in Canada.

The interim period that Estonian refugees spent in Sweden and Germany considerably strengthened the tradition of the folk dance. This was particularly true of the refugee camps in Germany where folk dancing, along with scouting, became one of the favourite youth activities. Hence, practically all of the younger people who immigrated to Canada had participated in folk dancing. What reinforced the Estonian folk dance in Canada was that, in addition to its social and recreational function, it could easily be used as an ethnic identifying device in an entertaining and easily comprehensible manner.

The earliest Estonian folk dance troupes in Canada were formed in 1948, in Vancouver, Montreal, and St. Catharines. From 1949 and into the early 1950's, the folk dance was introduced to Toronto, Hamilton, Kitchener, London, Kirkland Lake, Winnipeg, Port Arthur – in short, wherever there was an Estonian Association, and even to places where there were only a few Estonian families. But the history of the Estonian folk dance is uneven. Some of the original troupes lasted only a year or two, and when new ones were formed after a hiatus of several years they, too, ceased to exist after only a short period. This uneven picture has characterized the Estonian folk dance in Canada even in some of the larger Estonian communities. Toronto has been the exception. In general, however, the total number of Estonian folk dancers in Canada increased steadily from about 100 in 1950 to about 240 in 1958. After a temporary decline to about 150 folk dancers in 1961 the number again rose to an all-time peak of over 300 in 1963-64.[4] Thereafter there has been a steady decline, to about 160 in 1980, of whom 100 may be found in Toronto. The higher figures in 1956-58 and 1963-64 came about as a result of preparations for the North American Estonian Festivals in Toronto in 1957 and 1964. Preparations for the festivals drew new recruits to the ranks of the folk dance troupes and reactivated some troupes that had become moribund. Similarly, the Estonian World Festival in Toronto in 1972 again rejuvenated the folk dance groups and brought the numbers almost up to the 1964 levels. Estonian festivals held outside Canada have also had a rejuvenating effect on folk dance groups in Canada but not nearly to the same extent as those held in Canada.

It must be emphasized that folk dancing is exclusively a youth activity; hence, there is always a considerable turnover as older dancers drop out and new ones have to be recruited to replace them. This is particularly difficult due to the relatively small size of some of the Estonian communities, for when too many young people of folk-dancing age leave the community either for jobs or for university, it is difficult to maintain a minimum size to keep the troupe viable. Moreover, both the formation and the viability of a folk dance group depend on the availability of devoted leaders and instructors. Two good examples of the extremes of the factors making for the viability of a dance troupe are Kandali of Hamilton and Vikerlased of Montreal; the former maintained its strength evenly over two decades, and the latter was a highly acclaimed but short-lived phenomenon.[5]

In Hamilton at one time there were actually two groups. The Folk Dance Club was affiliated with the Hamilton Estonian Association and reached its peak around 1956, mainly as a result of preparations for the first North American Estonian Festival in Toronto, but interest subsided rapidly thereafter and the club disbanded. The other Hamilton dance group was the Estonian Folk Dance Club of the Boy Scouts and Girl Guides formed in 1954. This club became one of the best-known folk dance clubs in Canada. In 1970 it adopted the name Kandali and has performed for both Estonians and non-Estonians across Canada, as well as at all the major Estonian festivals in Canada and abroad, and has appeared several times on television. Kandali has not limited itself to Estonian dances only: it has also learned and presented dances of other ethnic groups, such as the Scottish sword dance, with remarkable success. Part of its success is undoubtedly due to the continuity of leaders and instructors, despite the normal turnover of dancers that has taken place.

The Montreal story is the opposite. Vikerlased was formed by about twenty young people in 1963 and had a very small turnover until it disbanded in 1970. Its activity, though, was phenomenal, with new recruits being added so that the group actually reached a total of between thirty and forty. It was led and coached by two professional engineers, one also a well-known musician and the other with varied skills in the theatrical arts. Hence, Vikerlased cultivated not only the folk dance but also folk music, folk customs, and other performing arts. In fact, they were a choir as well as a folk dance troupe and their performances were largely musicals based upon themes of folk dance and folk music. They performed before Canadian and Estonian audiences and on television, and issued records of their performances. But when both their mentors moved to Toronto and many of the core left Montreal, Vikerlased ceased to exist within a very short time.

Toronto has the most richly varied scene in dance of all the Estonian communities. The oldest of the various dance groups in Toronto is the Estonian Folk Dance Club Kungla, which was formed in February, 1949, with only three couples. It was affiliated with the Toronto Estonian Association until 1951 and in 1968 it adopted its present name. In 1962 another dance troupe was formed because one could not accommodate all who were interested. And later there have been up to seven troupes of different ages and different skills. In 1954 the Gymnastics and Folk Dance Section of the Estonian athletic club, Kalev, was formed. This was a signal event in that the Kalev dance group introduced musicals based on folk dance and gymnastic movements to both Canada and the United States. But when in 1960 the women gymnasts left Kalev to establish their own group, Kalev Estienne, most of the folk dancers joined Kungla, which continued the tradition of folk dance musicals. The highlight of the year for Kungla is its annual May Ball. Usually held in one of the largest ballrooms in Toronto and attended by many hundreds of people, it is one of the annual cultural events of the Estonian community.[6]

The secret of Kungla's success is that it is not only a folk dance club but also a social club for Estonian youth. Parties, summer outings, camping, and dances provide outlets for youthful enthusiasm and comradeship. The older guiding hands also make certain that new leaders and instructors are trained systematically. Kungla also provides its youthful members opportunities to travel: it makes regular trips around North America and has made two tours of Europe, in 1973 and 1977.

Kandali's and Kungla's success seems to indicate that the cohesion and endurance of a folk dance troupe does not depend solely on interest in folk dancing; the stronger and longer-lasting clubs interweave social activities and entertainment with folk dancing. Hence, the young members are kept together not only to learn to dance but to meet other young people from other communities and countries. Incidentally, dancing can also lead to marriage! Over thirty Estonian married couples reportedly met each other for the first time at Kungla's dance rehearsals.[7] There is yet another ingredient to attracting youth to the dance, and that is the enrichment of dancing activities with other arts – music, singing, acting – in the form of musicals. All three clubs dealt with above have successfully combined these talents.

The character of Estonian folk dances is quite different from many of the more widely known folk dances of Europe. In contrast to the folk dances of central, eastern, and southern Europe, which are in general excitement-generating and dramatic, the Estonian dances tend to be relatively slow-moving and complex with medleys of varied themes, nuances, rhythms, and movements. Hence, despite the richness of the content of Estonian folk dances, only a few can compete for attention in multi-ethnic audiences with the more exciting dances of other ethnic groups.

The art of the dance has improved much since the first folk dance troupes were formed thirty-five years ago. This is entirely due to the dedicated few students and teachers of the folk dance, such as Toomas Metsala of Kungla and Harnald and Regina Toomsalu in Hamilton, all of whom have studied the art of the folk dance systematically and continuously and have choreographed new dances and added new techniques. In fact the Estonian-Canadian choreographers and instructors are in the forefront of exile Estonians in dancing activities globally. They have been the ones to produce and choreograph the dance performances in musical shows at Estonian festivals in both the United States and Sweden, and they have also conducted preparatory courses for instructors from several countries prior to the Estonian World Festivals in 1972, 1976, 1980, and 1984.

Many of the new sources for Estonian folk dance development have been drawn from contemporary Soviet Estonia, where the folk dance is one of the few activities that is comparatively free from political control and direction.[8]

BOY SCOUTS AND GIRL GUIDES

In 1912, four years after Lord Baden-Powell formed the Boy Scouts in England, a scout troop was formed in Pärnu, Estonia, and a year later another was established in Tallinn.[9] But it took more than ten years for the movement to gather strength and become popular, and even then it was confined to the larger cities. In the 1930's, a rival home-grown youth movement, the Noored Kotkad (Young Eagles) and Kodu Tütred (Daughters of the Homeland), became popular and in a short time recruited a large part of Estonian youth all over the country, in the cities as well as in the countryside. It was more nationalistic, stressed patriotism, and was supported by both the government and civic organizatons. Indeed, many Boy Scout and Girl Guide leaders left to join the new organization.

With the Soviet takeover in 1940 both movements were suppressed and their organizations dissolved. After the expulsion of the Soviet armies in

1941 the German occupation authorities confirmed the dissolution of the movements. After the war the Soviets in Estonia replaced the pre-war youth movements with their own Communist youth organizations: the Little Oktobrists, the Pioneers, and the League of Young Communists.

But Estonian scouting lived on among the refugees in Sweden and Germany. In fact, scouting also replaced the competing indigenous national pre-war youth organizations and became more popular than ever among refugee Estonian youths. It is estimated that in 1949 there were between 2,000 and 2,500 Estonian Boy Scouts and Girl Guides among the refugees in Sweden and Germany. Subsequently, a very large proportion of them immigrated to other countries, including Canada. Once in Canada, scouting was promptly re-established, and also reorganized.

By 1950 there were already several Estonian Boy Scout and Girl Guide troops in southern Ontario and in Toronto, and others were in the process of formation in the Estonian communities elsewhere in Canada.[10] As in the case of all other Estonian-Canadian organizations, Toronto eventually became the centre of Estonian scouting. But whether in Canada or elsewhere, the movement never lost its worldwide cohesiveness and its Estonian orientation, even though the rapid emigration from Europe had thrown the Estonian scouting organization into disarray. In short order a new worldwide organization was formed, with the main divisions (in Estonian "Malev") established in the United States, Sweden, Canada, Australia, England, and Germany. A central bureau was created, which has rotated regularly among Toronto, New York, and Stockholm.

In 1953 the Estonian scouts in Toronto purchased 400 acres of Muskoka woodland surrounded by lakes from the Ontario government to be used for camping, hiking, and nature study. A campground was cleared and access roads were built by the scouts with the assistance of their patrons and supporters. The new campground was named Kotkajärve (Eagle's Lake). Some camping took place there already during that first summer. The next summer, in 1954, about 450 Estonian Boy Scouts and Girl Guides spent part of the summer camping at the new campgrounds.

During the 1950's a disagreement arose between the Estonian scout movement in Canada and the executive of the Boy Scouts of Canada. The Canadian executive did not want to recognize scouting groups in Canada that were organized on ethnic bases. Hence, when in 1955 the World Jamboree was held in Niagara-on-the-Lake in Ontario, Canadian Estonian scouts were not permitted to attend, although Estonian scout leaders from other countries did attend. Several years lapsed before the differences in approach were ironed out. Finally, the Boy Scouts of Canada recognized ethnic-group scouting in Canada and since then similar scouting organizations have been established by other ethnic groups, including the Latvians, Lithuanians, Hungarians, and Poles. However, the accommodation between the Estonian-Canadian scouting movement and the executive of the Boy Scouts of Canada required a formal integration of the Estonian Boy Scout troops with the Boy Scouts of Canada at the local level. Although this integration has been more formal than real, nevertheless, sound co-operation between the Estonian-Canadian and the indigenous Canadian national Boy Scout movement has taken place. Indeed, in 1975 Estonian-Canadian scouts represented Canada at the World Jamboree "Nord Jamb" in Norway.[11]

There were several reasons why the Estonian Boy Scouts insisted on maintaining a separate ethnic organization. First, it was argued that if scouting could not be ethnically based then the majority of the Estonian youth in Canada would not participate in scouting. Second, the Estonian scout leaders wanted to keep their close links with Estonian scouting in other countries for a number of reasons. They noted the differences in scouting practices in Canada and were convinced that their own practices were closer to the original intent of the international scouting movement. In particular, they emphasized the principle that scouting should be based on the initiative and independent activities of the lower levels of scouts rather than on guidance by the top echelons of older scouts and leaders. Another difference was the question of "individual scouts," a concept not recognized in Canada. In the Estonian scouting movement an individual scout is a lone scout living in a remote area who practises scouting and prepares himself for scouting examinations and periodic meetings and camping with a troop. The third main reason for the insistence on maintaining a separate Estonian scouting movement in Canada naturally was the desire to maintain the use of the Estonian language among the youth, including the use of scouting terminology in Estonian. And finally, it may be said that among Estonian scout leaders there were a number who had both outstanding experience and reputations in international scouting circles and they were reluctant to succumb to the local leadership of scouting in Canada.

Five scout groups have existed in Toronto, one of them a sea scout troop and another exclusively composed of senior scouts, the equivalent of Canadian scout leaders. Each of these groups has its own internal division of seniors, regular, junior, and cub troops and packs. The largest group in Toronto has had up to eighty scouts divided among the different levels. Other groups have been formed in Montreal, Hamilton, St. Catharines, Kitchener, London, Sault Ste. Marie, and Vancouver. In addition, Toronto, Montreal, Kitchener, Hamilton, St. Catharines, Sudbury, and Vancouver have had Girl Guide groups. In total more than 5,000 Estonian boys and girls in Canada have actively participated in Estonian scouting over the years. This is a much higher proportion than among Canadian youth at large. In fact, almost every Estonian boy or girl has at some time participated in scouting.

On a program basis Estonian scouting has been closely linked with ethnocultural activities, such as folk dancing, athletics, and commemoration of Estonian national holidays. The most visible of these ethnocultural activities has been the mandatory participation in Independence Day celebrations by scouts in uniform. The main link between

111

scouting and cultural activities has been simply the simultaneous or subsequent participation in other, non-scouting, youth activities such as the supplementary schools, folk dance troupes, academic or student organizations, choirs, sports clubs, and so on. This linkage has provided the Estonian scouting movement in Canada with a sense of Estonian national cohesion; and scouting has been regarded as simply another, but important, means for the cohesion of Estonian youth. Thus the Estonian scouting in Canada has been globally oriented, with strong linkages to Estonian scouting in other countries.

The total participation at the Kotkajärve camps between 1953 and 1972 was 9,648 Boy Scouts and Girl Guides, many of them from other countries. [12] In 1962 the first Estonian Jamboree in Canada was held at Kotkajärve with 552 Boy Scouts and 382 Girl Guides in attendance, mostly from Canada and the United States but with more than 100 from overseas, from Sweden, England, Germany, Australia, and South America. Another Estonian Jamboree held in Canada in 1972, a week after the Estonian World Festival in Toronto, brought a total attendance of 1,000, including 450 from overseas. Estonian scouts from the United States are frequent participants at the Kotkajärve camp, and Estonian scouts from Canada regularly attend Estonian camps in the United States. In addition, Estonian scouts from Canada have attended camps and Estonian jamborees in Sweden, Germany, England, and Australia, as well as world jamborees in different countries.

The heyday of Estonian scouting in Canada took place during the 1950's and 1960's; the 1970's saw a decline, which will continue in the 1980's and may even become a very sharp one. At the end of the 1970's only the larger Estonian communities – in Montreal, Hamilton, and Vancouver, in addition to Toronto – still maintained scout troops. And there has also been a decline in Toronto: in 1960 there were about 500 Boy Scouts and 400 Girl Guides there, but in 1979 there were only 300 and 200 respectively. [13] The decline in numbers has been particularly drastic at the lower levels of scouting, at the wolf cub and junior scout levels. The number of senior scouts, particularly the exceptionally knowledgeable and experienced leadership, is still comparatively high. Clearly, scouting is not as self-evidently attractive an activity as it used to be. In other words, scouting does not carry the priority among the social values of Estonian youth that it did during the first two decades after immigration to Canada.

SPORTS ORGANIZATIONS: KALEV OF TORONTO

Since large numbers of the Estonian immigrants who came to Canada at the end of the 1940's and the beginning of the 1950's were young people in their twenties and early thirties, considerable numbers among them were still active in amateur athletics or sports. In Estonia amateur sports had been very popular. The school system and numerous sports clubs promoted amateur athletics of all kinds, especially volleyball, basketball, and track and field, although the range of popular sports was very wide and included soccer, weightlifting, wrestling, gymnastics, skiing, swimming, tennis, yachting, target-shooting, and even chess. Estonians have always been proud of the achievements of Estonian athletes at international competitions, but especially in the sports of the Olympic Games, in rifle-shooting, and in chess. [14] Outstanding athletes acquired the aura of national heroes who consequently inspired the youth by example. As a result of the various social, organizational, and cultural values, very few Estonian youths missed active participation in amateur sports.

The war interrupted most athletic activities, but they were again taken up in the refugee camps in Germany and Sweden. In Germany frequent tournaments were held in volleyball and track and field, and in Sweden gymnastics, especially, were actively pursued. When the amateur immigrant athletes moved to Canada it would have been natural for them to join Canadian athletes in using the amateur sports facilities in Canada. After all, sports is one of the most international of activities; there are no ethnic reasons for drawing boundaries, especially if the larger community can enhance competition and make better facilities available for training. However, this did not happen, because the amateur sports with which Estonians were familiar were not very popular in North America and even elementary facilities for training were missing in most areas in Canada and the United States. For example, there were very few clubs that promoted track and field, and there were none for gymnastics or soccer. Nor were there any clubs or training facilities for cross-country skiing or ski jumping at that time. The YMCA and YWCA were about the only organizations in Canada that promoted those amateur sports that the Estonians were interested in. Hence, many Estonian athletes joined the Y or used its facilities to train and represented this organization in Canadian competitions. For example, it was an Estonian men's volleyball team representing the Toronto Central YMCA that held the Canadian volleyball championship uninterruptedly from 1953 to 1959; the Estonian women's volleyball team representing the Toronto YWCA was Canada's women's volleyball champion in 1957 and 1958; and the Estonian women's volleyball team representing the Montreal YWCA was the national champion in 1954 and 1955. [15] Moreover, a number of Estonian men and women found employment with the Y as instructors or organizers of athletics and amateur sports. Most of these were simply amateur athletes and not professional teachers; very few had ever belonged to the Y in Estonia.

During the 1950's and into the early 1960's, several Estonian athletes distinguished themselves in Canadian amateur sports by winning Canadian championships and by representing Canada in international competitions in the Summer Olympics, the Pan American Games, and the Commonwealth Games in track and field, wrestling, rifle-shooting, and swimming. [16] It also happened that in the early 1950's a few top achievements of Estonian athletes in Canada were not officially recognized as Canadian records because the athletes themselves either were not Canadian citizens yet or were not members of recognized sports organizations.[17] As a result two world records in shooting passed without official recognition.[18] A number of recognized athletes, nevertheless, did find employment in Canada as coaches or instructors of Canadian amateur teams or sports organizations.

But for the majority of Estonians, participation in sports meant playing and competing with other Estonians; hence, Estonian sports clubs emerged already in 1950 and 1951 in every Estonian community, large or small. The objective of these clubs was not to establish ethnically separate sports but to continue playing one's favourite sport and to find and create facilities to play these sports.

Historically, the first Estonian sports efforts were the soccer and basketball teams in the southern Alberta Estonian settlements and after the war the very first Estonian sports club was the Toronto Estonian Chess Club, founded in September, 1950. The reason for this was that chess was very popular in Estonia and does not require the expensive equipment or facilities of most other sports. The Estonian sports association Kalev was founded in Toronto in May, 1951, by a few former members of the Kalev Club of Tallinn, Estonia. In 1952 an Estonian Sports Club was founded in Montreal and in short order clubs were established in other Estonian communities, in Vancouver, Port Arthur, Hamilton, and Sault Ste. Marie. Most of the latter do not exist any more but during their heyday in the 1950's they were important centres promoting amateur sports among Estonian youth as well as among the Canadian public at large who came in contact with them.

Individual sports have been promoted both by clubs formed for the purpose and by the Toronto Kalev organization. For example, the Estonian Riflemen's Club was founded in 1953 in Toronto, and two others were established at about the same time, one in Montreal and another in southern Ontario. Later, the Estonian Yacht Club and two ski clubs were founded in Toronto.

Sports play an important role in Estonian summer camps and in scouting organizations as well. The regular day program for children ten years and up in the summer camps includes not only hiking, swimming, canoeing, and games, but also track and field and volleyball. The Seedrioru campsite includes track and field facilities and a rifle range used by both teen-age campers and the Southern Ontario Estonian Rifle Club. The scouting organizations have also actively promoted sports, particularly skiing and orienteering and, in Montreal, riflemanship. Among the summer camps it is customary to hold competitive meets both within individual summer camps and between teams from different Estonian summer camps in track and field, swimming, and volleyball.

The Kalev sports club has been the most important among the different Estonian sports organizations in Canada. In form it is a federation of a number of special sports clubs operating formally as sections of the parent club, specifically track and field, swimming, skiing, tennis, volleyball, basketball, and cross-country orienteering. In size it has been impressive; during the late 1950's and in the 1960's the total membership of Kalev amounted to over 1,000. One of its main functions was to arrange competitive meets with the sports clubs of other ethnic groups in Canada and with the Estonian athletes in the United States. In 1962 the Baltic Olympic Games in Canada were held at the new stadium with Estonian, Latvian, and Lithuanian athletes from the United States and Canada competing in track and field events.

In addition to track and field, the Kalev organization has also actively promoted two other sports in Canada, cross-country skiing and orienteering. The Kalev Ski Club was in fact the first cross-country ski club in Toronto and was the initiator of the Ontario Loppet cross-country ski competition. Kalev was also responsible for introducing cross-country orienteering to Canada, which, however, is still little known beyond the other north European ethnic groups in Canada.

In 1954, Kalev established a section of gymnastics and folk dance. This section combined gymnastics and folk dance as an art form that could be presented to various, mainly Estonian, audiences in Toronto, the rest of Canada, and the United States. Unfortunately the male gymnastics section of Kalev disappeared in 1966 because of lack of interest among young Estonian boys in gymnastics, although experienced and willing coaches and instructors were available. The story was entirely different with the women's rhythmic gymnastics, which attracted new recruits and grew in size. But even here a realignment took place and the women gymnasts withdrew from Kalev and founded the Kalev-Estienne Gymnastics Club and the folk dancers joined Kungla. The fate of the gymnastics and folk dance section of Kalev is symptomatic of the fate of Estonian sports clubs in general. As already mentioned, with the aging of the "old guard" the Estonian sports clubs in Canada either ceased to exist one after another during the 1960's and early 1970's or a specialization took place. The latter, of course, was confined to Toronto. Of the original sports clubs only Kalev of Toronto is still going strong at the beginning of the 1980's, but it, too, has suffered both an overall decline in participation and a splitting off of its sections.[19] The basic reason for this decline is that different sports than those that attracted the original immigrants attract their children. Moreover, amateur sports have made enormous progress in Canada during the 1960's and 1970's and are now supported and promoted by federal, provincial, and municipal governments to an extent unknown in the 1950's. Young Canadians of Estonian descent have joined Canadian athletic organizations and a number have distinguished themselves as outstanding athletes on Canadian school and university teams.

In conclusion, one might ask to what extent the Estonian athletes and sports clubs have promoted amateur sports in Canada? Although there is

115

no question of their influence, it is extremely hard to assess the impact of Estonians and their organizations. The main reason for this is the small number of Estonians in Canada, which meant that the resources of the original immigrants were already exhausted during the 1950's because of aging of the athletes. In fact, since the 1960's there have been no Estonian names among outstanding Canadian athletes. Moreover, it can be said that amateur athletics have not attracted the younger generations of Estonians in Canada nearly as much as they interested the first generation of immigrants. This is clearly shown by the fate of volleyball, traditionally a top sport among Estonians: far from winning national tournaments, as was the case in the 1950's, there are in fact no Estonian volleyball teams in existence any more, although by tradition the Estonian fraternities and sororities carry on their annual tournaments in volleyball and basketball with scratch teams. There has been a much greater promotional impact in Alpine skiing, a sport newly acquired by Estonians in Canada and promoted by the ski clubs and by Estonians who were among the original developers of ski resorts in central Ontario,[20] and in cross-country skiing, which the Estonian ski clubs in particular have emphasized by holding regular competitions among themselves and with other ethnic groups, as well as by organizing open competitions.

Perhaps the greatest Estonian impact on amateur sports in Canada has been through the original influx of Estonian coaches and instructors in Canadian athletic organizations and at Canadian schools and colleges. In fact, the size of this group in relation to the size of the Estonian population in Canada has been remarkable and their input has continued throughout the past three decades – in most cases increasing, rather than decreasing, with aging.

However, in one field of athletics the Estonian input in Canada continues to be highly visible and prominent – women's modern rhythmic gymnastics.

GYMNASTICS: THE TIIDUS GIRLS AND KALEV-ESTIENNE

Modern rhythmic gymnastics (MRG) originated as a non-competitive sport in western Europe at the beginning of this century. Originally it emerged as a criticism of the gymnastics of the turn of the century, which did not distinguish between men's and women's gymnastics. Hence, it may be regarded as a movement specifically aimed at women's physical fitness. Over time, rhythmic gymnastics also had an impact on men's gymnastics by modernizing and reforming it. MRG consists of exercises of movement arranged to music and thus combines the dance and athletics with the aim of attaining an aesthetic harmony displayed by control of body movement. The total impact of MRG on the body is extensive, going far beyond the benefits conferred by other aerobic exercises. MRG develops muscular strength, physical dexterity, controlled co-ordination of movement, and self-discipline.

116

MRG is still primarily a European sport, but Cuba, Japan, and now Canada also belong to the top competitors in the field. It has also caught on in the Third World, where fast progress is being made in catching up to the leaders. In world championship contests the best ten teams representing different countries are invited to compete; since 1969 Canada has been one of those. The International Olympic Committee recognized MRG as a demonstration sport and in the 1984 Olympics at Los Angeles rhythmic gymnastics was included in competition for the first time.

The first rhythmic gymnasts in Canada were members of a Finnish women's club in the 1930's; in the 1940's and 1950's the Czech Sokol (1945), the Finnish Sinikat (1949), and the Finnish Sisu (which still exists) were the clubs that had rhythmic gymnasts among their members. The gymnastics of these clubs were confined to their ethnic groups. It was only in the 1960's that the Estonian gymnasts made a breakthrough, broke down ethnic boundaries, and made MRG a nationally recognized and promoted sport in Canada.

In Estonia, MRG was introduced during the 1920's and gathered momentum in the late 1930's. Ernst Idla, a leader and instructor of MRG, acquired international fame during the 1930's as the developer of a new style that emphasized rhythmic gymnastics as a means of self-expression. In 1944 Idla fled to Sweden, where he continued to teach gymnastics and established the Idla Institute of Gymnastics in Stockholm, which was financially supported by the Swedish government.

Some of Idla's students immigrated to Canada and became mentors of MRG. The first Estonian teacher of MRG in Canada was Helene Tiidus, who in 1949 founded a private studio of gymnastics with four Estonian girls as students in Toronto. She had studied ballet in Estonia, had graduated in physical education from the University of Tartu, and had studied with Idla in Sweden. In the following year, twelve of her advanced students demonstrated MRG to an Estonian audience in Toronto, and by 1957 a group of 110 Tiidus Girls performed at the North American Estonian Festival in Toronto. In the 1960's the studio had about 300 students and her select gymnasts presented MRG to many audiences in Canada and the United States, including the highly acclaimed appearances at the World Exhibition in New York in 1965, at Expo in Montreal in 1967, and at all of the Estonian festivals in Canada and United States during the 1960's.

The sports association Kalev had both male and female gymnasts in its roster during the 1950's. The men's gymnastics at Kalev were mainly instrumental, but the women's gymnastics, as in the Tiidus studio, consisted mainly of modern rhythmic gymnastics. The women gymnasts were coached by Ingrid Saar in the advanced classes and by Evelyn Koop in the regular classes; both instructors had been former students of Idla and students in physical education at the University of Toronto. Women's gymnastics was attracting greater interest throughout the 1950's so that in 1960 the women gymnasts of Kalev found it convenient to establish their independent organization, Kalev-Estienne. Throughout most of the 1960's gymnasts of non-Estonian origins were hardly to be found in the membership of Kalev-Estienne and the group performed in public mainly to Estonian audiences. However, Evelyn Koop, the mentor and leader of Kalev-Estienne, had set as her aim the popularization of modern gymnastics in Canada. The road was rocky and included some detours. For example, commercial physical fitness centres were interested for a time in the application of MRG and actually employed some Kalev-Estienne instructors. But eventually Kalev-Estienne rejected the idea of commercialization and of turning MRG into something that it was not. In the meantime, some smaller MRG clubs emerged outside Toronto and Montreal, in St. Catharines, Sault Ste. Marie, and elsewhere, led by gymnasts with Estonian or Finnish MRG backgrounds. In addition, some instructors were employed by the YWCA and others, who were school teachers, taught MRG in their physical education classes.[21]

The breakthrough occurred in 1967. In connection with centennial year celebrations, Kalev-Estienne gave over fifty performances of MRG coast to coast and attracted interest. Special seminars were held at schools and universities to explain MRG. When the performances attracted the attention of the mass media Kalev-Estienne gymnasts were deluged with invitations for performances. The elite gymnasts were invited to perform for the visit of the Queen Mother in Toronto, and Governor General Roland Michener invited Kalev-Estienne to perform at the official reception of Queen Elizabeth at Ottawa. The publicity of the official invitations and the television performances of the centennial year lifted MRG and Kalev-Estienne to the very forefront of athletic news in Canada.[22]

This has resulted in increasing numbers of non-Estonian gymnasts joining Kalev-Estienne. Another breakthrough came in 1968 when Kalev-Estienne gymnasts were included in the international team that demonstrated MRG at the Olympic Games in Mexico City. The participation there convinced the leaders that their gymnasts had reached international standards and so Kalev-Estienne decided to participate at the international Gymnastrada held in Basel, Switzerland, in 1969, where the ten teams to compete at the next world championship contest in Havana to be held in 1971 were to be selected. But such trips are expensive, and after all the publicity of 1967, Kalev-Estienne expected financial support from the governments of Canada and Ontario. However, both governments declined to help. Undaunted, Kalev-Estienne launched a fund-raising campaign in Toronto and raised sufficient money to send a team of twelve gymnasts, smaller than they had hoped to send, to Basel to represent Canada at the contest. The team placed among the top ten, to the surprise of most other countries with long MRG traditions.[23]

The year 1969 was an important year in another way. In that year, under the leadership of Evelyn Koop, both the Ontario and the Canada Federations of Women Gymnasts were founded and the latter received its first federal grant. The founding of the Ontario and Canadian organizations was necessary in order to co-ordinate the increasing number of clubs and the increasing activities. A number of new clubs had to be founded in Toronto because Kalev-Estienne simply could not accommodate any more gymnasts, 300 to 400 being considered the maximum size of a club. In 1979 the Canadian Federation of Women Gymnasts consisted of over fifty clubs in eight provinces, with thirty-three located in Ontario. The total number of MRG gymnasts in Canada tops 7,000. Currently Kalev-Estienne is still the largest of the MRG clubs – most others have no more than 100 members.[24] And the leading gymnasts, coaches, and leaders are still overwhelmingly Estonian or Finnish.

At this point the history of MRG is no longer a history of the Estonians in Canada but of Canadian athletics. Indeed, MRG has become so "Canadian" that it and the Musical Ride of the Royal Canadian Mounted Police were selected to be the main attractions at the Canada Day celebrations at the Osaka World Fair in Japan. Also, Canadian coaches have achieved such international acclaim that they have been invited to demonstrate and coach MRG in Brazil and in the People's Republic of China, once to a Chinese audience of 200,000 in 1979.

NOTES

1. K. Arro in *Vaba Eestlane*, July 11, 1953.
2. K. Aun *et al.* (eds.), *Seedrioru 1955-1980* (Toronto, 1980).
3. *Ibid.*, p. 27. In the 1950's the fee per child per week at Seedrioru was only half of the fee at YMCA and Kiwanis summer camps. In 1979 the Seedrioru fee had risen to about 70 per cent of the fee in other camps because of the increasing cost of personnel.
4. Kurlents *et al.* (eds.), *Eestlased Kanadas*, p. 574.
5. *Ibid.*, pp. 575-6; *Sillas*, No. 4(9) (1978); Aun *et al.* (eds), *Seedrioru 1955-1980*, pp. 61-5, 88-9, 128-9.
6. *Kungla 1949-1979*, (Winnipeg: Josten's National School Service, 1979), a compendium of 144 pages of pictures and text in Estonian and English published on the thirtieth anniversary of Kungla.
7. P. Einola in *Ajakiri*, no. 1 (1979).
8. Estonian festivals outside Estonia never have deployed more than 600 folk dancers at the same performance. At a youth festival in Tallinn, Estonia, in the summer of 1979 more than 7,500 folk dancers participated.
9. H. Michelson, *50 Aastat Skautlust* (50 Years of Scouting) (New York, 1962); G. Mitt, *Estonian Scouting* (Toronto, 1979).
10. In the autumn of 1953 there were 299 Estonian Girl Guides and 318 Boy Scouts in Canada. Kurlents *et al.* (eds.), *Eestlased Kanadas*, p. 366.
11. Interviews with Heino Jõe, an Estonian scout leader in Estonia and Canada, on December 20, 1979, and January 10, 1980. On September 8, 1983, a written agreement was signed by the Boy Scouts of Canada and

the Estonian Boy Scouts in Canada outlining mutual relations and guaranteeing an autonomous existence of the latter. *Meie Elu*, September 15, 1983; *Vaba Eestlane*, September 15, 1983.

12. Kurlents *et al.* (eds.), *Eestlased Kanadas*, p. 387.

13. Interview with Heino Jõe on December 20, 1979.

14. Estonia placed eleventh in 1935, seventh in 1937, and third in 1939 in World Chess Team Championship competitions. The Estonian riflemen's team twice won at the World Shooting Championship Contest, the much coveted Argentine Cup, in 1937 in Helsinki, Finland, and in 1939 in Lucerne, Switzerland, and revolutionized sharpshooting in the whole world.

15. Kurlents *et al.* (eds.), *Eestlased Kanadas*, pp. 546-7. In the same and other years Estonian teams held also Ontario, Quebec, Toronto, and Montreal championship titles. Cf. Robert D. Bratton, *Canadian Volleyball: a history to 1967* (n.p.: Canadian Volleyball Association, 1972).

16. Mentioned should be Ergo Leps (800- and 1500-metre runs), Hans Moks (javelin), Ain Roost (discus), Toomas Arusoo (100- and 200-metre swimming), Arvo Vahtras and Felix Parum (wrestling). Kurlents *et al.* (eds.), *Eestlased Kanadas*, pp. 543-5.

17. Valdo Lillakas (3000-metre, 3-mile, and 6-mile runs) in 1951 and 1952. *Ibid.*, p. 542.

18. E. Tiilen and J. Hennock in 1968. *Ibid.*, p. 555.

19. Interview with the president of the Estonian sports club Kalev, Margus Tae, on November 10, 1979.

20. Horseshoe Valley, seventy kilometres north of Toronto, by V. Lohuaru, and Moonstone (Devil's Elbow), seventy kilometres northeast of Toronto, by V. Holmberg and H. Reigam.

21. E. Koop, *The Basics of Modern Rhythmic Gymnastics* (Toronto: Canadian Rhythmic Gymnastics Federation, 1977); also, interview with Evelyn Koop on December 10, 1979.

22. *Toronto Daily Star*, July 14, 1967: *Ottawa Citizen*, July 17, 1967; *Toronto Telegram*, August 18, 1967.

23. *Toronto Globe and Mail*, May 29, June 11, 1969; *Toronto Telegram*, July 19, 1969.

24. In Toronto a new club, Ritmika, was founded by Siina Kasekamp and Annely Riga in 1980 and has also grown to the size of 350 gymnasts, of whom about 100 are Estonians. *Meie Elu*, June 16, 1983.

NINE

Other Organized Activities

CO-OPERATIVE ENTERPRISES:
TORONTO ESTONIAN CREDIT UNION

Historically in Estonia the co-operative movement was the primary means whereby the economic standard of the middle classes, both in the cities and in rural areas, was quickly raised to west European levels by the beginning of this century. Indeed, the co-operative movement was the only means available to raise capital in a small society devoid of investment capital. Because of its early success the co-operative movement remained strong and popular in Estonia throughout the independence period, to the extent that it dominated the economy.

This experience in Estonia has been the main reason why the Estonian immigrants in Canada have repeatedly turned to co-operative enterprise here. The Estonian farmers in southern Alberta formed a number of co-operatives soon after arrival, such as the Mutual Fire Insurance Co-operative in 1910 and the Co-operative Telephone Company in 1916, as well as co-operatives for marketing, cattle breeding, and consumer goods purchasing and distribution. An example of both the necessity for and success of co-operative activity is the purchase in 1911 by the Medicine Valley Estonian Co-operative of a gasoline-driven threshing machine, the first in the area, for the then immense price of $3,825 – a sum far beyond the means of any single farmer.[1] However, none of these early co-operatives in the farming West lasted very long because the early Estonian immigrants were a mobile group, always moving from one area to another, in particular to the cities. Hence, all the Estonian co-operatives either dissolved or merged with other farmer co-ops in Alberta.

The Estonian immigrants of the post-war period were mostly urban dwellers and thus turned to different kinds of enterprises. The initial objective was the building of homes. Soon after their arrival, in the 1950's a number of co-operative housing projects were planned in Toronto and elsewhere, but only two were actually built in Toronto. Since housing co-operatives were virtually unknown in North America at the time, the banks were not interested in extending the necessary loans for these purposes, while credit was easily available for the purchase of family dwellings. Consequently, many Estonians, especially in Toronto, took advantage of the easy availability of mortgage money from the banks and purchased multi-family houses or, in a number of cases, apartment buildings. The two housing co-ops that successfully built apartment buildings were formed in the early 1950's in Toronto. The first was established in 1950 by Estonians who had emigrated from Sweden and had been able to take with them small personal savings. In the following year they built two modern apartment complexes in a wooded area in the east part of Toronto overlooking Lake Ontario, one of twenty apartments and the other containing fourteen apartments. The cost of the total project was $336,000, an immense sum for immigrant families in 1951. However, to qualify for a bank loan the co-operative legally had to register as a corporation, although co-operative rules were implemented internally. A second housing co-operative built an apartment building with thirty-two units in the Mount Pleasant-Broadway area in north Toronto in 1955 for a total cost of $400,000. [2]

In contrast to the atmosphere surrounding co-operative housing, the climate for credit unions was favourable during the early 1950's. Indeed, several factors encouraged and supported the growth of the Estonian Credit Union in Toronto. First, in Toronto the Ukrainian and Polish ethnic groups had already established their credit unions in the 1940's; the Lithuanian Credit Union was established a year before the Estonian one, and the Latvian one a year later. Second, the number and popularity of credit unions were growing in Ontario and new legislation was passed giving greater scope and opportunities for investment of the existing capital in credit unions.

In Estonia, credit unionism had built up a history of success over half a century, to the extent that in 1939 half of the volume of all banking operations was carried out by credit union-type co-operative banks. The immigrants brought with them both the memory of the positive experience with co-operative banking and a number of former Estonian credit union leaders. During the mid-1950's the new immigrants had reached the point where they had accumulated small depositable savings on the one hand, but on the other hand they needed loans for the purchase of cars, houses, household items, summer cottages, study in universities, and even for starting new businesses. Thus, many different factors, both external and internal to the ethnic group, had a cumulative effect on the astonishingly rapid growth of the Estonian Credit Union in Toronto immediately after its establishment in 1953.

The idea of establishing a credit union in Canada arose at a meeting of a number of former Estonian credit unionists at Niagara Falls on the occasion of the fiftieth anniversary of Estonian credit unionism in 1952.

The following year the former secretary of the Council of Co-operative Enterprises in Estonia, Arthur Ekbaum, reported favourably on the feasibility of establishing an Estonian credit union in Toronto. An organizing committee was created from former credit unionists and bankers. In December, 1953, the Estonian (Toronto) Credit Union Limited (EÜP) was incorporated. Although membership originally was limited to Estonians and their spouses living in the Metropolitan Toronto area, it was later extended to include all Estonians within a 150-mile radius of Toronto. The EÜP was opened with fifty-eight chartered members and capital of $390, which consisted of $5 membership fees and a savings deposit of $100. In January of 1954 the EÜP began its regular operations, opening two weekday evenings, one evening in the fellowship room of St. Andrew Church and another evening at the office of the Estonian weekly newspaper *Meie Elu*. For the first two years, until May, 1955, when a part-time manager was hired and an office was acquired, the EÜP consisted of a board of directors and a peripatetic "yellow suitcase" belonging to one of the directors in which the EÜP documents and cash were carried each business evening from the home to the place of business. All work, including accounting, was carried out by the directors without compensation.[3]

But its growth was astounding. At its first anniversary in December, 1954, the EÜP already had 248 members, $40,358 in deposits, and $31,813 in loans outstanding. During the second year, membership increased to 426 and transactions tripled. Five years later, in December, 1959, the annual report showed a balance of $1 million. In 1959 business machines were acquired. In 1960 the EÜP moved to its permanent home in Estonia House, where its offices include a conference room and a library. By this time the EÜP already had ten employees. During the 1960's membership increased by an average of 150 per year and the business balance grew by about $1 million each year. At the end of 1979 the EÜP had 5,143 members, including 231 Estonian organizations, and assets of $11.2 million.[4]

Nevertheless, the EÜP is still a small credit union. In fact, it does not even rank among the top 100 of the 4,000 credit unions in Canada. Its size is comparable to the Lithuanian and Latvian credit unions in Toronto, and its capacity to grow has reached its upper limits because of the size of the Estonian ethnic group. Its main problem during the 1980's is to attract new members from among the younger generation of Estonian Canadians.

Two factors bear emphasizing about the activities of the Estonian Credit Union: first, its role in the Canadian economy and within the Canadian credit union movement; and second, its role within the Estonian ethnic group in Toronto. The two roles are, of course, mixed just as the EÜP was a reflection both of economic growth that took place in Canada during the 1950's and 1960's and of the wealth-accumulation among the Estonian ethnic group. But the EÜP was also an important factor in this growth, particularly among the Estonian ethnic group – it facilitated capital flow. In addition, it contributed in several ways to the development of credit unionism in Toronto and in Ontario. For example, Estonian credit unionists, drawing parallels between credit unions in Estonia and in Canada, early came to the conclusion that the new credit union could not succeed unless it had the privilege of using cheques and having them cleared within the banking system. This privilege Canadian credit unions did not yet have in 1953. EÜP became a strong supporter of the Ontario Co-op Credit Society (later renamed the Ontario Credit Union League) in endeavouring to acquire that privilege. After the new Credit Union Act was passed in 1955, the EÜP became the first credit union in Toronto to implement chequeing privileges. For the first time credit union transactions were modernized; instead of merely cash deposits and withdrawals, cheques could now be drawn on savings balances and cleared through the banking system. Without the chequeing privilege credit unions would have been an anachronism in the increasingly cashless but credit-oriented society of the 1950's and the 1960's.

In addition, the EÜP was the first to provide both automatic and free insurance to its clientele and term-deposit service, and it installed a modern computer system in 1973. As a service to the Estonian community EÜP has published literature on the Canadian economy and on credit unionism, and since 1957 it has issued the yearbook titled *Ühispanga Uudised* (Credit Union News). In 1962 it introduced a credit union seminar offering academic-level courses in economics and credit union problems to its younger members. The two-year course was taught by university professors, well-known economists in the business sector, and credit union leaders and was completed by twenty students.

Naturally, the most important service that EÜP has performed has been to facilitate capital flow among Estonians and in the Toronto economy. There is little doubt that many savings deposits came to the EÜP that otherwise would not have been accumulated at all. However, the main attraction of the Estonian Credit Union was not that it could pay higher interest on savings and charge lower interest rates on loans than the commercial banks – the difference was not great and recently there has been none. It was rather the ease with which the transactions could be made and the mutual trust and community feeling among the Estonians on which the EÜP was based that made the difference. It cannot be overemphasized that the EÜP has not only functioned as a financial institution; its role has been far wider. In fact, it has added the all-important financial dimension to the social and psychological cohesion of the Estonian community. This cohesion originally permitted the EÜP to extend loans based only on personal knowledge of the applicant and of those who co-signed his loan, which commercial banks would have turned down on simple credit bureau ratings. Community cohesion also led to the punctual repayment of loans – after all, personal reputations were at stake in a tightly knit ethnic community. Hence, a trip to deposit savings or repay loans to the EÜP was not only a commercial undertaking, it was a trip to the community because the EÜP was an integral part of the community.

As the community supported the EÜP so the EÜP supported the community, both directly and indirectly. Its main contribution was the financial advice it gave often and freely to any Estonian who asked for it. But EÜP has also been an important financial supporter of both Estonian youth and Estonian ethnic cultural activities. Some of these stipends, extended by loans, made the difference between students being able to continue studying or having to leave university, particularly during the 1950's. In addition, many small businesses have been started by EÜP loans. And, of course, the most outstanding example of the EÜP's financial contribution to the community is the $3.5-million short-term loan it arranged through the Ontario Credit Union League for building the Eesti Kodu.[5]

COMMUNITY HALLS AND RECREATION AREAS

As early as 1950 a need was felt in Toronto for an Estonian community centre, but although the fund-raising began the following year it took almost ten years until Eesti Maja (Estonia House) was actually opened. Before 1957 contributions accrued at a very slow rate and totalled no more than an average of $2,500 per year, mostly from surpluses from ethnic events and festivals. In 1958 the largest contribution to date (over $6,000) came from the surplus of the North American Estonian Festival held in Toronto the previous year. Another reason for delay in building the community centre was conflicting opinion about the proposed centre. For example, the purchase was expected to take into account the following considerations: location in Toronto, neighbourhood, transportation and parking facilities, and, most important, the usage of the centre by specific organizations according to their particular wishes. The committee charged with acquiring a centre was far from idle: before 1960 over 100 parcels of real estate were considered and two offers were made. One offer was unsuccessful; the other was successful but the land was resold after the committee learned that it was located in a dry ward of Toronto.[6]

A special fund-raising campaign increased the fund to $115,000 and in the spring of 1960 a former schoolhouse on Broadview Avenue near the Bloor viaduct was bought for $101,000. The schoolhouse sat on a reasonably large parcel of land but the building was in a dilapidated state. During the summer the necessary renovation work was done, partly by voluntary unpaid labour, and in September Estonia House was opened prior to the beginning of the school year so that the supplementary school could already use it that year. In 1963 a new hall seating about 400 people, rooms for the supplementary school, and a cafeteria were added. In 1976 a new facade was added to the building, which included rooms for the shop of the Estonian Relief Committee, for the archives, and for offices. Estonia House currently houses the Estonian (Toronto) Credit Union, the offices of the weekly *Meie Elu*, the Estonian Central Council, the Estonian Federation, the Estonian National Foundation, the Estonian Relief Committee, the Estonian Arts Centre, the supplementary school, and the Boy Scouts and Girl Guides. In addition, it has three halls of different sizes, storage space for the archives, the cafeteria, and a number of private commercial offices. There is also an indoor rifle range in the attic built by the Estonian Riflemen's Club.

Of course, not all activities of the Estonian community take place in Eesti Maja. Toronto has a number of other Estonian community buildings, including Tartu College and three Estonian churches, which are used intensively by the community. Theatre performances, concerts, lectures, and seminars, for a variety of reasons, are more often than not in other places, including on the campus of the University of Toronto and in the halls of the St. Lawrence Centre. Indeed, during the major festivals the importance of Estonia House is always overshadowed by other festival locations. Nevertheless, since 1960 Estonia House has provided the Estonian community with an indispensable focus for its activities, both physically and organizationally. In legal structure Estonia House is a shareholding company, with a capitalization of $148,000, of which $27,000 belongs to Estonian organizations and the rest to 1,921 individual shareholders.[7] Thus, in structural form Estonia House is a communal enterprise of a large number of small investments, averaging $60 per shareholder. Operationally, Eesti Maja is a self-supporting enterprise with rent as its sole source of income, the largest tenant being the Estonian Credit Union.

No other Estonian community in Canada has succeeded in building its own community hall, except the one in Vancouver that was built jointly by the Estonian Lutheran Church and the Estonian Association. As mentioned, however, a number of Estonian church buildings are used as community centres as well. Also, it should be mentioned that practically all larger Estonian communities have built their own summer recreational areas in the countryside.

TARTU COLLEGE, TARTU INSTITUTE, AND METSAÜLIKOOL

The term "academic organization" in Estonian designates a club-like organization, with lifetime membership of both university undergraduates and alumni. The University of Tartu in Estonia had more than twenty such Estonian academic organizations plus a number of German, Russian, and Jewish ones. These varied widely in style and form: some were German-style Studentenverbindungen (fraternities) and included only men; others included only women; and some included both men and women. All, however, had interdisciplinary membership, that is, the membership was not restricted to any specific faculty nor were there any geographic restrictions. The main criterion for membership was university status and personal acceptability. Besides the development of personal friendship, the aim of these clubs was the promotion of intellectual interaction. Some of these organizations, in fact, worked primarily as intellectual or literary clubs.

In 1940 the academic organizations were disbanded by the Soviets and their properties, other assets, and archives were confiscated. Many of the leading members were arrested and persecuted or died during war years. In 1944 about a quarter of the former members of the various academic organizations succeeded in escaping to Western countries, mainly Sweden and West Germany. Between 500 and 600 of these ended up in Canada, mostly in Toronto.[8] Very soon after arrival these former members established local chapters of their organizations, and as Estonian students entered Canadian universities new members were recruited, with the twin results that most Estonian-Canadian university graduates are members of the Estonian academic organizations and that the overwhelming majorities of their memberships are now made up of those who have been admitted since the war.

Although these academic organizations attempt to carry on the old traditions by formal meetings, membership parties, and celebrations of anniversaries of their organizations, the fact is that the activities are but a reflection of the former ones in Estonia very simply because these organizations do not play the seminal role on the campus and among university graduates in Canada that they played in Estonia. Moreover, the community of Estonian university graduates in Canada is dispersed about the country and not concentrated in a small area as was the case in Estonia. As time goes on regular participation by the younger members has been declining, although recruitment is still holding up and, for instance, four of the seventeen academic organizations in Toronto have purchased their own clubhouses near the University of Toronto.

Although the members of the academic organizations participate in the various ethnocultural activities of the Estonians in Canada as individuals, and not as representatives of their clubs, the participation rate of the members of the academic organizations is very high. In fact, this group performs the central role of leadership among the Estonian communities across Canada. The personal relationships established as a result of common membership and across generations, as well as across the different academic disciplines, forms an invisible informal network that cements the cohesion of the other more community-oriented Estonian ethnic organizations to an invaluable although indeterminable extent. These personal connections penetrate all the important organizations of the Estonian ethnic groups in Canada and reach out to all the other Estonian communities in the Western world. Moreover, the chapters of the different academic organizations in the different countries are in constant touch with each other and frequent meetings of members of the different academic organizations take place. In Toronto, Tartu College is the outstanding example of the collaboration among the Canadian Estonian academic organizations.

Tartu College, an eighteen-storey student residence adjacent to the University of Toronto campus, was built in 1969 at a cost of over $3 million. It was financed primarily by a long-term loan from the Central Housing and Mortgage Corporation, as were also two other student residences in Toronto and one in Ottawa at the same time.[9] After completion the buildings were turned over to committees of resident students for management, except in the case of Tartu College, where management was turned over to a joint council of the seventeen Estonian academic organizations that had partially financed the building. Tartu College's main aim has been to provide inexpensive but good housing and an appropriate environment for students close to the campus of the University of Toronto. In 1971, 67.7 per cent of the residents were undergraduates and 32.3 per cent graduates; 31.4 per cent were from the Toronto area, 49.8 per cent from western Ontario, and 18.9 per cent from the other provinces of Canada or from other countries, including the United States, Israel, Poland, Australia, and a number of African and Asian countries.[10] Tartu College also has housed some administrative offices of the University of Toronto and has the space for Estonian academic organizations and for the Tartu Institute.

Tartu College is a unique venture in Canada. As a co-operative student housing project it has been eminently successful. This success can be explained only by the firm traditions of the Estonian academic organizations and the long past experience of co-operative enterprises that Estonia and Estonians have had.

The Tartu Institute is a non-profit organization established to promote the study and research of Estonian history. It was established in 1971 and is governed by a twenty-one-member board of directors, of whom four are nominated by Tartu College and the rest must be either professors of a recognized university or recognized scholars.

The activities of Tartu Institute have been limited by lack of financial resources, since its only income is a subsidy from the Tartu College and donations, which have not been sought very actively. Since 1971, six to ten annual public lectures on academic topics, most often in Estonian but sometimes in English, have been given to audiences ranging in size from thirty to 200. The lecturers have been divided almost equally among those from Canada, those from the United States, and those from overseas. No fees or travel costs have been paid to any lecturer; the secretary of the institute has snared Estonian scholars when their conference and research travels bring them to or through Toronto. The institute has given small research grants or stipends to Estonian students and has supported financially the Estonian-language advanced course given by the University of Toronto at Tartu College. The institute has managed to build a modest library and archives and has initiated projects in compiling a bibliography of books and articles on Estonia, including Estonians in Canada.[11]

The Metsaülikool, colloquially known as the Mü among Estonians, is a creation of the younger Estonian academic community in Toronto, established in 1967 and copied abroad. Mü is an annual one-week seminar for Estonian university graduates and students held in the last week of August at the Kotkajärve Boy Scout camp in Muskoka. Although the Mü was the first week-long seminar instituted among Estonians abroad, it had a number of youth conferences as forerunners, including the KLENK (Kesk Lääne Eesti Noorte Koondis – the Mid-West Estonian Youth Association) annual conference held since 1958 over the American Thanksgiving weekend in November and the cultural youth conference held more or less regularly over the Easter weekend in New York City.

At the Mü, lectures and discussions are given by acknowledged Estonian experts in their fields, and the seminar is conducted exclusively in Estonian. The fields of study of the seminar are centred on Estonian language and literature, the problems of modern and current Estonian history, folklore, music, and the fine arts.

Most of the students (annually about 100) come from Canada and the United States but each year there are a few who come from Europe. Most of the lecturers are from North American universities but each year at least one scholar has been invited from Europe. For example, in 1980 two lecturers came from Australia and one from the University of Salzburg in Austria. Between 1967 and 1980 more than 700 Estonian university graduates had attended Mü and about fifty academics conducted lectures or discussions, most of them on a repeat basis.

The Mü is a "retreat" from the disturbances and distractions of everyday life to the "forest" to study Estonian culture intensively. The students, lecturers, and discussion leaders live together for a week and learn to know each other personally, which is possible given the small number of participants. Although the formal program is heavy, time is left over for swimming, hiking, sports, and campfire entertainment.

The Mü has had a strong impact on the younger generation of Estonian intellectuals. The seminars have emphasized intellectual integrity and honesty in dealing with current political problems, in addition to the basic discussions of the background and continuing trends of Estonian cultural development. But Mü is also an intensive experience of Estonian culture and language at an advanced level, for here young Estonian intellectuals live and practically breathe Estonia and the problems of Estonia day and night for a week while cut off from the everyday world.

Mü has also travelled. In 1974 it was held in Finland to emphasize the common cultural heritage of Finns and Estonians, to attract students from Europe, and to spread the concept. In this it was successful, for the following year a similar week-long seminar-retreat was started in

Sweden, called the Metroo, and subsequently another similar seminar was started in Australia. All three have continued annually and interest in all has increased from year to year.

Strangely, despite its success, Mü has no structured organization. Each year the Mü leaders and organizers are selected from among former Mü leaders and students and the new group gets together to plan the next year's program. In fact Mü operates, and always has, on an informal and year-to-year basis. But Mü's influence and impact have been far-reaching, and its leadership core and its former students can be found in all of the Estonian academic and intellectually oriented organizations. And the Mü group has organized two important additions to the intellectual life of the Estonians in Toronto. The Society of the Friends of Estonian Literature in Toronto, although an independent organization, consists largely of the Mü group, and the bi-monthly *Ajakiri*, published in Toronto, is a periodical and information bulletin of Mü, which spreads the concerns of the younger intellectuals across the Estonian communities not only in Canada but also abroad.

PROFESSIONAL ASSOCIATIONS AND SOCIAL CLUBS

No history of Estonian organizations in Canada would be complete without mentioning the Estonian professional associations and interest clubs. Although they have numbered a few dozen, more important than their number is the way in which the adjustment of the post-war refugee-immigrants in their new country is reflected in a typology of these groups. Estonian professional associations were founded in Canada in the 1950's by former members of these associations in Estonia. Thus there were associations of Estonian jurists, teachers, physicians, agronomists, civil servants, army officers, and artists, to mention only those that also had branches or members in Estonian communities outside Toronto. The aim of these associations was to unite the members of the Estonian professional groups abroad not only in Canada but also in other countries where similar associations existed.

It is of interest to note that Estonian engineers, by far the largest professional group among Estonians in Canada, never established their association. The reason seems simply to be that engineering was still a comparatively new profession in Estonia and not as well organized as some of the more traditional ones. In contrast, Estonian agronomists, a comparatively small group in Canada, were traditionally well organized in Estonia and thus a worldwide federation of their associations in different countries emerged in a short time. A similar global orientation can be noticed in other professional groups that had a strong organizational background in the home country. This brings us to the conclusion that these associations were primarily fragments of the associations in the former homeland that were re-established in the other countries. Furthermore, in the 1950's the hope of returning to Estonia remained and this may be seen as the main raison d'être of the professional organizations of Estonia abroad.

However, most of these associations could find no professional or any other relevance in their new environment; they not only failed to recruit new members but many of their members did not continue in their former professions. Thus, most of the professional associations gradually became inactive or had disappeared altogether by the 1970's. The Association of Estonian Artists in Toronto has survived mainly because it recruited new members and has maintained its function: an annual exhibition of new works of Estonian artists in Canada and the organization of art exhibits for Estonian festivals. Similarly, the association of Estonian physicians, which has recruited almost all younger Estonians who have graduated from the medical schools in Canada into its membership, continues. The association regularly arranges for lectures and discussions to Estonian audiences and performs an additional function by assigning Estonian doctors to weekend duties for the Estonian community in Toronto.

Various special-interest clubs emerged later than the professional clubs, in the 1960's and 1970's. They are the product of the post-adjustment period and function very much as any of the social clubs. Those in Toronto include the Estonian Economics (Businessmen) Club, the Estonian Horticultural Club, and the Estonian Ethnographic Club, all of which have enjoyed a stable membership. Added should be the provincial clubs, something akin to the Newfoundland clubs in various Canadian cities, which consist of Estonians who themselves, or whose parents, came from one of the provinces of Estonia. These clubs have been founded at various times from the 1950's to the early 1980's and vary considerably in size and internal cohesion. The oldest and strongest are the clubs of those whose homes were on the Estonian islands in the Baltic Sea.

Since the beginning of the 1970's an increasing number of post-war Estonian immigrants has reached retirement age, the result being that Estonian pensioners clubs now can be found in all major Estonian communities in Canada. The Estonian Pensioners Club in Toronto has over 700 members and is active in many recreational and special-interest fields and also has a choir.

NOTES

1. Kurlents *et al.* (eds.), *Eestlased Kanadas*, p. 308.
2. *Ibid.*, p. 310.
3. *Ühispanga Uudised* (The News of the Credit Union), Toronto (Estonian) Credit Union, XXIII (1979).
4. *Ibid.*, XXIV (1980).
5. *Ibid.*, XXIII (1979).

6. K. Eerme (ed.), *Eesti Maja Torontos* (Estonia House in Toronto) (Toronto, 1965).
7. *Ibid.*, p. 24. Only three shareholders had an investment over $1,000; twenty-one had less than $10.
8. Kurlents *et al.* (eds.), *Eestlased Kanadas*, p. 414.
9. The others were the Rochdale and Neill-Wycik Colleges in Toronto, and the Pestalozzi College in Ottawa.
10. E. Mägi in *Verbum habet Sakala* (Sakala has the Floor) (Toronto: Sakala, 1974), p. 69.
11. *Annual Reports* of the secretary of the Tartu Institute.

TEN

Ethnic Festivals

Estonian ethnic festivals in Canada have ranged widely, both in program and attendance, from the traditional midsummer festivities with a few score participants at the local community level all the way to the Estonian World Festival with thousands of Estonians attending from many countries. All festivals, however, are rooted in traditions brought from Estonia and all have the same objective: to maintain an Estonian ethnocultural community abroad.

The traditional midsummer festivity in Estonia, historically the oldest Estonian festival, as in the other north European countries centred on a bonfire, Jaanituli, which in Estonia was customarily a burning barrel of tar on top of a pole. For centuries the event was a spontaneous merry-making affair at the communal level and included singing, dancing, drinking, eating, and social games. The Alberta Estonians at the beginning of the century celebrated midsummer in this traditional way. But in later years the merry-making became organized, as it did in Estonia, and programs included choir singing, athletic competitions, and plays. Some Alberta Estonian summer festivals during the 1930's attracted several hundred participants, including many non-Estonians from neighbouring villages.

THE TORONTO ESTONIAN SUMMER FESTIVAL

Similarly, but within the framework of a community picnic, Estonians living in the Toronto and Niagara Peninsula areas held midsummer gatherings near St. Catharines. The post-war immigrants joined these gatherings and in 1949 the midsummer celebrants numbered about 1,000, mostly newcomers.

As the Toronto immigrant community grew they soon took over and in 1951 they replaced the St. Catharines midsummer gathering with the midsummer festival of the Toronto Estonian community, which henceforth was held at various locations north of Toronto. In 1952 attendance at the Toronto midsummer festival reached 3,500. The main thrust of the festival revolved around the planned program, as the case had been in Estonia during the 1930's, and it included choir singing, games, folk dance, gymnastics, and other group performances.

The record of the Toronto Estonian Summer Festivals, however, was uneven. During the 1960's attendance ranged from a low of 1,000 to a high of 3,000, and in some years the festival was not held at all because of adverse weather, priority given to other ethnic events, and the lack of a permanent location for the festival. In the late 1960's it disappeared. Nevertheless, the Toronto festival did play an important role in building the community spirit of the Estonians in Toronto for almost twenty years, and many cultural programs – including two open-air theatre performances, one in 1963 and another in 1968 – were produced and presented.

THE MIDSUMMER FESTIVALS AT SEEDRIORU

An "Estonian Song Festival" was held in the summer of 1956 at the newly purchased Seedrioru summer campgrounds near Elora. The event attracted about 2,500 Estonians and marked the beginning of summer festivals there that have continued for over twenty-five years. The main reason for the continuing success of these festivals has been the quality and the popularity of the programs presented. In five years the festival has been a song festival of Estonian choirs in North America, in fifteen summers open-air theatre performances have been presented by the Toronto Estonian National Theatre, and in the remaining years there have been performances of original musicals based on popular songs, music, folk dance, and ethnic customs or mythology. Because of its location near Toronto and comparative closeness to a number of Estonian communities in the United States, the Seedrioru Festival quickly became not only an Ontario-Estonian but also an American-Estonian festival. The date of the festival, the first weekend in July, encourages attendance by Estonians from both countries. Many Estonians, especially the youth, who come from farther away usually pitch their tents on the grounds at Seedrioru and camp there for several days during the festival.

The open-air theatre performances have been impressive. Around the core of former actors and singers of the National Opera House and other professional theatres in Estonia a cast of around 100 amateur actors and youths has often been assembled. Two of the performances have been gala performances of original works and many have had their first open-air presentation at Seedrioru. With two exceptions, all of the presentations have been works by Estonian playwrights and composers. In 1963 *Hamlet* was presented, the cast including actors and actresses who had played the same roles in Estonia.[1]

The Seedrioru Festival program has always been complemented by concerts presented by soloists and by folk dance or gymnastic performances. The formal program is followed by popular entertainment and dancing.

ESTONIAN FESTIVALS ON THE WEST COAST

The West Coast Festival has been held every second summer since 1953 in either July or August. It differs from the festivals discussed above in that it is a city festival rotating among university campuses in Los Angeles, San Francisco, Seattle, Portland, and Vancouver. Because cities have facilities far beyond anything available in the summer campgrounds, the West Coast Festivals also include fine art and/or ethnographic exhibitions, indoor theatre performances, solo concerts, and other indoor events. The main program usually consists of either choir concerts or performances of folk dance and gymnastics, or both. Often, choirs, folk dance groups, gymnasts, and soloists from Toronto and the eastern United States are the main attractions. In contrast to the Seedrioru approach, the West Coast organizers have sought publicity in the English-language mass media and solicit participation by local non-Estonians. In 1969, for example, in Vancouver over half of the 2,000 tickets sold for the main event were purchased by people who were not Estonians.[2] Most, however, were members of other ethnic groups originating either in northern or central Europe. Although the main programs of these festivals are usually concentrated on a Saturday, the other events stretch over several days of a long weekend.

THE "MEETING DAY" AT MONTREAL IN 1967

During the World Exposition in 1967 an Estonian festival called a "Meeting Day of Estonians" was held on the Expo grounds in Montreal for the special purpose of presenting Estonians and their cause as Second World War political refugees. This festival was really a political manifestation presented by cultural means. Originally the event was to take place at the Pavilion of Nations and the Republican Estonian blue-black-white flag was to be flown; however, at the last moment the Expo management moved the event to the Sports Stadium, located some distance from the centre of the Expo grounds, and the use of the Republican flag was prohibited. Nevertheless, the event took place and the gymnasts exhibited the Republican colours in using blue-black-white dress and large tri-coloured ribbons as their exercise equipment.[3]

An audience of about 3,000 attended the program, which consisted of choir presentations, folk dance, and women's rhythmic gymnastics. Four choirs from Toronto and Montreal sang, as did soloists from both the United States and Canada. The Estonian Orchestra from Toronto played and 150 folk dancers and a select group of women gymnasts performed. The event was closed, as are all Estonian festivals, by the singing of the Republican Estonian national anthem.

THE ESTONIAN CENTENNIAL SONG FESTIVAL
IN TORONTO, 1969

To commemorate the centennial of the National Song Festival in Estonia a North American Estonian song festival was held on May 31, 1969, at Varsity Arena on the grounds of the University of Toronto. A record twenty-eight choirs with more than 600 singers, divided almost equally between Canada and the United States, were the main attractions; five orchestras, three from the United States, and a special concert by a 400-voice children's choir were included in the program.[4] On the following Sunday, June 1, the Toronto Estonian Male Choir and the University of Rochester (New York) Symphony Orchestra presented a concert of exclusively Estonian music at Convocation Hall of the University of Toronto.

THE ESTONIAN INDEPENDENCE DAY CELEBRATIONS
IN TORONTO

The most important event in all Estonian communities abroad is the celebration of the Estonian Independence Day in February. The program of this ceremonial day consists of concerts by choirs and soloists, performances by folk dancers or gymnasts, declamations by Boy Scouts and Girl Guides, and speeches in both Estonian and English. Because of the size of the Toronto Estonian community the celebration in Toronto must be ranked as one of the main Estonian festivals in Canada. The event takes place on the afternoon of the Sunday closest to February 24, the official Estonian Independence Day, and is attended by representatives from the federal and Ontario governments and from the city of Toronto, as well as by representatives from other ethnic groups and some foreign diplomats. For thirty years the city council of Toronto has hoisted the Republican Estonian flag in front of the City Hall for the duration of the celebrations.

THE KILLAMÄNGUD (PROVINCIAL GAMES)

After a hiatus of a decade the Provincial Games, a replacement for the Toronto Estonian summer festivals, were proposed. Many groups who orginated from various provinces of Estonia had organized summer festivals separately. A national festival called Killamängud, claiming to revive the festivities of Estonian antiquity, had been held in Tallinn in the 1930's. The new resurrected Killamängud took place in August, 1978, at the Devil's Elbow Ski Resort and was repeated in 1980 and 1982 in other locations near Toronto. Each provincial group presented its own program, which usually included exhibits of provincial costumes, handicrafts, models of architectural landmarks, and performances of provincial folk dances. The most popular and/or the typical and unique foods of the provinces were also served.

THE NORTH AMERICAN ESTONIAN FESTIVALS

As early as 1953 discussion for "a new type of Estonian festival" began to appear in the Estonian press but no definitive proposal came forward before 1955.[5] The many arguments advanced in the Estonian community in Toronto may be grouped into three categories. First, it was observed that Estonians, although well organized in their local communities, nevertheless had no goals or activities that would unite all Estonians in Canada. Hence, something had to be done to mobilize Estonians to an awareness of their ethnic identity across Canada as well as in the local communities. It was also observed that most Estonians already had cars and travelled long distances for pleasure, so that distance, hitherto the bane of Estonian cohesion in Canada, was no longer a problem.

Second, it was argued that the festivals organized locally, and even by the Toronto community, were mainly social gatherings that offered popular entertainment with no respectable cultural content. For example, the midsummer festivals in the countryside did not have facilities for art exhibitions, theatre, conferences, or even stages for larger song festivals and folk dance presentations, nor stadia for athletic games. Such facilities would be available in the "cultural environment" of a large city. Thus, the new type of festival had to be held in a city that had those facilities. It is almost needless to add that in these arguments the national festivals in Estonia in the 1930's were often referred to as the model.

Finally, it was argued that one of the shortcomings of Estonians had been their closed and inward-looking character; no effort had been made to reach the Canadian public at large "to show who we are and why we are here." This was obviously a political objective; during the 1950's the Estonian community still hoped for the liberation of Estonia and felt obligated to bring their case before the Canadian public. The political argument later receded into the background while the cultural and ethnic mobilization took over as preparations began in earnest for the festival.

The preparations for the first North American Estonian Festival were set in motion by a meeting of delegates of twenty-four Estonian organizations in Toronto on January 29, 1956. A main committee was struck and authorized to create subcommittees as necessary to carry out the preparations for the festival. The preparations were extensive; invitations and information were sent to all Estonian choirs in North America; several seminars were held for local leaders and instructors of folk dance, in both Canada and the United States, and Professor Juhan Aavik of Sweden, a distinguished Estonian composer and veteran director of choirs at large Estonian National Song Festivals, agreed to be the chief conductor.

The program of the festival was extensive. At the CNE Arts Building ninety works by thirty Estonian artists living abroad were shown in one exhibition; ninety-five works of Eduard Wiiralt, the most eminent twentieth-century Estonian artist, who died in 1954 in Paris, were displayed in another; and there was a special exhibition of the history of Estonia since the 1917 Russian Revolution. In addition, there were several specialized exhibits showing Estonian youth activities, supplementary school work, and books.

On the second day of the festival, May 31, 1957, theatre performances were held in Eaton Auditorium. The following day a congress comprised of delegates from 106 Estonian organizations in North America took place, and in the late afternoon were the song festival and Estonian games, at the stadium on the CNE grounds. A mass choir, composed of sixteen individual choirs with 500 singers, 400 folk dancers, and 100 male and female gymnasts performed. This was brought to a conclusion by a "People's Party," a dinner with entertainment held in the Automotive Building of the CNE. Sunday began with three church services, two Lutheran and one jointly held by other Protestant denominations, followed in the afternoon with the last item of the festival, a soccer match between Estonian and Latvian teams at Kew Beach Stadium.

The festival was a resounding success: the Estonian press was jubilant and financially the festival had produced a $6,000 surplus. Nevertheless, in succeeding weeks an adverse note began to surface – the festival had not caught the attention of the Canadian public and press to the extent that had been hoped. But this was immediately explained away by reference to the summer doldrums when people are away from cities and by arguments of the "different tastes" of the Canadian public.

The self-criticism must be taken with a grain of salt, since both the CBC and the CBS networks made film clips of the festival that were shown across North America. Moreover, the Toronto English-language dailies reported and commented on the festival, though not on the front pages. But it was also true that attendance at the festival was almost entirely Estonian, which had been expected.

In summary, considering that the festival was put on by people who had arrived in Canada and the United States only a few years earlier, the enterprise, which attracted up to 8,000 Estonians from across North America, takes on gigantic overtones. Nevertheless, the plaintive comment by one Estonian, that "in Canada still nobody knows us, nor pays any attention to what we do," held some truth.[6]

The second North American Estonian Festival was held three years later (1960) in New York. The third North American Festival was held in Toronto again, May 14-18, 1964. This time the various exhibitions were held in the newly acquired Estonia House and consisted of an art exhibition, and an exhibition called "Twenty Years Abroad." This was divided into twelve sections, with each section depicting an aspect of the life of Estonians since 1944, in Germany, in Sweden, and especially in Canada.

The main aspects covered were music, theatre, sports, church, publishing, handicrafts, economic advancement, and education.

The main event of the festival, the song, dance, and gymnastics program, took place at Maple Leaf Gardens. This time more than 2,000 performers participated in the program.[7] This was the biggest festival that Estonians had ever put on outside Estonia and was attended by 9,000, half of whom came from the United States.

A complete film of the festival was shot by professional cameramen, and the dailies in Toronto covered the festival more thoroughly than they had done seven years earlier. Nevertheless, the Toronto Estonian press still found that "Canadians are not much interested in what we are doing."[8] There was some point to this criticism since one of the Toronto dailies reported the Estonian festival in the entertainment section while giving front-page coverage to a rowdy but much smaller rock-and-roll festival at the Toronto Islands.[9] The fourth, and last, North American Festival was held in New York in 1968.

THE ESTONIAN WORLD FESTIVALS

The North American festivals fulfilled another important function: the promotion of ethnic solidarity. Many who attended the festivals did so to meet friends, relatives, acquaintances, schoolmates, former neighbours, or members of the same organization they had not seen for years, perhaps not since during the war in Estonia. They now lived scattered across the huge North American continent. It was only normal human curiosity to discover how old friends, acquaintances, and relatives had managed and how well they were doing economically, especially when different countries were involved. Indeed, the festival often was included as part of a planned tour of visiting relatives and friends around North America. Young Estonians also liked to see new places and meet their Estonian contemporaries in other countries, often joining a folk dance troupe, choir, or gymnastic group in order to travel and meet other Estonian youth. All these factors contributed to the success of the North American festivals as much as or perhaps more than the formal ethnic idealism.

The desirability of a joint American-European festival was therefore a natural extension of the North American Festival. But neither side of the Atlantic believed in the feasibility of such a venture. So it was that in 1968 one Estonian festival was held in Stockholm and another in New York only a week apart.

The main reason for scepticism on both sides of the ocean was the cost of air travel: in the mid-1960's it was calculated that not more than a few hundred Estonians would undertake travel for festival purposes across the Atlantic. However, with the 1960's came faster and progressively cheaper air travel, and group flights could cut the cost of travel even further. Moreover, during the late 1960's many Estonians from Europe flew to North America to visit friends and relatives and combined these visits with tours of the United States and Canada; and many Canadian and American Estonians joined the North American middle-class discovery of Europe. Hence, when the next North American Estonian Festival was planned in Toronto for 1972, the Estonians in Sweden were naturally consulted. The reaction was positive and the festival was tentatively planned as an Estonian World Festival.

When the first Estonian World Festival was held in Toronto, July 8-16, 1972, it surpassed all previous festivals in attendance and in the variety of programs presented. In addition to a record attendance from the American west coast and in general from both Canada and the United States, more than 3,000 came from Europe, mainly from Sweden, and several hundred came from Australia, as well as a few from the Latin American countries. Indeed, Estonians from all over the world – except from the Estonian homeland – came together in Toronto.

The festival followed the familiar patterns, but more events were scheduled and the program was expanded to eight days. Separate exhibits were held for fine art in Tartu College; books and publications were displayed at the Ontario Institute for Studies in Education (OISE); ethnic costumes and handicrafts were shown at the Royal Ontario Museum; and smaller specialized exhibits about "Life of Estonians abroad" – Estonian schools, churches, scouting, summer camps, and stamps – were shown in Estonia House.

The festival was also a theatre festival. Estonian theatre groups from Toronto, the United States, and Stockholm presented eight performances altogether at the St. Lawrence Centre and Estonia House, in addition to an open-air performance at Seedrioru. Musically, a dozen concerts were presented, mainly by soloists, but there was also a church concert of soloists, choirs, and orchestras, as well as a special "young talent" concert at the St. Lawrence Centre.

On July 14 a congress of delegates from 350 Estonian organizations met at OISE. The main themes of the discussions concerned Estonian ethnic and language retention, relations with Estonians in the homeland, and attitudes toward the Soviet occupation of Estonia. A declaration condemning the Soviet occupation of Estonia was adopted in both Estonian and English and was read in front of the City Hall the next day. On the evening of July 11 a garden party was held by athletes and youth organizations at Casa Loma. Another dinner evening, the traditional "People's Party," was held on the evening of July 14 in Moss Park Armoury.

Other events of this first Estonian World Festival included a procession of Estonian organizations from Queen's Park to Nathan Phillips Square at City Hall. The declaration adopted on the previous day was read in both Estonian and English and former Prime Minister John G. Diefenbaker gave the main speech to 15,000 participants in the procession. Music was provided by five Canadian army bands. The demonstration concluded by the massed participants singing the Estonian national anthem. A song festival was held on the afternoon of July 15 at the CNE stadium. Despite a heavy rain before the festival an audience of 10,000 showed up to hear the concerts, which began with a procession of forty-eight choirs from Canada, the United States, and overseas. A folk dance and gymnastics festival was held at the CNE stadium that evening and attracted a record attendance of over 20,000, of whom about a third were not of Estonian ethnic origin. The show, a single, continuous, and integrated performance based on folk dance, choreographed movements, and folklore motifs, was arranged by Toomas Metsala and Evelyn Koop and included 600 folk dancers and 700 women rhythmic gymnasts, the latter mainly from Canada and Sweden.

The festival was closed formally on the morning of Sunday, July 16, by an ecumenical service at St. Paul's Cathedral, with the Archbishop of the Estonian Lutheran Church and seventeen other ministers of the Estonian Lutheran, Orthodox, and other protestant denominations officiating.

The second world festival was held four years later at Baltimore, Maryland, and the third one at Stockholm in 1980. Estonians from Canada participated in both; Stockholm attracted over 1,500 Canadian Estonians.

The fourth Estonian World Festival was held in Toronto again, July 7-15, 1984. In format it resembled that of 1972, only the number of events had grown to a total of about 140, ranging from dozens of concerts and many organizational congresses and meetings to reunions, balls, and disco dances at the CN Tower restaurant. There were also specialized exhibits of book plates, stamps, and coins at the Eaton Centre, and an exhibit of Estonian ethnography housed in the Royal Ontario Museum. The main events – the opening ceremonies at Ontario Place, the song festival, ESTO-Vision (a folk dance and gymnastics performance) at Maple Leaf Gardens, and the procession from Queen's Park to Nathan Phillips Square at City Hall – drew crowds of 10,000 to 20,000; and 6,000 sat down to dinner at the Toronto International Centre. Two major concert performances took place, one of Estonian contemporary music at Roy Thomson Hall and another of the music of Estonian (E. Tubin, A. Pärt) and Finnish (J. Sibelius) composers at Ontario Place performed by the Toronto Symphony Orchestra and Estonian choirs with the internationally acclaimed Estonian conductor from Sweden, Neeme Järvi, conducting. Paradoxically, at a time when many grassroots organizations are in sharp decline, the global festivals are gathering momentum.

NOTES

1. Aun *et al.* (eds), *Seedrioru 1955-1980*, pp. 77-8.
2. *Meie Elu*, July 16, 1969.
3. Kurlents *et al.* (eds.), *Eestlased Kanadas*, p. 613.

4. This was only a weak echo of the centennial celebration held in Tallinn, Estonia, on June 28, 1969: about 1,000 choirs with over 30,000 singers, and an audience of more than 250,000.
5. *Meie Elu*, July 5, 1967; also an interview with R. Kreem in *Meie Elu*, May 14, 1964.
6. *Vaba Esti Sõna*, June 6, 1957; H. Johani in *Meie Tee*, No. 5/6 (1957).
7. Kurlents *et al.* (eds.), *Eestlased Kanadas*, p. 605.
8. *Vaba Eestlane*, May 20, 1964.
9. *Toronto Daily Star*, May 19, 1964.

PART THREE

The Past and the Future

ELEVEN

Cultural Conflict and Exchange

CULTURES IN CONFLICT

Paradoxically, the successful integration of Estonian immigrants after the Second World War into the Canadian economy and society did not lead to a desire to integrate socially and culturally with the prevailing cultural patterns of Canada.[1] Although the adult immigrants experienced the usual cultural shock, this did not bring about a sense of bewilderment or a questioning of their past culture. Instead, it led to a rejection of many of the Canadian cultural values and patterns. As well, a few of those who had immigrated earlier, and who were already acclimatized to the Canadian-North American culture, returned to the fold of Estonian cultural communities in the 1950's. As a result the identity of the Estonian ethnic group in Canada remained strong and cohesive for over three decades. And although the younger adults and the children who immigrated in 1947-52 later adopted the prevailing Canadian cultural patterns of the 1970's and 1980's, the dualism whereby distinctive Estonian cultural patterns are being propagated has continued among the second generation. Thus, to a significant extent, the original conflict between the immigrant and the dominant Anglo-Canadian cultural patterns is evident even today, although words such as "unacceptable" or "incompatible" are no longer used. Instead, reference is made to a distinct Estonian heritage, behavioural patterns, and cultural richness distinct from the North American popular culture. The coexistence of the two is simply assumed as a necessity of life or as a matter of fact.

Language, it should be noted, did not lead to the original cultural conflict. While language provided an initial impediment to communication, it was not a serious hindrance. Nearly all Estonians at immigration had some knowledge of English, which they had learned at school in Estonia, or in Germany or Sweden in preparation for immigration. Of course, very few were fluent in English, except those who had previously lived in England or had held positions where English was required, as for example in the service of the British and American occupation authorities in Germany. Lack of fluency reduced job prospects for a time for many adult immigrants in occupations that demanded good oral and written English, but this certainly was not a factor in restricting social contacts or in the cultural conflict that arose. Moreover, the fact that nearly all Estonians immigrated to English-speaking communities in Canada played no role whatever in this conflict. Since there were very few French-speaking Estonians it is possible that the linguistic adjustment in French Canada would have been different and would have led to different cultural relations. However, this is most unlikely if we use the experience of Estonians in Sweden as a guide, for Swedish was a language that no Estonian knew before arrival in Sweden yet Estonians learned it quickly within a few years.

During their first decade in Canada the Estonian post-war immigrants set themselves up in judgement of Canadian cultural patterns, were critical of them, and rejected many of them. Although the rejection of the socially dominant Canadian cultural patterns was somewhat selective, in general that which was regarded as "North American" or, in other words, that which was "not European" was questioned or rejected. Part of this rejection was based on the judgement that North America, including Canada, was culturally less advanced than Estonia had been. More specifically, there were a few matters that the Estonian immigrants found particularly "un-European." Perhaps the most recurrent was the materialist thinking that Estonians found pervading many aspects of Canadian life. Canadians, so the Estonians found, did not seem to be concerned with other values than material well-being.

One of the most irksome questions that was always asked by Canadians was whether Estonians were now happy in Canada, having left behind war-torn Europe for this land of peace and plenty. The question was asked usually in a way that presupposed an affirmative answer. Indeed, often it was not a question, but a statement to be confirmed. But the refugee was not happy being in Canada. He considered himself lucky that he had escaped the many dangers and survived the hardships of war and its dislocations; he was satisfied that he could earn his living and have a more-or-less normal life without fear and want. But how could he be happy when he had been deprived of his friends and relatives? He had been forced out of his homeland to which he was emotionally attached, and a brutal destruction of this land and its people – his people – still went on. This, he hoped, would some day come to an end so that he could return home again.

Often he was unhappy because he was in a foreign country where his education and experience counted for little or nothing, where lifestyles were strange and different. But this Canadians or emigrants from the British Isles seemed neither to understand nor to have any interest in. Moreover, when the plight of the war and its injustices were described, the Canadian would compare them to the plight of the depression of the 1930's in Canada and reply that Canada also had been involved in the war. But how could domestic economic troubles be equated with destruction in the war, with the killing and torture of thousands of innocents, forcible loss of homes, and the ideological clashes between nations? To the refugee it seemed unmistakable that Canadians thought only in terms of personal well-being and material things while refugees thought in terms of justice and injustice. Their minds did not meet.

It was not only the question of war and its experience that showed that the minds of Canadians were more bound with material things, for their main interests, to judge by their conversation, were about their cars, family matters, "making money," and what "money can buy" – or at least so the Estonian refugees felt. "Money matters" seemed also to dominate social organizations, charitable work, future planning, business, and the entertainment enterprises with their everlasting fund drives. Neither did political campaigns raise any of the broader ideological issues. Even the churches in Canada continuously solicited pledges and special contributions, whereas in Estonia there had been an annually fixed church membership fee. Thus to the Estonians there was evidence without end to confirm that in North America "money was king." They felt that they could neither approve nor adopt the same thinking, though they felt confident that they, too, could "make money" with hard work and some luck. Many were bitter that in this materialistic world their former experience and personal abilities did not count when looking for jobs; the materialist society was interested only in immediate returns.[2]

Another aspect of Canadian society that was strange to Estonians was "American commercialism." By this they meant not only commercialized professional sports, which were unknown in Estonia and in Europe before the war, but also broadcasting dependent on advertising and its programs interrupted by commercials, huge sections of ads in newspapers and magazines, billboard commercials, and aggressive advertisement of anything from entertainment to drugs. In addition, there were commercial-like fund drives of voluntary organizations and institutions, as if everything could, and must, be done by selling. Then there was "the commercialization of the Christmas season" – just one single day of holiday preceded by several weeks of commercial sales. In Estonia Christmas had been a three-day holiday, plus Christmas Eve as another half-day holiday, a quiet and serene season for family reunions, visits, and church services of which the most memorable was the Christmas Eve service, which hardly anyone missed. The paradox, in the eyes of Estonians, was that in Estonia the Communist regime did away with Christmas and other Christian holidays, for its own ideological-political reason; now almost the same was done by other means, by business greed! The paradox raised the question in the minds of Estonians of which was true: that which was preached or that which was done?

145

Though Estonians found the commercial aspect of life lively and fascinating, they found it disgusting as well. Perhaps that was the reason why very few Estonians entered the sales and service professions.

Canadians were found not much interested in such cultural aspects of life as the performing arts, fine arts, literature, music, and amateur athletics as a form of physical culture. Some Estonians were shocked when they discovered that the major English-speaking metropolis of Canada, Toronto, had no opera house, no ballet company, and no well-established repertory theatre. There was a small art gallery run by an amateur committee and a small symphony orchestra, both struggling with shortages of funds, and some touring Broadway productions and an annual visit by the Metropolitan Opera touring company from New York. In the smaller cities the situation was much worse, and in Montreal it was not much better either. Clearly this was not the result of lack of finances but the result of lack of interest and tradition. By contrast, little Estonia had more than one opera house and half a dozen professional repertory theatres supported by both the public and governments, and music and amateur sports had been a way of life. The contrast seemed too much to be believable.[3]

Moreover, articles and reviews in the Canadian press were limited to visiting artists and Hollywood movies. There was no literary or art journal in Canada and a literary tradition seemed to be missing. True, there were plenty of American books available, but mostly of an entertaining nature, and movie houses showed almost exclusively Hollywood movies – and were commonly called "theatres," a misnomer to Estonians.[4] Neither were there European-type coffee houses where intellectuals and artists could meet, nor any live music in restaurants, which were also found uniformly dull in decor and cuisine. Sometimes, so it was believed, even educated Canadians were uninterested in the theatre, music, literature, and art. The conclusion by Estonians was that in the Canadian value system cultural aspects had a low priority and that they were treated basically as entertainment. Hence, cultural enterprises had to compete with the entertainment industry without any special support from the public or governments. In the judgement of Estonians this confirmed, once more, the dominance of materialist thinking and commercialism in Canada. Although the friendliness of Canadians was exemplary and Estonians could reassume their personal and family lives in Canada better than they had expected, the roots of their traditions and those of Canada were so different that they had no wish to adopt Canadian cultural behavioural patterns. The social behaviour of some Canadians they also found provincial, superficial, and in some senses artificial, as for instance in the extended and meaningless use of first-names and the Canadian avoidance of controversial issues in social discourse. Thus Estonians were driven back even more on their own cultural and social ethnocentrism.

In this judgement of Canadian society and the "Canadian way of life" much was true, but much should be taken with a grain of salt. These were the perceptions that the Estonian immigrants acquired through experiences and channels closest to them. The educated cultural, social, and political leadership of the home country hardly ever succeeded in establishing close social or cultural contacts in Canada with their counterparts. Most were thrown into different occupations, at least initially, and had to live in neighbourhoods where they were far removed from their Canadian equals. Even for professionals whose qualifications were quickly accepted in Canada, such as the physicians, architects, and engineers, it took time before meaningful social ties developed. Thus, many of these perceptions were generalizations from immediate experiences. There is also an element of bitterness in refugee psychology that tends to reject and resist anything that was not in the lost homeland on the one hand; on the other, there is a tendency to overemphasize the losses.

Yet these were collective judgements often shared with other post-war political refugees, and a majority of the Estonians had lived in other countries besides Estonia and Canada, which enabled a lot of comparisons. And all the refugee group of 10,000-strong continued their contacts with other Estonians by visits and correspondence in the United States, Sweden, Germany, England, Australia, and many other countries. Much of what was rejected in Canada was taken as the impact of America, and, as a matter of fact, any comparison between Canada and the United States usually redounded to Canada's credit, especially in cultural matters.

However, it must be remembered that the above evaluation was of the Canada of the late 1940's and early 1950's; the Canada of the 1970's and 1980's is far different. And after all, not all aspects of social and cultural life in Canada were criticized or found unacceptable. For instance, there was no criticism of the political system, although not only the common people but also the politicians were sometimes found naive concerning the international political realities and on economic and welfare issues.[5] In contrast, common-law legal and court systems were accepted as a matter of course though they were profoundly different from the continental European legal and court systems. And although the educational and school systems were also different, they were accepted and the easy accessibility to various kinds of educational institutions, including universities, was applauded and made use of to upgrade former education or to learn new professions. A list of these positive aspects would be as long as the negative one. Nevertheless, there was a deep conflict of cultures that took time to overcome.

CULTURAL EXCHANGE

It is a truism to say that whenever different cultures meet cultural exchange takes place. But the process of exchange depends on many factors, two of which – the comparative size of the culture groups and the extent of the cultural contacts – are of decisive importance. In Canada, where (with the exception of the province of Quebec) the dominant English-speaking community has absorbed and assimilated most immigrant groups, the duration of this process has depended on such variables as cultural and linguistic affinity, social and economic pressures, and frequency of cultural contacts. In contrast, the retention of an ethnic culture has been assisted by the size of the immigrant group and its isolation either as a result of geographic concentration (localization) or internal cohesion (segregation).

The obverse of the cultural exchange process is the impact of minority cultures upon the main culture of the country: their contributions to and enrichment of the latter. Many of these contributions are only attitudinal or behavioural and thus are not visible. As well, a contribution to the culture of Canada by a member of an immigrant group may or may not be a contribution of the ethnic culture.[6] Moreover, there is a considerable difference in the impact that different ethnic minorities have in the consciousness of the majority – usually the larger the group the greater the visibility.

In the case of the Estonians, if we keep in mind the smallness of the early immigrant group, we may assume that with the arrival of the post-war refugee immigrants the assimilation process of Estonians in Canada slowed down, and that the greatest impact of the Estonians as a group on Canadian culture took place during the 1950's and early 1960's. On the other hand, individual contributions by Estonians to the Canadian society and culture increased thereafter, when economic, educational, and social accommodation and integration had taken place.

The small number of Estonian immigrants before the Second World War who lived scattered among the people of Canada had no hope, nor had many any real wish, to maintain their Estonian cultural patterns. Their aim was to integrate into the surrounding social and cultural milieu as quickly as possible. A very few made personal contributions to the culture of Canada, among them an artist, an Arctic explorer, and a seminary professor.

In the Estonian settlements of rural Alberta, Estonian culture and language survived for the period of about the lifetime of one generation mainly because in the empty Prairies culture contacts were slow in developing. But with the growing economic and social mobility of the 1930's and increased outgroup contact even these ethnic communities dissolved rapidly. Although these Estonian communities represent a historic segment of the multicultural heritage of Alberta, they have left hardly any imprint on the surrounding culture. The second generation of these communities nearly all left for the cities and were quickly absorbed into the mainstream of Canadian culture.

The story of the post-war Estonian immigrants is different, mainly because of the size of the group, the timing of their arrival, and their settlement patterns. The group was almost four times larger than the total number of Estonian immigrants during the previous five decades and they came to Canada in the short period of about four years. They were adamantly devoted to the idea of "remaining Estonian" and formed strong and cohesive ethnic communities: in Toronto a community of 10,000 and in Montreal, the Vancouver area, and southwestern Ontario communities of about 2,000 Estonians each. Moreover, during the 1950's and 1960's because of the unprecedented growth in the Canadian economy there was little economic pressure for cultural integration, nor was there much social pressure because of the multi-ethnic nature of the surrounding immigrant population.

They settled in the large industrial cities where the outgroup contacts were extensive and grew rapidly. While those who immigrated in their adult years stubbornly clung to the Estonian language and cultural patterns, most of the younger generations who grew up and attended schools in Canada associated with non-Estonians and adopted the value systems and behavioural patterns of their peer groups. This is not to say that they became alienated from other Estonians or the Estonian community, only that most of their social contacts were outside the ethnic community. It was a slow but progressive development in which the youth adjusted to the cultural environment of this country.

Perhaps the most reliable indicator of this development is the loss of the native mother tongue and its use as the home language. According to the 1971 census data only 49 per cent of Estonians in Canada used Estonian as their main language at home, whereas 45 per cent used English. After making proper allowance for the pre-war Estonian immigrants and their descendants, whose home language was already mostly English, the loss of the Estonian language by the post-war group during this twenty-year period is considerable, an estimated 30 to 40 per cent. The main reason for this loss is marriage outside the ethnic group, but because almost 70 per cent of married Estonians were married to Estonians (and only 11 per cent to spouses of British ethnic origin) it must be concluded that English was spoken in many homes where both spouses were of Estonian origin.

At the same time (1971) a still comparatively high 79 per cent of Canadians of Estonian ethnic origin reported Estonian as their mother tongue. Ten years later it had dropped to 68 per cent. Although an accelerated decline in the mother tongue is to be expected as a consequence of the loss of Estonian as the home language,[7] the decline in the mother tongue affects negatively the ability to participate in Estonian cultural activities, with a resultant decline in Estonian culture in Canada.

Estonian communities are too small ordinarily to have any impact upon the culture of their host communities. But in this respect Estonians are not alone. They are one among about a half dozen similar refugee groups from Europe, such as the Latvians, Lithuanians, Poles, and Ukrainians – joined by refugees from Hungary and Czechoslovakia after

149

1956 and 1968 respectively – with whom they share not only a European background but also an outlook and experience of cultural matters. Even more important is the fact that Estonians were among the first arrivals of the great influx of post-war immigrants from continental Europe who settled mostly in the same industrial cities. Under the impact of this large-scale immigration many economic, social, and cultural patterns and attitudes in Canada changed. It was not only that the ethnic composition changed in these cities but the general street picture and the prevailing habits and value systems also became diversified. Toronto in particular became essentially a multi-ethnic city and grew into a metropolitan and cosmopolitan centre of North America. Similar changes took place in other cities in Canada, although on a smaller scale. It may be assumed that Estonians played a supportive role, albeit a small one, in bringing about these changes, especially in Toronto where their numbers are most substantial.

Here we are alluding to contributions that are mainly attitudinal, that do not bring about any dramatic change but are supportive and contributory in nature and are thus seldom visible. Nevertheless, Estonian bakeries and food stores, for example, were among those that triggered changes in food marketing and eating habits. Similarly, Estonian Boy Scouts were among the other ethnic units in Canada that had worldwide grassroot connections of that movement; Estonians built the first cooperative housing blocks in Toronto, and Estonian volleyball teams held several Canadian championship titles in the late 1950's and early 1960's. More specifically, in amateur athletics and sports, in architecture and arts, and in music, contributions by Estonians as a group may be seen.

Between the 1950's and 1980's attitudes to amateur sports and physical fitness in Canada changed dramatically and irreversibly. In this development innumerable Canadians and members of many ethnic groups participated, among them Estonians. By the traditions prevalent in Estonia many young Estonian immigrants remained amateur sports enthusiasts and a few of them distinguished themselves in various activities in Canada. But even more than the athletes, it was the Estonians who found employment as coaches, instructors, organizers, and advisers with Canadian amateur sports organizations, the YMCAs and YWCAs, the schools and the sports equipment industries who had an impact on amateur athletics in Canada.[8]

Estonians have made a visible contribution to Canadian culture in the fields of architecture and painting. Beginning with the construction boom of the 1950's, architects, engineers, builders, and designers had ample opportunities to implement new ideas and innovative designs. Among them were a number of Estonians who had obtained their training, experience, or inspiration from Europe. Their innovations contributed to the modernization of the architectural landscape of Canadian cities. Among the first were new and innovative church building designs in Toronto and Vancouver followed by many other private and public buildings in Toronto, Vancouver, Hamilton, Sault Ste. Marie, and other cities. Estonian architects designed the Skylon in Niagara Falls, the innovative pre-stressed concrete Seaway Tower Hotel in Toronto, the Bank of Montreal tower in Toronto, and the first Canadian concave, cone-shaped building, the Prince Arthur high-rise apartment building in Toronto, subsequently built all over Canada. The skyline of Vancouver was changed by the high-rise apartment, office, and hotel buildings in English Bay built by Estonian developers and partly designed by Estonian architects. Of the score of Estonian architects involved in the above projects two should be singled out for their visibility in the Canadian architectural fraternity, both winners of several Canadian and international prizes: Elmar Tampõld and Ants Elken, the latter a professor of architecture at the University of Toronto.

Few painters and artists could remain "professional" in Canada, but some found their opportunities in commercial and applied arts. Three Estonian post-war immigrants, Oswald Timmas, Ruth Tulving, and Vello Hubel, have become members of the Royal Canadian Academy of Arts. A number of professional artists among the younger Canadian-educated generation of Estonians are also known in Canada as well as internationally, such as Andres Kingisepp.

The third visible contribution of Estonians to Canadian culture is in music. In the early 1950's there were few choirs in Canada and most were church choirs. The number of choirs and the popularity of choir singing since have increased conspicuously and to the extent that in the 1970's the Canadian Federation of Choirs was founded. In this process the promotional role of Estonian choirs has been an important contribution, and many Estonian composers have enriched the music repertory not only of Estonian communities in Canada and abroad, but also in the music of Canada as a whole. Among the most prominent of these are Udo Kasemets, one of the avant garde music critics and composers of Canada, Roman Toi, Kaljo Raid, and Lembit Avesson. Armas Maiste and Ovid Avarmaa in Montreal, teachers and performers of music, have been leading names in Canadian jazz music. Other Estonians have taught music in Canadian secondary schools, music schools, and universities and have given public concerts and conducted orchestras or choirs. All have, in addition to the regular repertory of teaching and performing, also introduced their students and audiences to Estonian compositions, both of the folk and modern genres.

Other cultural areas of value in the Estonian community have made little impact on the majority culture of Canada. Among these are drama and literature, because of the language barrier. In the 1950's the Estonian publishing house Orto was one of the largest publishers in Toronto, but all its publications were in Estonian and its market was restricted to the Estonian communities in Canada and abroad.[9] In fact, only one book by an Estonian writer has ever been published in both English and French in Canada.[10]

151

Though the quality of the Estonian theatre in Toronto and Montreal in the 1950's was high, only a couple of Estonian actors have been able to make a limited appearance on the non-Estonian stage. However, a number of younger-generation Estonians have made their contributions to the performing arts in Canada, for example, the opera singer Avo Kittask, the theatre critic and dramaturgist Yrjo Kareda, and TV producer Ain Söödor.

NOTES

1. This chapter draws heavily on information from interviews by the Oral History Project of the Estonian Federation in Canada.
2. A large number of lawyers, teachers, and other intellectuals among Estonian post-war immigrants could not continue in their professions.
3. Most vocal in their criticism of culture in Canada were the intellectuals who could not continue in their professions, but they were also those who made up the leadership of the ethnic group.
4. This seems rather a question of semantics, but in Estonia and in the Estonian language a clear distinction was made between serious drama, which meant professional theatre, including opera and ballet, and movies (cinema), which were considered mere entertainment.
5. Estonian economy had been largely a mixed economy with co-operative and government enterprises strongly competing with private enterprise; the social welfare system was one of the most advanced of its time.
6. For instance, a contribution to the Canadian culture by a singer of Italian descent may or may not be a contribution of Italian culture, whereas pizza is an Italian contribution. Likewise, a contribution by an Estonian architect may or may not be a contribution by the Estonian architectural tradition, whereas sauna is a Finnish-Estonian contribution.
7. Census data for 1981 on Estonian home language were not available in the published sources of Statistics Canada, where Estonian, Latvian, and Lithuanian have been lumped together as "the Baltic." However, it may be estimated that more than half of the post-war Estonian immigrants and their descendants in 1981 spoke English as their main language at home.
8. See above, Chapter Eight.
9. Orto Estonian Publishing House Ltd., MG28 V 24, Finding Aid No. 1328, Public Archives of Canada, prepared by Reet Kruus, n.d. [1982], p. V.
10. Arved Viirlaid, *Graves without Crosses* (Toronto: Clarke, Irwin & Co., 1972).

TWELVE

Generations in Conflict

Generational conflict may occur in any society where major economic, social, or cultural changes take place with the result that the next generation rejects the dominant values of its elders.[1] In an immigrant community such conflict is more likely because of the underlying cultural conflict between the immigrant culture and the culture of the host country into which the second generation immigrants are introduced. Hence, in the post-war Estonian ethnic community in Canada a generational conflict was to be expected as a normal and natural phenomenon. However, when it came it took on the political overtones characteristic of a community of political refugees. This, again, emphasizes the difference between the economic migrant and the political refugee and their respective value systems.

The driving force behind the vigorous cultural organizations and activities of Estonian refugee communities after the war was basically political. Its aim was not only to preserve Estonian culture but to keep the Estonian patriotic spirit and morale intact for a return to a homeland. As the hopes of a quick return dimmed and finally had to be abandoned, a liberated Estonia nevertheless remained the overriding goal of central ethnic orgizations abroad, as well as of the overwhelming majority of Estonians in Estonia.

But there was not much that either those in Estonia or those abroad could do to bring about this goal, even during the 1950's when the Cold War raised unrealistic hopes of speedy liberation. In Estonia all resistance against the political and economic sovietization of the country was promptly suppressed. Abroad, the only things the exiles could do were to continue to explain the plight of their native country to their host societies and to keep their Estonian communities and culture intact by bringing up the next generation in as firm a mould of patriotism as possible. In this, many community leaders misunderstood reality and overestimated the capability of the older-generation leaders to mould the younger. The young people who grew up in the Canadian environment could not be expected to devote their energies to the Estonian cause like their elders, or master the Estonian language perfectly, or marry only Estonians. Thus, "relapses" in "Estonianness" were soon noticed and deplored, and the young people and their parents were blamed. As time went on, decreasing numbers of youths took active interest in other than youth-oriented Estonian organizations and a number disappeared from the ethnic organizational scene after their youth activities, only to reappear some years later as passive spectators at community main events and festivals. Thus, activities in the smaller ethnic communities declined and the principal organizations became more and more dominated by the same older people whose energies became overstrained. The decline in youth participation cannot be blamed so much on the youth as on the many older leaders, because in many organizations it was not the moderates but those who believed in a fixed set of ethnic and political goals who commanded the leadership positions and used these to condemn any vacillation in patriotic attitudes and to morally castigate the youth.

In the 1950's the Estonians in Canada, old and young, formed a uniform community socially, culturally, and politically. Although there were people among them of different social and political backgrounds and views, all were united in their condemnation of communism, including those who had suffered under German rule. Their common experience had formed their dominant political attitudes: many had fled their homes primarily because they were frightened for their lives when the country was occupied by the Soviets again in 1944. The value system of pre-war Estonia ranked high; a number had belonged to the intellectual, social, and political elites of the country and thus had helped to form those very values themselves. For them a prolonged Soviet occupation meant a complete destruction of those values in Estonia along with the ruination of the country economically and the annihilation of the Estonian population. These beliefs were anchored in their personal experience of the Soviet occupation of 1940-41, and basically they were not wrong. In fact, an armed guerilla resistance against the Soviets had lasted into the late 1940's, when it was broken by the forced collectivization of the farmers and by mass deportations of Estonians. Several Estonian Communist Party leaders were also purged, deported, or liquidated for their "nationalist deviation" at this time.[2] These things were happening in the context of the war that had caused general devastation, an economy in ruins, and a population on the verge of starvation. The meagre information that reached the West reconfirmed the beliefs held by Estonian communities abroad.

After Stalin's death, changes took place in the Soviet Union in the 1950's that in general have been referred to as the "Thaw." Both abroad and in the homeland this meant that a very limited exchange of letters became possible, mostly between close relatives. On both sides it was understood that the letters were censored and therefore correspondents were very careful about what to write; some people in Estonia did not respond to letters from abroad at all. As a result, the information received through these letters was incomplete and spotty and questions naturally arose as to what extent these letters reflected the truth and to what extent they reflected what those in Estonia had to write or were ordered to write. However, as time went on and the correspondence gradually increased and expanded, some conclusions could be drawn: police repression had decreased; deportees to Siberia or other parts of the Soviet Union were returning; the economic situation was improving; and there was some intellectual freedom, although everything still had to be couched in Marxist-Leninist terms and within the framework of party control. However, a number of Estonians in Canada doubted that such changes were possible under the Soviet rule and attributed all such information to Soviet propaganda. They advised against any correspondence with Estonians, for this, according to them, could be used to intimidate or prosecute the recipients of correspondence simply because they had relatives abroad and exchanged letters with them. In the 1960's, these differing interpretations sharpened and formed the basis for a conflict in which the older and younger generations were the main protagonists.

Moreover, in the 1960's a new element entered the controversy, namely, meeting in person with people from Estonia. A few residents of Soviet Estonia could travel or visit their close relatives abroad and a few expatriate Estonians were permitted to visit their relatives or friends for short periods in Estonia. At the same time as these restrictions on travel continued, Estonians abroad, and especially the youth, were urged by Soviet Estonian publications to visit their homeland. Soviet Estonia was pictured as an advanced and progressive socialist country whereas Estonia of the 1930's was condemned for its "decadence," "fascist dictatorship," and "suppression of the working people." In fact, party functionaries and some party members were principally the ones allowed to travel abroad and visas to visit Estonia were rarely issued and then only for a few days, mainly to the capital city of Tallinn. Clearly, contacts between foreign Estonians and home Estonians were strictly controlled by the Soviet leadership because it was also known that visitors from Estonia had to report whom they had met abroad after their trip.

This kind of party and state control over contacts was taken by the Estonian community leaders in Canada as a Soviet offensive to undermine the anti-Soviet morale among the refugees and especially among the Estonian youth who did not have personal experience with communism. Therefore, the Estonian central organizations with political objectives of liberating Estonia from Soviet control flatly banned any visits to Estonia or meeting of visitors from Estonia. In addition, there was a widespread suspicion that the Soviet aim of encouraging controlled contacts with exile Estonians was to recruit spies from among the refugees.

Despite the ban and suspicion, the visits and contacts, though still limited in numbers and controlled by the Soviets, gradually increased because the ethnic organizations did not have any coercive powers to reverse the trend. The youth in particular rejected the notion that they must accept the dictate because they were not mature enough to make their own investigation in these matters. They countered the ethnic leadership with the argument that they did not visit Estonia because the Soviets invited them, but because they wanted to see their homeland, their relatives, young Estonians there, and the people and the culture of their land of origin. They suggested also that politics and culture should be kept apart, whereas the elderly diehards absolutely denied that culture could be separated from politics and referred to their own personal experience as evidence of this.

It is hard to evaluate even two decades later who was right and who was wrong in some of the detailed issues of this controversy. Moreover, to some degree the controversy was one-sided since the young people launched their own discussion groups, such as the Metsaülikool, and avoided any confrontation by simply ignoring their opponents. Objectively it can also be argued that culture and politics are not separable and that some of the youth, inexperienced as they were in the practical side of communism and sovietization, could overlook and misunderstand pertinent factors of Soviet propaganda. It may be argued also that Soviet propaganda prompted a more critical review of Estonia of the 1930's. Nevertheless, when all is said, there was the common experience that many of the youth returned from Estonia more anti-Communist and anti-Soviet than they had ever been before, especially in cases of repeated visits and longer stays. But the main message they brought back was their own deep interest in Estonian culture of both the past and the present and the news that there was an unusual cultural revival in Estonia. Despite the political oppression and low economic standards and homages to be paid to Marxism-Leninism and Soviet "advancements," creative activity in literature, art, music, intellectual inquiry into the cultural past, and a revival of ethnic festivals had reached a new height, perhaps as a counterweight to the political exhortations and an escape from the drabness of everyday life. When the younger generation compared this with the ethnocultural activities of scattered Estonian communities in Canada and the United States, and given that the youth did not have personal experience to compare with the 1940's or 1950's, many came to the conclusion that Estonian culture in Canada could survive only if supported by contacts with Estonian intellectuals in Estonia. The irony, however, was that these young people, genuinely interested in Estonia and its culture, were branded as victims of Soviet propaganda whereas those who had lost their interest and had quietly withdrawn from Estonian communities were left alone and ignored.

It must be conceded that this political controversy was not strictly bound by the generational lines and that many of the older generation of Estonians in Canada held similar views and gave support to the youth, and in the 1970's a few older Estonians also visited Estonia and invited and financed visits from there. Thus, at its peak the controversy split the whole Estonian community in Canada, especially in Toronto, and it must also be noted that these visits and travels never became large in scale, mainly because the Soviets limited them by visa restrictions.

Gradually the patriotic diehards in Toronto lost their credibility since their stance was untenable, though they still dominated the main ethnic organizations and influenced the Estonian-language press. The contacts could be condemned but not controlled. The changes in Estonia could be denied but the denials lost their credibility. To argue on the basis of personal experience of the 1940's became anachronistic. Nevertheless, the crisis in Canada lasted longer than in other Estonian communities, particularly those in Sweden. There seem to be two reasons for the difference between Sweden and North America. While the anti-Soviet stance in general was still strong in Canada after the Cold War and was shared by many other refugee groups, Sweden quite early asserted its independence by treating both the United States and the Soviet Union with a nearly even-handed criticism; moreover, Estonians were the only large refugee group from behind the Soviet line in Sweden. In Sweden the geographic proximity naturally enhanced more travel and more contacts, and thus more information from Estonia, partly also through intermediaries in Finland. Hence the greater openness of Estonian communities in Sweden toward the realities of Soviet Estonia.

In Canada the controversy meant the loss of many potential community leaders, especially from among the younger people who stayed aloof from the controversy or withdrew from contention for leadership. But when in the late 1970's the controversy finally quieted down without any formal agreement or reconciliation, the goal of the Estonian community of a liberated Estonia had not changed, only the approach and methods to deal with the issues of contacts with Estonia today had changed. In the meantime a new generation had grown up, Canadian by birth and education, and Estonian only by their ethnic origin and voluntary choice to participate in ethnic affairs. Not encumbered with the sentimental animosities of the past, they were also better equipped to deal with the Canadian society on ethnic matters. Already in the 1970's some of them emerged as new leaders in the Estonian Central Council and other central organizations, which provided a broader base and infused new vigour to these organizations.

In the Estonian Central Council community-wide elections held in 1981, the average age of the candidates was forty-seven and 20 per cent were under thirty years of age – in other words, they were Canadian-born. Participation in these elections was the highest in the thirty years they had been held, which also means that the majority of the voters belonged to the younger generation. Hence, although the legacy of the generational conflict of a weakened organizational structure was still remembered at the beginning of the 1980's, at the broad level of community awareness that participation in elections to the Estonian Central Council represents, the younger generation was clearly expressing an interest and a commitment to the Estonian community in Canada.[3] And the strictly intellectually oriented organizations, made up mainly of the younger generation, were as vigorous as ever in pursuing an understanding of Estonian culture and history in a broad sense.

To a certain extent this political controversy had cleansed the thinking about relationships with the home country and its people and about the goals of the ethnic community in Canada. Being forced to come to terms with these controversial issues had even enhanced the interest and awareness about ethnocultural matters, especially among the younger generation.

NOTES

1. This chapter draws chiefly on information from the Estonian-language press in Toronto and from personal conversations by the author with many Estonians in Canada from younger as well as older generations.
2. See R.J. Misiunas and R. Taagepera, *The Baltic States: Years of Dependence 1940-1980* (Berkeley 1983), pp. 126-94, 230ff.
3. *Meie Elu*, May 28, July 9, 1981; *Vaba Eestlane*, May 14, May 28, June 4, 1981.

THIRTEEN

Facing the Future

Estonians as a distinct group remained unnoticed in Canada until the post-war wave of immigration established them as one of the ethnic communities in Canada's multicultural society in the second half of the twentieth century. The change in the visibility of Estonians was due to two emerging factors: their suddenly increased numbers and their very active ethnocultural organizations. The visibility was enhanced by extensive contacts that many Estonians had with mainstream English-Canadian organizations and the contributions of Estonians to several sectors of the Canadian society and economy.

In the three decades since their rise to visibility as a distinct ethnic community, significant demographic and ethnocultural changes have taken place among the Estonians. These changes have affected the original structure of the community considerably and will determine the nature of the Estonian community as a distinct ethnic entity in Canada. The concluding pages of this book present a brief analysis of these factors and attempt to predict the structure of the Estonian community in the future.

DEMOGRAPHICS

The basic demographic factor is, of course, the small size of the Estonian ethnic group in Canada. According to the 1961 census, 18,550 Canadians were of Estonian ethnic origin and according to the 1971 census, 18,810. Although these figures approximate the Latvian and Lithuanian groups, they are simply not in the same league with such large ethnic groups in Canada as the Germans (1,317,200), the Italians (730,820), and the Ukrainians (580,660). Although the majority of the ethnic groups of Canada are small, Estonians comprise one of the smallest. As a matter of fact, in size Estonians rank about fortieth among the ethnic groups of Canada.

The most crucial demographic factor to be kept in mind is that the Estonian ethnic group is "frozen" in that, first, the group is too small to reproduce itself as a distinctive ethnic community, as for example the Germans and the Ukrainians have been able to do despite the standard attrition by "anglicization," and, second, no significant immigration of Estonians can be expected in the future. The simple fact is that, in contrast to the continuing immigration of some other nationalities to Canada, there has been a complete cutting off of immigration from the Baltic states since the Second World War. As we have pointed out above, since immigration of Estonians before the Second World War was negligible, the whole Estonian ethnic group in Canada consists virtually of the post-war immigrants of the late 1940's and early 1950's and their descendants. Statistically these facts may be seen in Tables 8 and 9. Table 9 also makes it very clear that because of the age pyramid little growth can be expected among Estonians. For example, in 1971, 53 per cent of Estonians in Canada were over forty years of age whereas the group in the reproductive age, the twenty- to forty-year-olds, represented only 21 per cent. Hence, instead of an increase, a decline in the statistical size of the Estonian ethnic group may be expected during the next decades. Moreover, this means that the percentage of Canadians of Estonian origin cannot keep up with the growth of the total population of Canada. In the mid-1950's there were about 130 Estonians to 100,000 Canadians, but in 1961 there were only 100 and the figure further declined to 87 by 1971 (0.0128 per cent in 1955, 0.0101 per cent in 1961, and 0.0087 per cent in 1971). The Estonian presence in Canadian society is thus statistically declining.

LANGUAGE

Although a cursory look at the language statistics in Table 10, which shows selected ethnic-group language retention in 1971, paints a positive picture of the Estonians, especially in comparison with most other ethnic groups, a more careful look and the analysis shown in Tables 11-13 suggest a different conclusion, especially for the future. Thus, while the 1971 census data show that language retention among Estonians is comparatively high, with 78.97 per cent giving Estonian as their mother tongue and 48.7 per cent giving Estonian as a home language, Table 11 shows that there has been a drop of 13.37 per cent in mother tongue among Estonians between 1961 and 1976 and a drop of 17.55 per cent in the five years between 1971 and 1976. This is in line with the reduction in mother tongue among all ethnic groups as selected, with the exception of the Portuguese and the Italians, which show increases because of their recent and continuing immigration to Canada. In fact, while the loss of mother tongue among the Estonians is comparatively moderate among the older ethnic groups in this country, the number of those with Estonian as their mother tongue in 1976 was less than 12,000, a minuscule group when compared to the Germans and the Italians with just under half a million each, the Ukrainians with just under 300,000, and the total of those with English as their mother tongue, just over 14 million. Indeed, in contrast to the decline in other mother tongues, apart from some recently arriving ethnic groups, the population in Canada with English as its mother tongue increased almost a third (32.48 per cent) between 1961 and 1976.[1]

Table 12 also confirms that among the Estonian ethnic group there is a language transfer to English: 34.5 per cent of those whose mother tongue was Estonian spoke English at home. This means that by 1971 one-third of those whose first language learned was Estonian normally spoke English at home. In addition, if we assume that most of those of Estonian ethnic origin who do not show their mother tongue as Estonian also speak English at home, then we may conclude that English is the home language of about half of those Canadians of Estonian ethnic origin. Clearly, English will be the mother tongue of the next generations.

In the pattern of language retention and transfer of Estonian to English among the Estonian ethnic group, three standard factors play significant determining roles: age, domicile, and marriage. Table 13 makes it clear that by 1971 the Estonian ethnic group in Canada could be divided into two distinct home-language groups: among those over forty-five less than a third had English as their home language, but among the younger age groups two-thirds had English as their home language. Domicile also makes a considerable difference in the pattern of language retention and transfer. Language retention in metropolitan areas is significantly higher among all age groups than in the rural areas. As Table 13 shows, in the rural areas only between 13 and 19 per cent of those under forty-five speak Estonian at home, in contrast to 36-37 per cent in the metropolitan areas and a significantly higher 42-47 per cent in Toronto. It is obvious that the larger the ethnic community and the greater the availability of other Estonians, the greater the language retention. Ethnic youth organizations, supplementary schools, family circles, and the cultural community cumulatively assist in retaining the mother tongue as the home language. The statistics thus bear out the earlier observations above that Estonian activities and organizations have generally been in decline in Canada since the 1960's. In contrast, only in Toronto have new youth-oriented organizations and cultural activities emerged in the 1970's. Clearly, the Estonian ethnocultural community will last in Canada as long as it lasts in Toronto.[2]

Marriage is the third and most significant factor in language transfer, since it is only in endogamous marriages that the ethnic home language is passed on as the mother tongue of the children. In contrast, exogamous marriages lead to language transfer to the dominant language of the host society. Table 14, taken in conjunction with Table 13, bears out these general observations in the Estonian case. About two-thirds of Canadians of Estonian ethnic origin under the age of forty are married to non-Estonians, whereas only about a third of those between the ages of forty to fifty, and only 20 per cent of those over fifty, are married to non-

Estonians. It should also be noted that the differences between male and female exogamy-endogamy statistics are slight, nor are there particularly significant differences in the ethnic origins of the exogamic unions, apart from the fact that about 12 per cent of the exogamous female and male marriages have a partner of British origin. However, there is a significant difference in the endogamous-exogamous marriage pattern in Toronto. There, in all age groups, the endogamous marriage share is higher than in the Canadian total although the age-group pattern is the same. In contrast to the Canada-wide total, in Toronto only about half of those under forty are married to non-Estonians. However, there is also a very significant jump in exogamy from the 30-39 age group to the under-30 age group, both among males and females: almost two-thirds of the males in the latter age group and 55 per cent of the females have married outside the ethnic group, in contrast to only 42 per cent of the males and 48 per cent of the females in the older age group.

Nevertheless, both the Toronto and the Canada-wide marriage statistics show a relentless trend toward exogamous marriages. This will, of course, mean an inexorable trend toward English as the home language in ever-increasing percentages of homes where one of the partners is of Estonian extraction and an increasing decline in Estonian as the mother tongue among their children. And, although because of the numbers involved there will be a core of Estonian homes with Estonian as the home language for some time to come in Toronto, the marriage statistics dictate an increasing decline in Estonian endogamous marriages with the consequence that Estonian will decline even there as the home language, only more gradually.

ETHNOCULTURE

When the 14,000 Estonian political refugees came to the shores of Canada after the Second World War, uprooted as they were from their homeland, they successfully established a facsimile of the ethnic culture they had left behind and operated an identifiable Estonian community. At first the ethnocultural community, scattered as it was across the vastness of Canada, flourished wherever a few Estonians settled. And although the smaller Estonian communities soon disappeared as Estonians moved to Toronto and Vancouver and Montreal from their initial settlements, they carried with them the overriding goal of retaining their Estonian identity and for almost two decades worked hard to build and maintain a flourishing Estonian culture in Canada. The refugees by the 1960's had become good Canadians, but they remained first and foremost Estonians in their sociocultural habits and value systems.

As time passed and as economic and social opportunities in the Canadian host society beckoned, the younger among them began to place their talents at the service of the host society and slowly became culturally integrated into it. Although it may not have been apparent at the time, the 1970's saw significant changes in both the attitudes and the composition of the Estonian community in Canada. In the 1980's these changes will become evident and will profoundly affect the viability of Estonian culture and identifiable communal enterprise in Canada. Whereas the 1970's saw the beginning of the passing away of yesteryear's carriers of the torch of Estonian culture and ethnicity in Canada, the 1980's will see the last of them; the 1970's also saw the rise of the new breed of Estonian – the Estonian Canadian. This Estonian Canadian, the new generation that has been brought up in Canada (and increasingly, also, has been born in Canada) has no ambition to return to Estonia. The new Estonian Canadian does not even have to think about being a Canadian first; instead, he has to make an effort to pursue his Estonian ethnicity actively if he also wants to be an Estonian. He realizes that Estonian culture in its full development can only flourish in the Estonian homeland and he knows that it is being actively developed there. Nevertheless, to the extent that he wants to participate in this Estonian culture and to carry on at least some of the traditions of his forefathers, he knows that he has to make a special effort to read or speak Estonian as his second or third language. Thus, in the 1990's it will be the new Estonian Canadian, who has deliberately chosen to maintain his Estonian heritage in a competitive environment, who will not only lead but dominate the Estonian ethnic organizations and activities in Canada.

The question to be asked is: is this assimilation? Unfortunately, the answer can only be imprecise and inconclusive. On the one hand, economically, educationally, and socially the younger generations of Estonians in Canada have become totally assimilated into the dominant English-Canadian patterns. In fact, most Estonians of the younger generations can now be identified by an outsider as members of the Estonian community only by their surnames. Nevertheless, many among the same younger generations have also pursued Estonian folk dancing, music, literature, art, and folk art and have continued to participate extensively in these activities on an avocational, free-time basis. None, of course, can live exclusively in the Estonian language and few can even spend most of their leisure time in the Estonian cultural community. In this sense, then, the Estonian Canadian actively pursuing his Estonian heritage is at the same time a totally assimilated Canadian and yet is a carrier of Estonian culture as well.

Although ethnicity is an elusive concept, it is very clear that as long as there is an active group of Estonian Canadians who still speak the language and actively pursue an interest in the main cultural patterns carried by the language, Estonian culture will be maintained in Canada. Beyond this there is little question that, even with the loss of language, some publicly visible and identifiable Estonian social and cultural patterns will be maintained in this country (led by the committed groups), much as there are Jewish, Scottish, and Irish ethnic communities in Canada although very little linguistic competence in the ethnic language exists in those

groups. In fact, language has never been a primary identifying characteristic of these ethnic groups in Canada. Hence it may be expected that
ethnic Estonian Canadians who no longer speak their ethnic language
will culturally and politically lend their sympathetic support to the Estonian cause jointly with Estonians in other countries.

Whatever the outcome, it can be predicted that the Estonian ethnic
community at the end of the century will be smaller and much less
Estonian-speaking than it is now; its main objective and raison d'être will
be social contact and the pursuit of Estonian culture on an avocational
basis. This will be in complete contrast to the Estonian community that
was established in Canada in the 1950's: a transplanted refugee community interested in maintaining a separate Estonian cultural identity and
cohesiveness in exile. Nevertheless, the Estonian ethnic group in Canada
is not a mere footnote to history but forms a positive contribution to
Canadian multiculturalism, and its impact will last for several generations.

NOTES

1. The 1981 census of Canada shows 13,070 reporting Estonian as their
   mother tongue, 6,240 males and 6,835 females. The breakdown by provinces is as follows: 10,265 in Ontario, 1,395 in British Columbia, 695 in
   Quebec, 415 in Alberta, 205 in Nova Scotia, 100 in Manitoba, 85 in New
   Brunswick, 45 in Newfoundland, 35 in Saskatchewan, 10 each in Prince
   Edward Island and the Northwest Territories, and 5 in the Yukon. (The
   data have been rounded.) Statistics Canada, *1981 Census of Canada,
   Population, Mother Tongue and Sex, for Canada and Provinces*, Cat.
   92-902 (Ottawa, October, 1982).
2. The 1981 census shows even greater concentration of Estonians in Ontario
   (and presumably also in Toronto) than before. Of 15,915 who reported
   their (single) Estonian ethnic origin, 11,800, or 74 per cent, lived in Ontario, 2,065 in British Columbia, and only 745 in Quebec. Eighty per cent
   of those who reported Estonian as their mother tongue lived in Ontario.
   See *ibid.*; Statistics Canada, *1981 Census of Canada, Population, Ethnic
   Origin*, Cat. 92-911 (Ottawa, February, 1984).

Appendix: Tables

TABLE 1

	Total Baltic	Estonian	Latvian	Lithuanian	Total Canada
Total population in Canada	61,525	18,810	18,180	24,535	21,568,000
As % of total Cdn. population	0.285	0.087	0.084	0.114	100
Total ethnic population in CMAS	50,020	15,935	15,075	19,010	11,876,000
% of ethnic group	81.30	84.72	82.92	77.48	55.06
% of Cdn. total	0.42	0.13	0.13	0.16	100
Total ethnic population not in CMAS	11,505	2,875	3,105	5,525	9,692,000
% of ethnic group	18.70	15.28	17.08	22.52	44.94
% of Cdn. total	0.12	0.03	0.03	0.06	100
Toronto, Ontario	25,030	9,365	7,980	7,685	2,628,000
% of ethnic population	40.68	49.79	43.89	31.32	12.85
% of CMA population	0.95	0.36	0.30	0.29	

Urban-Rural Population by Ethnic Origin, 1971[1]

1. Urban classified as living in the twenty-two central metropolitan areas (CMAs) of Canada.

SOURCES: (Baltic group) Statistics Canada, *Census of Canada*, 1971, unpublished data; (Canada) Statistics Canada, *Census of Canada*, 1971, Cat. #92-722, Bulletin #1-3.4, Table 5.

TABLE 2

Highest Level of Education Attainment by Selected Ethnic Origin and Age Groups for the Out-of-School Population Aged 25 Years and Over, Canada, 1971[1]

	Total[2] No.	Elementary[3] No.	%	Secondary[4] No.	%	Some Univ. No.	%	Univ. Degree[5] No.	%	Post.-Grad. Degree[6] No.	%
Total all groups											
Estonian	12,739	3,276	25.72	6,583	51.68	1,049	8.24	1,453	11.41	378	2.97
Latvian	12,366	2,567	20.76	6,801	55.00	1,247	10.08	1,368	11.06	383	3.10
Lithuanian	15,387	6,454	41.95	6,599	42.89	971	6.31	1,085	7.05	278	1.81
British Isles	5,013,935	1,489,055	29.70	2,379,865	47.47	182,000	3.63	330,840	6.60	51,940	1.04
French	2,992,415	1,631,515	54.52	925,705	30.94	72,135	2.41	118,845	3.97	25,595	0.86
German	706,840	289,445	40.95	270,595	38.28	19,945	2.82	37,135	5.25	6,785	0.96
Italian	366,010	261,410	71.42	75,910	20.74	6,330	1.73	7,820	2.14	1,130	0.31
Jewish	175,880	49,110	27.92	72,005	40.94	13,070	7.43	25,540	14.52	2,860	1.63
Ukrainian	332,585	163,940	49.29	118,540	35.64	8,480	2.55	14,675	4.41	2,105	0.63
Canada total	11,043,125	4,527,875	41.00	4,597,335	41.63	353,850	3.20	636,825	5.77	106,735	0.97
Age 25-34											
Canada total	2,802,775	656,300	23.42	1,396,955	49.84	131,740	4.70	255,065	9.10	37,650	1.34
Estonian	2,169	148	6.82	1,043	64.68	215	9.91	585	26.97	178	8.21
Latvian	1,674	37	2.21	829	49.52	220	13.14	449	26.82	139	8.30
Lithuanian	2,295	236	10.28	1,393	60.70	166	7.23	414	18.04	86	3.75

Age 25-44

British Isles	2,178,725	387,075	17.77	1,147,555	52.67	99,220	4.55	195,575	8.98	27,650	1.27
French	1,511,030	652,180	42.05	586,475	37.81	47,940	3.09	82,715	5.33	17,315	1.12
German	368,450	96,545	26.20	168,665	45.78	13,335	3.62	26,240	7.12	4,685	1.27
Italian	222,380	148,260	66.67	52,070	23.42	4,745	2.13	6,125	2.75	920	0.41
Jewish	64,725	5,545	8.57	25,895	40.00	7,365	11.38	17,070	26.37	1,845	2.85
Ukrainian	139,980	30,755	21.97	73,460	52.48	5,650	4.04	10,715	7.65	1,400	1.00
Canada total	5,302,665	1,566,240	29.54	2,522,505	47.57	213,660	4.03	414,175	7.81	65,385	1.23

Age 35-44

Canada total	2,499,890	909,940	36.40	1,125,550	45.02	81,920	3.28	159,110	6.36	27,735	1.11
Estonian	1,705	331	19.41	1,042	61.11	121	7.10	172	10.09	39	2.29
Latvian	1,708	202	11.83	1,164	68.15	113	6.62	191	11.18	38	2.23
Lithuanian	2,622	626	23.88	1,633	62.28	151	5.76	152	5.80	60	2.29

Age 45-64

Canada total	4,002,795	1,854,755	46.34	1,577,260	39.40	107,540	2.69	182,785	4.57	34,605	0.87
Estonian	6,786	1,766	26.02	3,751	55.28	608	8.96	537	7.91	124	1.83
Latvian	6,682	1,373	20.55	3,784	56.63	799	11.96	579	8.67	147	2.20
Lithuanian	7,514	3,302	43.95	3,042	40.48	602	8.01	465	6.19	103	1.37

Age 45 and over

British Isles	2,835,210	1,101,980	38.87	1,232,310	43.47	82,780	2.92	135,265	4.77	24,290	0.86
French	1,441,385	979,335	67.94	339,230	23.54	24,195	1.68	36,130	2.51	8,280	0.58
German	338,390	192,900	57.01	101,930	30.12	6,610	1.95	10,895	3.22	2,100	0.62
Italian	143,630	131,150	78.78	23,840	16.60	1,585	1.10	1,695	1.18	210	0.15
Jewish	111,115	43,565	39.19	46,110	41.48	5,705	5.13	8,470	7.62	1,015	0.91
Ukrainian	192,605	133,185	69.15	45,080	23.41	2,830	1.47	3,960	2.06	705	0.37
Canada total	5,740,460	2,961,635	51.59	2,074,830	36.14	140,190	2.44	222,650	3.88	41,350	0.72

TABLE 2

Highest Level of Education Attainment by Selected Ethnic Origin and Age Group for the Out-of-School Population Aged 25 Years and Over, Canada, 1971[1]

	Total[2] No.	Elementary[3] No.	%	Secondary[4] No.	%	Some Univ. No.	%	Univ. Degree[5] No.	%	Post.-Grad. Degree[6] No.	%
Age 65+											
Canada total	1,737,665	1,106,880	63.70	497,570	28.63	32,650	1.88	39,865	2.30	6,745	0.39
Estonian	2,079	1,031	49.59	747	35.93	105	5.05	159	7.65	37	1.78
Latvian	2,302	955	41.49	1,024	44.48	115	5.00	149	6.47	59	2.56
Lithuanian	2,956	2,290	77.47	531	17.96	52	1.76	54	1.83	29	0.98

1. Canada and non-Baltic ethnic origin data were not strictly comparable to the available Baltic data. The following discrepancies existed: (a) Age groups for non Baltic ethnic origin were only the 15-25, 25-44, and 45 and over groups. The under-25 age group was omitted as comparable Baltic data do not exist. (b) Baltic data were reported on the basis of the educational classifications above where university degree includes all degrees below the post-graduate level (below bachelor's, and first professional). Non-Baltic classifications of educational attainment at the degree level include all and any post-secondary education regardless of degree designation but not including vocational courses.
2. The sum of the individual groups for the Baltic data did not add to the total reported by Statistics Canada. Baltic totals were adjusted to reflect the sum of the group totals; Canada and non-Baltic ethnic origin totals were also adjusted to reflect the sum of the group totals rather than the "random rounded" totals reported by Statistics Canada.
3. Elementary includes all education prior to Grade 9.
4. Secondary is education at the Grades 9-13 level for the Baltic ethnic group as well as secondary education in combination with vocational training for the non-Baltic group.
5. University degree includes bachelor's, first professional, and university degree below the bachelor's level. See Note 1.
6. Post-graduate degree includes master's and/or doctorate degrees for the Baltic group. For the non-Baltic population, this grouping includes university degree in combination with other training at the university level (post-graduate education is assumed).

SOURCES: Statistics Canada, *Census of Canada*, 1971, unpublished data; *ibid.*, Cat. #92-743, Bulletin #1.5-3, Tables 4, 7.

TABLE 3

Experienced Labour Force and Participation Rates, 1971[1]

	Total Baltic	Estonian	Latvian	Lithuanian	Total Canada
Total population	61,525	18,810	18,180	24,535	21,568,310
Male	31,575	9,225	9,355	12,995	10,804,125
Female	29,940	9,585	8,825	11,530	10,764,185
Experienced labour force total	29,420	9,325	9,305	10,790	8,626,925
Participation %	47.83	49.58	51.18	43.98	40.00
Self-employed total	2,745	820	815	1,110	668,850
% of labour force (25 +)	9.33	8.79	8.76	10.29	8.87
Male labour force total	19,955	5,820	6,280	7,855	5,665,715
Participation %	63.19	62.61	67.13	60.45	52.44
Female labour force total	11,650	4,045	3,670	3,935	2,961,210
Participation %	38.91	42.40	41.59	34.13	27.51
Male self-employed total	2,240	670	645	925	586,130
% of male labour	11.25	11.51	10.27	11.78	10.34
Female self-employed total	500	150	170	180	82,720
% of female labour	4.33	3.71	4.63	4.57	2.79

1. Self-employed are over 25 and include both members and non-members of the labour force. Participation rates are determined as a % of total population. Experienced labour force includes those over 15 years of age.

SOURCES: Statistics Canada, *Census of Canada*, 1971, unpublished data; *ibid.*, Cat. #94-723, Bulletin #32-9, Table 8.

TABLE 4

**Average Earned Employment Income by Sex and
Selected Ethnic Origin, Canada, 1971**

	Total Baltic	Estonian	Latvian	Lithuanian	Total Canada
Total average earned employment income	$6,368	$6,477	$6,554	$6,115	$5,033
As % of Canadian average	126.53	128.69	130.22	121.50	100.
Male average employment income	7,556	7,866	7,783	7,142	6,538
As % of Canadian average	115.57	120.31	119.04	109.24	100.
Female average employment income	4,183	4,362	4,328	3,846	2,883
As % of Canadian average	145.09	151.30	150.12	133.40	100.

SOURCES: Statistics Canada, *Census of Canada*, 1971, unpublished data; *ibid.*, Cat. #94-768, Bulletin #3.6-10, Table 19.

TABLE 5

Major Occupational Group by Ethnic Origin, Canada, 1971

Occupational Group		Total Baltic	Estonian	Latvian	Lithuanian	Total Canada
Total all	No.	29,420	9,325	9,305	10,790	8,626,925
Occupations	%	100	100	100	100	100
Managerial	No.	1,165	425	415	325	372,240
grp. 1	%	3.96	4.56	4.46	3.01	4.32
Natural,	No.	2,510	955	910	655	313,185
social services	%	8.54	10.24	9.78	6.07	3.63
grp. 2, 3						
Religion, teaching,	No.	2,680	855	1,020	805	699,440
and medicine	%	9.11	9.17	10.96	7.46	8.11
grp. 4, 5, 6						
Clerical, sales	No.	8,770	2,985	2,605	3,180	3,974,970
and service	%	29.81	32.01	28.00	29.47	46.08
grp. 8, 9, 10						
Farming,	No.	1,540	425	360	755	665,750
fishing, hunting,	%	5.23	4.56	3.87	7.00	7.72
forestry, and mining						
grp. 11, 12, 13, 14						
Processing and	No.	1,950	450	625	875	540,580
material handling	%	6.66	4.83	6.72	8.11	6.27
grp. 15, 20						
Machining and	No.	2,350	620	805	925	688,210
equip. operate.	%	8.02	6.65	8.65	8.57	7.98
grp. 16, 19, 21						
Product fabric.	No.	2,915	910	785	1,215	634,350
and assembly	%	9.91	9.76	8.44	11.26	7.35
grp. 17						
Construction	No.	2,150	690	760	700	568,565
grp. 18	%	7.31	7.40	8.17	6.49	6.59
Other	No.	1,065	345	330	390	248,110
grp. 22, 7	%	3.64	3.70	3.55	3.62	2.88
Not stated	No.	2,320	665	700	955	737,270
grp. 23	%	7.87	7.13	7.52	8.85	8.55

SOURCES: Statistics Canada, *Census of Canada*, 1971, unpublished data; *ibid.,* Cat. #94-734, Bulletin #3.3-7, Table 4.

TABLE 6

Occupational Classification by Ethnic Origin, Canada, 1971

Occupational Classification		Total Baltic	Estonian	Latvian	Lithuanian	Total Canada
Total all	No.	29,420	9,325	9,305	10,790	8,626,925
occupations	%	100	100	100	100	100
Professional	No.	6,365	2,235	2,345	1,785	1,384,865
grp. 1, 2, 3, 4, 5, 6	%	21.61	23.97	25.20	16.54	16.05
Industrial	No.	9,360	2,670	2,975	3,715	2,431,705
blue-collar	%	31.89	28.63	31.97	34.43	28.19
grp. 15, 16, 17, 18, 19, 20, 21						
Sales and services	No.	9,210	3,145	2,765	3,300	4,055,450
grp. 9, 10, 8, 7	%	31.32	33.73	29.72	30.58	47.01
Primary	No.	1,540	425	360	755	665,750
industry	%	5.23	4.56	3.87	7.00	7.72
grp. 11, 12, 13, 14						
Not classified	No.	625	185	170	270	167,630
grp. 22	%	2.12	1.98	1.83	2.50	1.94
Not stated	No.	2,320	665	700	955	737,270
grp. 23	%	7.87	7.13	7.52	8.85	8.55

SOURCE: Data and classifications of groups derived from Table 5.

TABLE 7

Estonian Professionals in Canada, 1950-1980

	(1) Immigrated after Second World War	(2) Graduated in Canada, 1950-1979	(3) January 1, 1980
Agriculturalists[1] [a]	49	ca 10	ca 30
Architects[b]	8	ca 40	ca 50
Artists[2]			
Performing Arts[c]	18	30 (est.)	20 (est.)
Fine arts	ca 10	20 (est.)	20 (est.)
Chemists	ca 10	ca 40 +	50
Dentists[3]	3	ca 15	ca 15
Economists and			
accountants	ca 30	80 (est.)	70 (est.)
Engineers[4]	100 (est.)	400 +	500 +
Journalists[d]	17	ca 30	15 (est.)
Lawyers[5] [e]	120-140	ca 20	ca 20
Army officers[6] [f]	ca 30	ca 5	ca 5
Ministers[7]			
Lutheran[g]	21	5	14
Others	ca 15	ca 5	ca 15
Musicians[8]	ca 20	30 (est.)	30 (est.)
Natural scientists	15 (est.)	50 (est.)	55 (est.)
Nurses[9]	100 (est.)	80 (est.)	130 (est.)
Pharmacists	ca 10	ca 20	ca 25
Physicians[10] [h]	31	ca 50	ca 80
Teachers[11] [i]	115	260 (est.)	260
Others[12]	50 (est.)	200 (est.)	200 (est.)
TOTAL	600-700	1,500 + [j]	2,000 + [j]

Concerning immigrants, there is some overlapping in professions, with the same person holding more than one profession such as lawyer/army officer, teacher/musician, journalist/economist, and some odd combinations like lawyer/engineer or lawyer/musician, but there are not many and where known the overlap has been eliminated by discarding the secondary profession.

Since many immigrants graduated in Canada anew either in the same or in different fields, they are counted in both column (1) and column (2), but in column (3) they are counted as they were in column (2).

Concerning column (3), it has to be reckoned that many immigrants have died between 1950 and 1980, and all graduates in Canada are not engaged in the field of their graduation; for instance, some arts graduates are either teachers or government employees, some economists have turned into entrepreneurs, etc. Most of these are counted under "others" in column 3.

Column (2) and column (3) include, as far as it was known, the descendants of the pre-Second World War immigrants. Column (1) also includes those who immigrated later in the 1960's and 1970's, but there were very few – for example, three pastors, three physicians, etc., from England, Australia, Sweden, or the Latin American countries. Some engineers and chemists also left Canada for the U.S. during the 1960's and 1970's.

1. Includes horticulturalists, but not foresters.
2. Graduates of the School of Theatrical Arts or the Academy of Fine Arts.
3. University graduates.
4. Civil, mechanical, electrical, and chemical engineers.
5. Includes the judiciary and civil servants with university education.
6. Military Academy graduates.
7. All Lutheran and most other ministers had university education.
8. Higher music school graduates.
9. Graduates of schools of nursing.
10. Includes specialists in medical sciences.
11. Elementary and secondary school teachers. In Estonia an elementary school teaching certificate required either the six-year Teachers Seminary or five-year gümnasium (secondary school) and the two-year Pedagogical Institute in Tallinn; a secondary school teaching certificate required university graduation in the discipline and pedagogy courses (equivalent to one year) at the University of Tartu.
12. Includes veterinarians, foresters, social scientists, librarians, linguists, etc.

SOURCES:
(a) Mainly from a letter by A. Irs, president of the Society of Estonian Agriculturalists in Canada, December 7, 1979.
(b) Mainly from a letter by A. Elken, professor of architecture at the University of Toronto, January 25, 1980.
(c) Interview with L. Vohu, director of the Estonian National Theatre in Canada, November 7, 1979.
(d) Mainly from a letter by K. Arro, editor of *Vaba Eestlane* in Toronto, November 21, 1979.
(e) Information from Estonian academic organizations in Toronto, and A. Peel, secretary of the Society of Estonian Jurists in Canada, interviews in November and December, 1979.
(f) Information from Estonian Officers Corps in Toronto.
(g) Mainly from a letter by Bishop K. Raudsepp, September 26, 1979.
(h) Letter and information from Dr. H. Sepp, president of the Estonian Medical Scientists in Canada, November 23, 1979.
(i) Interview with H. Leivat, secretary of the Estonian Supplementary School in Toronto and Estonian Teachers Association in Canada, November 8, 1979.
(j) Totals have been checked against information available in a study by Professor O. Träss on Estonian university graduates in Canada from 1950 to 1972 in *Eestlased Kanadas,* pp. 480-6, 494-6; a study by R. Antik, archivist of the Estonian Central Archives in Canada, on membership of Estonian academic organizations in Canada, in *Eestlased Kanadas,* p. 413; and Canada census data for 1971 on the occupational distribution of Estonians in Canada.

According to O. Träss, 1,170 Estonians had graduated from Canadian universities from 1950 to 1972, but he adds that this figure includes only direct data and the actual figure may be closer to 1,300. If we assume that the educational attainment of Estonians in Canada continued from 1972 at the rate of the late 1960's and early 1970's, then the figure given here is rather modest. Träss's figures also include 143 M.A. and twenty-seven Ph.D. degrees. According to R. Antik, 2,734 members of Estonian academic organizations left Estonia in 1944. Since about 25 per cent of all Estonian refugees finally immigrated to Canada, about 600 to 700 of them should have come to Canada. From the 1971 census data we retrieved a figure of about 2,200 Estonian professionals. In 1980 this figure should be substantially higher, but the census figures were based on broad types of occupations whereas ours here are based on professional preparation. If anything, our derivations in this table are very modest; the actual figures are probably 10-20 per cent higher.

174

TABLE 8

Ethnic Origin by Census Years, 1941-1971
(Selected Ethnic Groups)

	1941	1951	% 1941-51	1961	% 1951-61	1971	% 1961-71
Total Canada	11,506,655	14,009,429	21.75	18,238,247	30.19	21,568,310	15.26
Total Baltic	n.a.	n.a.	n.a.	64,373	n.a.	61.525	-4.42
Estonian	n.a.	n.a.	n.a.	18,550	n.a.	18,810	1.40
Latvian	n.a.	n.a.	n.a.	18,194	n.a.	18,180	-0.08
Lithuanian	7,789	16,224	108.29	27,629	70.30	24,535	-11.20
Finnish	41,683	43,745	4.97	59,436	35.87	59,215	-3.72
German	464,682	619,995	33.42	1,049,599	69.29	1,317,200	25.50
Italian	112,625	152,245	35.18	450,351	195.81	730,820	62.28
Jewish	170,241	181,670	6.71	173,344	-18.16	296,945	71.30
Norwegian	100,718	119,266	18.42	148,681	24.66	179,290	20.59
Portuguese	n.a.	n.a.	n.a.	n.a.	n.a.	96,875	n.a.
Ukrainian	305,929	395,043	29.13	473,337	19.82	580,660	22.67

1. n.a. = data not available.

SOURCES: Statistics Canada, *Census of Canada*, 1961, Population Bulletin 1, 2-5, Table 34; *ibid.*, 1971, Bulletin 1, 3-2, Cat. #92-723, Table 1.

TABLE 9

Estonian Ethnic Origin by Age Groups, 1971

Age	Number	% of Total	Group Characteristics
0- 9	2,050	26.33	
10-19	2,905	(4,955)	born in Canada
20-29	2,370	20.99	almost all born abroad, 1 to
30-39	1,580	(3,950)	20 years old when came to Canada
40-49	3,055	34.43	overwhelmingly immigrants,
50-59	3,425	(6,480)	21 to 40 years old when came to Canada
60-69	2,375	18.25	mostly immigrants, 41 years
70 or over	1,060	(3,435)	old or older when came to Canada
TOTAL	18,820[1]	100%	

1. Difference with the total figure in Table 8 is due to the rounding of data.

SOURCE: Statistics Canada, *Census of Canada*, 1971, unpublished data.

TABLE 10

**Ethnic Origin, Mother Tongue, and Home Language
Selected Ethnic Groups, 1971**

	Ethnic Origin	Mother Tongue Ethnic	% of Ethnic Origin	Home Language Ethnic	% of Ethnic Origin
Estonian	18,810	14,855	78.97	9,160	48.70
Latvian	18,180	14,225	78.25	8,305	45.68
Lithuanian	24,535	15,195	61.93	8,280	33.75
Finnish	59,215	36,375	61.43	16,520	27.90
German	1,317,200	558,965	42.44	196,875	14.95
Italian	730,820	538,765	73.72	399,630	54.68
Jewish/Yiddish	296,945	50,320	16.95	18,845	6.35
Norwegian	179,290	27,650	15.42	1,825	1.02
Portuguese	96,875	86,925	89.73	68,630	70.84
Ukrainian	580,660	309,855	53.36	129,9?0	22.39

SOURCES: Statistics Canada, *Census of Canada*, 1971, Cat. #92-723, Table 2; *ibid.*, Cat. #92-821, Table 1; *ibid.*, Cat. #92-776, Table 1.

TABLE 11

Mother Tongue, 1961, 1971, and 1976
Selected Ethnic Groups

	1961	1971	Gain/Loss 1961-71 %	1976	Gain/Loss 1971-76 %	Gain/Loss 1961-76 %
Estonian	13,820	14,520	5.07	11,975	-17.55	-13.37
Latvian	14,062	14,140	0.55	11,150	-21.21	-20.65
Lithuanian	14,997	14,725	-1.81	11,065	-24.90	-26.21
Finnish	44,785	36,725	-18.0	28,470	-22.49	-36.42
German	563,713	561,085	-0.47	476,715	-15.04	-15.43
Italian	339,626	538,360	58.52	484,050	-10.09	42.53
Norwegian	40,054	27,405	-13.58	18,070	-34.06	-54.89
Portuguese	n.a.	86,925	n.a.	126,535	45.58	n.a.
Ukrainian	361,496	309,855	-14.29	282,060	-8.97	-21.97
Yiddish	82,448	49,890	-39.46	23,435	-53.07	-71.53
English	10,660,534	12,973,810	21.70	14,122,770	8.87	32.48
French	5,123,151	5,793,650	13.09	5,887,205	1.61	14.91

SOURCES: Dominion Bureau of Statistics, *Census of Canada*, 1961, Bulletin 1, 2-9, Table 63; Statistics Canada, *Population: Demographic Characteristics: Mother Tongue*, February, 1978, Cat. #92-821, Table 1.

178

TABLE 12

Mother Tongue and Home Language, 1971
Selected Ethnic Groups
(Language Retention and Language Transfer)

	Mother Tongue	Home Language	% of Mother Tongue	Home Language English	% of Mother Tongue	Home Language other than Ethnic or English	% of Mother Tongue
Estonian	14,855	9,160	61.66	5,125	34.50	570	3.84
Latvian	14,225	8,305	58.38	5,280	37.12	640	4.50
Lithuanian	15,195	8,280	54.49	6,095	40.11	820	5.40
Finnish	36,375	16,520	45.42	19,115	52.55	740	2.03
German	558,965	196,875	35.22	352,750	63.11	9,340	1.67
Italian	538,765	399,630	74.18	117,915	21.87	21,220	3.94
Norwegian	27,650	1,825	6.60	25,415	91.90	410	1.48
Portuguese	86,925	68,630	78.95	13,585	15.63	4,710	5.42
Ukrainian	309,855	129,990	41.95	176,655	57.01	3,210	1.04
Yiddish	50,320	18,845	37.45	30,305	60.22	1,170	2.33
English	12,967,455			12,812,770	98.81	154,675	1.19
French	5,792,710	5,436,775	93.86	347,345	6.00	8,590	1.48

1. Derived from "Mother Tongue" minus "Home Language Ethnic" minus "Home Language English."

SOURCE: Statistics Canada, *Census of Canada*, 1971, Population: Statistics on Language Retention and Transfer, Special Bulletin, August, 1975, Cat. #92-776 (SP-6), Table 1.

TABLE 13

**Home Language Estonian or English
Ethnic Origin Estonian, by Age Groups, 1971[1]**

(1) Canada

Age Group	Total	Estonian	%	English	%
0-24	5,550	1,850	33.33	3,700	66.67
25-44	3,600	1,180	32.78	2,420	67.22
45-64	6,480	4,675	72.15	1,805	27.85
65 or over	1,925	1,480	76.88	445	23.12
TOTAL	17,555	9,185	52.32	8,370	47.68

(2) Central Metropolitan Areas (incl. Toronto)

0-24	4,570	1,665	36.43	2,905	63.57
25-44	3,040	1,105	36.35	1,935	63.65
45-64	5,525	4,175	75.56	1,350	24.44
65 or over	1,665	1,325	79.58	340	20.42
TOTAL	14,800	8,270	55.88	6,530	44.12

(3) Toronto

0-24	2,555	1,195	46.77	1,360	53.23
25-44	1,673	708	42.23	965	57.77
45-64	3,420	2,825	82.60	595	17.40
65 or over	1,040	915	87.98	125	12.02
TOTAL	8,688	5,643	64.95	3,045	35.05

(4) Non-Metro (Rural) Areas[2]

0-24	980	185	18.88	795	81.12
25-44	560	75	13.39	485	86.61
45-64	955	500	52.36	455	47.76
65 or over	260	155	59.62	105	40.38
TOTAL	2,755	915	33.21	1,840	66.79

1. Excluded are (a) Ethnic Origin Estonian but Home Language neither Estonian nor English, and (b) Home Language Estonian but Ethnic Origin not Estonian. Both groups exist but they are too small to be of any significance.
2. Non-Metro (Rural) Areas (4) figures derived from Canada (1) less Central Metro Areas (2).

SOURCE: Statistics Canada, *Census of Canada*, 1971, unpublished data.

TABLE 14

Endogamy and Exogamy,
Ethnic Origin Estonian[1]

(1) By Ethnic Origin of Spouse

Ethnic Origin of Spouse	Ethnic Origin of Wife: Estonian	%	Ethnic Origin of Husband: Estonian	%
Total	4,890	100.0	4,800	100.0
Estonian	3,405	69.42	3,405	70.86
British Isles	555	11.31	630	13.11
German	165	3.36	165	3.43
Baltic	120	2.45	30	0.62
French	55	1.12	90	1.87
Other	590	12.03	480	9.99

1. Differences in totals are due to the rounding of data by Statistics Canada.

SOURCE: Statistics Canada, *Census of Canada*, 1971, unpublished data.

TABLE 14—Continued

Endogamy and Exogamy, Ethnic Origin Estonian[1]

(2) By Age Groups:

Canada:

Age	Total	Married: Male				Total	Married: Female			
		Endogamy	%	Exogamy	%		Endogamy	%	Exogamy	%
Up to 29	425	135	31.76	290	68.24	395	135	34.18	260	65.82
30-39	600	260	43.33	340	66.67	660	260	39.39	400	60.61
40-49	1,165	770	69.09	395	33.91	1,160	770	66.38	390	33.62
50-59	1,375	1,210	88.0	165	12.0	1,480	1,210	81.76	270	18.24
60+	1,195	1,060	88.70	135	11.30	1,220	1,060	86.89	160	13.11
TOTAL	4,760	3,435	72.16	1,325	27.84	4,915	3,435	69.89	1,480	30.11

Toronto (Metropolitan)

Age	Total	Married: Male				Total	Married: Female			
		Endogamy	%	Exogamy	%		Endogamy	%	Exogamy	%
Up to 29	215	80	37.21	135	62.79	175	80	45.71	95	54.28
30-39	225	130	57.78	95	42.22	250	130	52.0	120	48.0
40-49	575	450	78.26	125	21.74	555	450	81.08	105	18.92
50-59	685	640	93.43	45	6.57	720	640	88.89	80	11.11
60+	590	575	97.46	15	2.54	595	575	96.64	20	3.36
TOTAL	2,290	1,875	81.88	415	18.12	2,295	1,875	81.70	420	18.30

1. Differences in totals are due to the rounding of data by Statistics Canada.

SOURCE: Statistics Canada, *Census of Canada*, 1971, unpublished data.

Bibliography

BOOKS AND ARTICLES

Aun, Karl, *et al.*, eds. *Seedrioru 1955-1980*. Toronto, 1980.

Bruce, Jean. *After the War*. Don Mills, Ontario: Fitzhenry & Whiteside, 1982.

Burnham, R.E. *Who are the Finns?* London: Faber and Faber, 1946.

Cronmiller, Carl R. *A History of Lutheran Church in Canada*. Toronto: Ev. Lutheran Synod of Canada, 1961.

Dirks, Gerald E. *Canada's Refugee Policy: Indifference or Opportunism?* Montreal: McGill-Queen's University Press, 1977.

Eerme, Karl, ed. *Eesti Maja Torontos* (Estonia House in Toronto). Toronto, 1963.

Estonian World Festival: A Collection of Press Clippings. Toronto: The Estonian World Festival Committee, 1973.

Green, Alan G. *Immigration and the Postwar Canadian Economy*. Toronto: Macmillan, 1976.

Hajdu, Peter. *Finno-Ugrian Languages and Peoples,* translated (from the Hungarian) and adapted by G.E. Cushing. London: Deutsch, 1975.

Hawkins, Freda. *Canada and Immigration: Public Policy and Public Concern*. Montreal: McGill-Queen's University Press, 1972.

Holmes, John W. *The Shaping of Peace: Canada and the Search of World Order, 1943-1957*, vol. I. Toronto: University of Toronto Press, 1979.

Holborn, L.W. *Refugee: A Problem of Our Time*. Metuche, N.J.: The Scarecrow Press, 1975.

Homesteads and Happiness. Eckville, Alberta: Eckville and District Historical Society, 1979.

Hutchison, I.W. *Arctic Nights Entertainment*. London: Blackie & Sons, 1935.

Inno, Karl, and Felix Oinas. *Eesti Teatmeteos* (Source Book on Estonia), vol. II. Geislingen/Steige: ERS & EUKS, 1949.

Jackson, J. Hampden. *Estonia*. London: Allen and Unwin, 1948.

183

Kala, August, ed. *Toronto Eesti Võitlejate Ühing* (Estonian Veterans' Association of Toronto). Toronto, 1979.

Kalbach, Warren E. *The Impact of Immigration on Canada's Population.* Ottawa: Dominion Bureau of Statistics, 1970.

Kareda, Endel, comp. *Estonia the Forgotten Nation.* Toronto: Estonian Central Council in Canada, 1961.

Karni, Michael G., ed. *Finnish Diaspora I.* Toronto: The Multicultural History Society of Ontario, 1981.

Kilbourn, William, and Rudi Christl, eds. *Toronto.* Toronto: McClelland and Stewart, 1977.

Klesment, Johannes. *The Estonian Soldiers in the Second World War.* Stockholm: The Estonian National Council, 1948.

Koop, Evelyn. *The Basics of Modern Rhythmic Gymnastics.* Toronto: Canadian Modern Rhythmic Gymnastics Federation, 1977.

Kork, Arvi (A. Tinits). *Tammiraiujad* (The Dam Builders). Lund: EKK, 1966.

Kungla 1949-1979. Winnipeg: Josten's National School Service, 1979.

Küng, Andres. *A Dream of Freedom.* Cardiff: Boreas Publishing, 1980.

Kurlents, Alfred, *et al.*, eds. *Eestlased Kanadas* (Estonians in Canada). Toronto: KEAK (Canadian Estonian History Commission), 1975.

Lewis, E. Glyn. *Multilingualism in the Soviet Union.* The Hague: Mouton, 1972.

Lootsma, Elmar, *et al.*, eds. *Eestlased Londonis* (Estonians in London). London, Ontario, 1979.

Lord, John B. *Aleksander Tamsalu 1891-1960: A Botanist in Exile.* Hamilton, Ontario: Royal Botanical Garden, Bulletin No. 11, 1980.

Mitt, Gunnar. *Estonian Scouting.* Toronto: Estonian Boy Scout Federation, 1979.

Mägi, Arvo. *Estonian Literature.* Lund: EKK, 1972.

Michelson, Herbert. *50 aastat skautlust* (Fifty Years of Scouting). New York, 1962.

Misiunas, Romuald J., and Rein Taagepera. *The Baltic States: Years of Dependence, 1940-1980.* Berkeley: University of California Press, 1983.

Naan, Gustav, ed. *Nõukogude Eesti* (The Soviet Estonia). Tallinn: Valgus, 1975.

Palmer, Howard. *Land of the Second Chance: A History of Ethnic Groups in Southern Alberta.* Lethbridge, Alberta: Lethbridge Herald, 1972.

Parming, Tõnu. *The Decline of Liberal Democracy and Rise of Authoritarianism in Estonia.* Berkeley: Sage Publications, 1975.

Parming, Tõnu, and Elmar Järvesoo, eds. *A Case Study of a Soviet Republic: The Estonian SSR.* Boulder, Colorado: Westview Press, 1978.

Pennar, Jaan, *et al. The Estonians in America 1627-1975.* Dobbs Ferry: Oceana Publications, 1975.

Pullerits, Albert, ed. *Estland.* Tallinn: [Estonian Bureau of Statistics], 1938.

Raud, Villibald. *Estonia: A Reference Book.* New York: The Nordic Press, 1953.

Royal Commission on Bilingualism and Biculturalism, Book IV, *The Cultural Contributions of Other Ethnic Groups*. Ottawa, 1969.

Saagpakk, Paul. *Estonian-English Dictionary*. New Haven: Yale University Press, 1982.

Saarniit, Joann. "Voyage to Freedom," in Milli Charon (ed.), *Between Two Worlds: The Canadian Immigration Experience* (Toronto: Quadrant, 1983), pp. 17-26.

A Thousand and One Facts about Estonia. Tallinn: Perioodika, 1977.

Uibopuu, Valev. *Meie ja meie hõimud* (The Estonians and the Finno-Ugrians). Lund: EKK, 1984.

Uustalu, Evald, ed. *Aspects of Estonian Culture*. London: Boreas Publishing, 1961.

Uustalu, Evald. *For Freedom Only: The Story of Estonian Volunteers in the Finnish War of 1940-1944*. Toronto: Northern Publications, 1977.

____. *The History of Estonian People*. London: Boreas Publishing, 1952.

Veedam, Voldemar. *Sailing to Freedom*. London: Hutchinson, 1961.

Võõbus, Arthur. *Studies in the History of Estonian People*. 9 vols. (to date). Stockholm: ETSE, 1969-84.

Wukasch, P. "Baltic Immigration in Canada 1947-1955," *Concordia Historical Institute Quarterly*, 1 (1977), pp. 4-22.

Wheat Heart of the West: A History of Barons and District. Barons, Alberta: Barons History Committee, 1972.

PERIODICALS

Journal of Baltic Studies, 1969- .

Meie Elu (Our Life), Toronto, 1950-.

Meie Tee (Our Way), New York, 1931-.

Sillas, Bulletin of the Estonian Federation in Canada, Toronto, 1975-. Irregular.

Teataja, Stockholm, 1945- .

Tulimuld, Lund, Sweden, 1950- .

Vaba Eestlane (Free Estonian), Toronto, 1952- .

Vaba Eesti Sõna (Free Estonian Word), New York, 1948- .

Ühispanga Uudised (Credit Union News), yearbook of the Toronto Estonian Credit Union, 1957-.

OTHER SOURCES

Estonian Central Archives in Canada, Toronto.

Canadian Estonian History Commission Archives, in the Estonian Central Archives, Toronto.

Oral History Project, interviews by the Estonian Federation in Canada, 1976-79.

Department of Citizenship and Immigration, *Quarterly Immigration Bulletin*, 1958-71.

Department of Manpower and Immigration, *Quarterly Statistics: Immigration*, 1972-80.

Statistics Canada, *Census of Canada, 1961, 1971, 1981*.

Tartu Institute Archives, Toronto.

Index

187

GENERATIONS: A HISTORY OF CANADA'S PEOPLES